Advance Acclaim for
The Alignment Effect

"The companies that will get ahead and stay ahead in today's inter-connected business environment will be those that take control of technology, not those that let technology take control of them. Business leaders who want grab the reins and steer IT in the same direction as the rest of the business must read this book."
> – **Charles B. Wang**, *Founder and Chairman of the Board,*
> *Computer Associates International, Inc.*

"I found this book an enlightening and valuable read. The real world stories coupled with the author's interpretation of the CIO's business role today should make every business leader sit up and take notice. Everyone in a position of leadership should read this book before they set next year's IT budget."
> – **Phil Fasano**, *Senior Vice President,*
> *Global Technology Group, JPMorgan Chase and Company*

"*The Alignment Effect* paints a vivid picture of information technology's worst-kept secret: IT cannot, by itself, solve your business problem. To solve your problem, any new technology must be carefully aligned with your business objectives and processes. Otherwise, save your money. Read this book if you want to ensure the success of your own technology implementation!"
> – **Don Peppers** *and* **Martha Rogers, Ph.D.**, *authors of the One to One series of books on managing individual customer relationships*

"Faisal Hoque demonstrates that technology is no longer just the realm of engineers and programmers. *The Alignment Effect* challenges 'C' level executives to drive IT value and provides them the pathway to smart, integrated business decisions."
– **Randolph C. Blazer**, *Chairman and CEO, KPMG Consulting, Inc.*

"The strength and appeal of *The Alignment Effect* is that it provides a flexible but actionable approach that, if interpreted and applied well, can greatly increase the probability that alignment will—over time—occur."
– **Bob Zmud**, *prolific author, Research Director for the Advanced Practices Council of the Society for Information Management, and Professor and Michael F. Price Chair in MIS, Michael F. Price College of Business, University of Oklahoma*

"The examples of business/technology alignment and misalignment speak to every reader. Rarely have horror stories been explained so clearly, and Hoque shows how to ensure alignment so that next year's horror stories don't involve your company."
– **Don Tapscott**, *International best-selling author and Co-Founder of Digital 4Sight*

"Faisal Hoque's assertion that capturing the value of IT requires synchronizing business, process, and technology issues is right on. My own sense in my field of research is that many companies need to do exactly what the author describes as important."
– **V. Sambamurthy**, *widely recognized researcher on business-IT alignment and Eli Broad Professor of Information Technology, Eli Broad College of Business, Michigan State University*

"Top executives have realized for years that closing the gaping distance between technology and business can provide their organization with a strong, defensible, competitive advantage. However, knowing it and executing it are very different. *The Alignment Effect* finally clearly lays out a process of how to do it, and do it right."
– **Chuck Martin**, *Author, Managing for the Short Term*

"It occasionally happens that the producer of an innovative technology reaps rewards even if the customer fails to realize the promised benefit. It never happens that the customer reaps rewards under such circumstances. If you want to avoid being that customer, get to know BTM as defined in *The Alignment Effect*."
– **Isaac Applbaum**, *Partner, Lightspeed Venture Partners*

THE ALIGNMENT EFFECT

How to Get Real Business Value
Out of Technology

FAISAL HOQUE

FINANCIAL TIMES
Prentice Hall

Prentice Hall PTR
Upper Saddle River, NJ 07458
www.ft-ph.com

Library of Congress Cataloging-in-Publication Data

Hoque, Faisal
    The alignment effect : how to get real business value out of technology / by Faisal (i.e., Faisal] Hoque
      p. cm.
  Includes bibliographical references and index.
  ISBN 0-13-044939-3 (alk. paper)
    1. Information technology--Management. 2. Economic value added. I Title.

HD30.2 .H664 2002
004'.068--dc21

2002027866

Production Supervisor: Wil Mara
Acquisitions Editor: Jim Boyd
Editorial Assistant: Allyson Kloss
Marketing Manager: Bryan Gambrel
Manufacturing Manager: Alexis Heydt-Long
Buyer: Maura Zaldivar

The jacket, interior pages, figures, and tables were designed by Lance Sperring
The author photo on the jacket was taken by Peter Baker Studios

© 2002 Faisal Hoque
Published by Financial Times Prentice Hall
An imprint of Pearson Education, Inc.

The publisher offers discounts on this book when ordered in bulk quantities. For more information contact: Corporate Sales Department, Prentice Hall PTR, One Lake Street, Upper Saddle River, NJ 07458. Phone: 800-382-3419; FAX: 201-236-7141; E-mail: corpsales@prenhall.com.

Company and product names mentioned herein are the trademarks or registered trademarks of their respective owners.

Printed in the United States of America

10 9 8 7 6 5 4 3 2 1

ISBN 0-13-044939-3

Pearson Education LTD.
Pearson Education Australia PTY, Limited
Pearson Education Singapore, Pte. Ltd
Pearson Education North Asia Ltd
Pearson Education Canada, Ltd.
Pearson Educación de Mexico, S.A. de C.V.
Pearson Education—Japan
Pearson Education Malaysia, Pte. Ltd
Pearson Education, Upper Saddle River, New Jersey

FINANCIAL TIMES PRENTICE HALL BOOKS

For more information, please go to www.ft-ph.com

D. Quinn Mills
Buy, Lie, and Sell High: How Investors Lost Out on Enron and the Internet Bubble

Dale Neef
E-procurement: From Strategy to Implementation

John R. Nofsinger
Investment Blunders (of the Rich and Famous)…And What You Can Learn From Them

John R. Nofsinger
Investment Madness: How Psychology Affects Your Investing… And What to Do About It

Tom Osenton
Customer Share Marketing: How the World's Great Marketers Unlock Profits from Customer Loyalty

Richard W. Paul and Linda Elder
Critical Thinking: Tools for Taking Charge of Your Professional and Personal Life

Matthew Serbin Pittinsky, Editor
The Wired Tower: Perspectives on the Impact of the Internet on Higher Education

W. Alan Randolph and Barry Z. Posner
Checkered Flag Projects: 10 Rules for Creating and Managing Projects that Win, Second Edition

Stephen P. Robbins
The Truth About Managing People…And Nothing but the Truth

Fernando Robles, Françoise Simon, and Jerry Haar
Winning Strategies for the New Latin Markets

Jeff Saperstein and Daniel Rouach
Creating Regional Wealth in the Innovation Economy: Models, Perspectives, and Best Practices

Eric G. Stephan and Wayne R. Pace
Powerful Leadership: How to Unleash the Potential in Others and Simplify Your Own Life

Jonathan Wight
Saving Adam Smith: A Tale of Wealth, Transformation, and Virtue

Yoram J. Wind and Vijay Mahajan, with Robert Gunther
Convergence Marketing: Strategies for Reaching the New Hybrid Consumer

Dedication

Tom, this one is for you. For your unyielding faith, your sincere support, your continuous inspiration, and most importantly for your true friendship.

In memory of Faez.
  – Faisal

In memory of Dennis.
  – Ryan

Acknowledgments

THIS BOOK COULD NOT HAVE BEEN WRITTEN without the special talents and determination of Ryan J. Sheehan, Christine Aruza, Zoe Sochor, and Lance Sperring. A heartfelt thanks goes out to them for their patience and perseverance in seeing this project through to the end. I am also especially grateful to my entire company, enamics, Inc., for never losing its resolve in the quest to help others recognize and achieve the benefits of Business Technology Management (BTM). Through their tireless efforts my vision for BTM has been realized.

I will be forever indebted to the following for their personal support and for sharing their industry insights: Randolph C. Blazer, Chairman & CEO, KPMG Consulting, Inc.; Patrick F. Flynn, vice president and CIO, PACCAR, Inc.; Scott Hayward, managing director, JPMorgan Chase and Company; Dale Kutnick,

chairman, CEO & research director, META Group, Inc.; Dr. Jerry
Luftman, best-selling author of *Competing in the Information Age*
and Distinguished Service Professor, Stevens Institute of
Technology; Chuck Martin, best-selling author of *Managing for the
Short Term* and *Net Future* and former associate publisher,
InformationWeek; Jack Mollen, senior vice president, Human
Resources, EMC Corporation; Honorio J. Padron, president and
CEO, Business Services, Exelon Corporation; Don Peppers, best-
selling author of the *One to One* book series and founding partner
of Peppers and Rogers Group; Chris Perretta, CIO, GE Capital
Card Services, Kevin Poulter, head of Business Integration, British
American Tobacco; John Sievers, president, Consumer and Small
Business Group, Southern New England Telecommunications;
Howard Smith, CTO, CSC Europe; Tom Trainer, former CIO,
Citigroup, Inc., Eli Lilly & Co., and Reebok International Ltd.;
and Carl Wilson, executive vice president and CIO, Marriott
International, Inc. The candor with which they recount their
experiences provides us all with a rich set of didactic cautions,
lessons, and guidance. I hold each of these individuals in the high-
est regard.

I am also grateful to my editor, Jim Boyd, for the direction and
continual support that he gave me throughout the entire process.
No matter what unconventional request I made or zany idea I
proposed to him, he always listened with a receptive ear and
responded with patient suggestions that considered any alternative
possibilities. Without his guidance and the efforts of the folks at
Financial Times Prentice Hall, this book would never have made
it from brainchild to bookstore.

Special thanks go to Frank Ovaitt and Paul Berg for the innu-
merable hours they have spent in support of this project. Time
and time again, they kept me headed on the right path with
their reliable and experienced counsel. They always have my
deepest respect and I consider myself a fortunate recipient of
their sage advice.

I also wish to extend my gratitude to the members of enamics'
board of directors and advisory board in addition to the numerous
customers, partners, and investors that have helped shape our
thinking and validate our direction. It is through their feedback,

contributions, and encouragement that BTM has been able to successfully forge ahead in the marketplace.

Dale Kutnick and Meta Group also deserve special recognition for their commitment and support. From day one, they have demonstrated their belief in these concepts. The same also holds true for Sathish Reddy and the hard work of his team at Itreya. We wouldn't be able to pursue our vision without their dedicated labors, nor without those of Paul Daversa and his company, Resource Systems Group.

I am deeply grateful for having been blessed with a wonderful family and a few special friends. To my family, thank you for instilling in me, from the earliest days, the passion required for taking on a project of this magnitude and the drive needed to succeed. To my friends, thank you for touching my life and cheering me on.

Most importantly, I am eternally thankful for my wife and best friend, Christine Hoque, whose faith has inspired me to never give up all these years. She has encouraged all of my radical ideas and has endured with me the ups and downs, the 4 a.m. conversations, the lost evenings, and the delayed plans, that often come hand-in-hand when you decide to chase your dreams. She makes living worthwhile. Lastly, I welcome our son with my arms open wide as the finishing touches are being put on this book.

May, 2002
Faisal Hoque

Introduction

MY OBSERVATIONS OF BUSINESS AND TECHNOLOGY over the last 15 years compel me to write this book and to answer this question: Why aren't we getting real business value out of technology? One thing is sure—companies that continue to repeat the mistakes of the past will never reap the rewards of the future. Most companies fail to capitalize on the technologies they already have; and many more are poised to meet this same fate with the next big technology fad spawned in Silicon Valley and propelled by venture capitalists. Whether it's wireless, Web services, or the latest and greatest in nanotechnology, companies will never get value—real or perceived—without first solving the business/technology disconnect.

This book will begin by illustrating some of the ways the disconnect can manifest itself in the enterprise. These examples reveal an unequivocal truth: In order to understand, communicate, and plan how they should utilize technology in the enterprise, companies first need to align three key areas—business, process, and technology. But to achieve alignment among these areas requires a fundamentally different approach than those used before—one that brings these disciplines together in a way that all can understand. This approach creates unprecedented visibility into how business and technology decisions are made, and provides the means for tracing decisions back and forth between the two, so that companies can discover and communicate interdependencies.

This approach is called Business Technology Management, or BTM. In the pages that follow, the principles, activities, and governance that make up BTM will unfold to provide the structure and the mindset to help any company in any industry get real business value from IT.

I am not alone in my views on the disconnect, or in my ideas about what's necessary to solve it. Many chief executive officers (CEOs), chief information officers (CIOs), industry gurus and academics—such as the contributors to this book (some of whom have been grappling with the disconnect since the earliest days of IT)—believe that the time has arrived for companies to adopt a structured approach to aligning business and technology.

What's to Come?

Whether you accept this premise or not, one thing is obvious: The approaches that companies have been relying upon to close the disconnect aren't getting the job done. So what needs to be different in the way companies go about solving it?

To answer this crucial question, the approach should follow several guidelines. First, the approach should view the problem primarily from the perspective of the business. IT has a long history of considering itself an island apart from the rest of the enterprise. But, like every other business function, IT should service the bottom line first, and then its own needs. This doesn't mean that IT is only about dollars and cents; one of the biggest mistakes that companies have made in the past is failing to recognize the intangible benefits that can come from IT—benefits such as improved customer relationships and better communication between business units. The people who are most likely to recognize and advocate these benefits are business professionals, since they are often the end-users of technology. It is a mistake not to get this crucial group sufficiently involved in making decisions about how technology can and should impact the business. If IT is to become focused on the business, this trend needs to change.

Second, the approach should focus specifically on the business/technology disconnect, and leave other, more narrowly focused techniques (such as scorecarding or systems design) out of the equation. This means that the solution should zero in on the three key areas that need to be aligned—business, process, and technology—and specifically the connections between them. Often the easiest way to understand this is by forming a picture in your mind similar to what appears in Fig. I.1:

Figure | I.1

The three areas that need to be aligned in order to close the business/technology disconnect: business, process, and technology

Third, the approach should enable disparate groups of people with different interests, capabilities, and objectives to visualize and communicate about IT. This includes everyone from the CxO suite on down to programmers and developers. To close the disconnect, all of these people need to be on the same page.

Finally, the approach should solve the problem up front, before the disconnect is cast in stone by expensive and irreversible IT implementations. The logical place for this to happen is in the design stage, where disconnects can be diagnosed, examined, and cured—all before the first line of code gets written.

Obviously, these guidelines leave a lot of room for interpreting how to go about closing the business/technology disconnect. Filling in these gaps is what *The Alignment Effect* is all about.

———————

This book begins with *Part I: The Business/Technology Disconnect*, which introduces the disconnect and uses real-world examples to show the profound effect that it can have upon the enterprise. These examples, which include scenarios from integrated financial systems to human resources to call reporting, illustrate some typical conditions that can result in disconnects, as well as some of the material losses that they can produce. To begin closing the business/technology disconnect, IT departments need to address several emerging challenges. These challenges point to the need for a new approach to align business and technology: the principles, activities, and governance that make up BTM.

Part II: The Principles of BTM, examines three underlying principles that must be in place in order to perform BTM. These principles include predictive modeling, which allows project teams to create blueprints that improve design decisions and facilitate alignment; collaborative decision-making, which includes a broad range of stakeholders to make sure that competing needs are balanced; and making knowledge and assets reusable, which maximizes the value of both intellectual and physical capital.

In *Part III: The Activities of BTM*, we explore business model definition, process optimization, and technology automation—the three activities that companies undertake to align business and technology. The purpose of these activities is to create an end-to-end blueprint of the enterprise architecture that is relevant to a given IT project. In order to create this blueprint, the project team relies on predictive modeling and the other principles of BTM. The activities of BTM begin by capturing a model of the current enterprise architecture, including business, process, and technology. The next step is creating multiple scenario models that correspond with the directions that the project could take. After selecting a final scenario, the final step is implementing the design created in the corresponding model and updating the current model to reflect the changes.

Part IV: Governing With BTM, illustrates how the enterprise should administer BTM to achieve two goals. First, the blueprint developed during the activities of BTM helps senior decision-makers (including the CIO) to set strategic direction for how the business should put technology to work by managing the IT portfolio. Second, the design decisions captured in the blueprint become an important ingredient for helping the company maintain tactical control over their IT projects, including control over quality and cost management. Finally, since governance implies a concerted effort to incorporate BTM into the workplace, I will introduce some key roles and responsibilities for helping BTM make the jump from promise to practice.

The Sum Total

Together, these building blocks add up to a structured approach—BTM—which aligns business and technology so that companies can get real value out of IT. This is the key message of BTM, and also of this book. So even if you decide not to read a word beyond this sentence, remember this point: "BTM aligns business and technology to get real value out of IT."

The Business/ Technology Disconnect

"The study of error is not only in the highest degree prophylactic, but it serves as a stimulating introduction to the study of truth."
– *Walter Lippman*

IMAGINE FOR A MOMENT that you want to build your dream house. After some research, you select Janet, a prominent architect, and Robert, a respected contractor, for the job. To kick things off, you invite them over to your apartment to discuss the project. After brief introductions and some cursory small talk, the three of you sit down at the kitchen table and get to work:

YOU: As the two of you know, I'm interested in building a house.

THEM: [Nodding]

YOU: Not just any house. My dream house.

THEM: [More nodding]

YOU: For years now I've been picturing this house in my mind, so I know exactly what I want. First, it's got to feel like home. I'd like a breakfast nook, a whirlpool tub in the master bathroom...

THEM: [Jotting down notes]

YOU: ...a deck off the family room. And a dramatic two story entrance, of course. Also, I just love our neighbor's fireplace...

THEM: [Scribbling furiously]

YOU: ...So what do you think?

THEM: [Pause]

JANET: It sounds to me like you'd love the colonial revival style. We could include a portico with ionic columns, and a dentil band to add an air of sophistication...

YOU: A "dentil" what?

ROBERT: And I know an importer who gets beige breccia marble direct from Karnezeika...

YOU: "Karne"-where?

JANET: ...and a hipped roof...

ROBERT: ...cantilever walls in the family room...

JANET: ...with sidelights and transoms...

ROBERT: ...tensile strength, ASTM A615...

At this point, you're probably lost. Or, at the very least you feel like you're no longer in charge of the conversation. How does all of this technical jargon relate to your vision of a dream house? What do "tensile strengths" and "dentil bands" have to do with "feeling like home"?

The problem here is common: you've hired two skilled associates who instinctively view the project from their own specialized perspectives—which you definitely don't share. But despite all of this, you're still the boss, and you need to figure out a way to make sure that everybody comes together to achieve your vision—no matter how limited your architectural and structural engineering vocabulary may be.

But not to worry. Architects and builders have faced this problem as long as they've been building for style as well as for shelter. To help communicate issues and align their expertise, Janet and Robert will follow an established approach that helps them to collaborate and ultimately, to capture the design for your dream house in the form of an architectural blueprint. The three of you will then use this blueprint to bridge the gaps between their technical knowledge and your general objectives: Janet could point out the portico and the simple yet elegant design of its ionic pillars; Robert could explain how advanced structural engineering allows continuous open spaces throughout multiple rooms; and you could envision what it would be like to actually live in the home. Without this approach, designing your house would mean ceding control over the project to Janet and Robert; the end result would presumably look impressive and be structurally sound, but there would be no way to ensure that it matched your vision of a dream house.

Now let's revisit this scenario, but with a twist. Picture the same scene, with you, Janet, and Robert sitting at your kitchen table. Imagine a Hollywood-style special effect in which that scene morphs into another. Instead of being a prospective homeowner, you've become a senior business executive. And instead of building a house, you're managing a corporation.

Your company is an aggressive market leader, quick to adopt the latest tools and practices to achieve competitive advantages. In recent years this has meant embracing technology to provide the infrastructure you need to do business. To plan, deploy, and manage these IT investments, you've hired Janet (now a high-powered consultant) and Robert (now a respected CIO). Like before, the three of you are sitting together at a table—but now it's in a corporate boardroom rather than in your kitchen:

YOU: As the two of you know, we're beginning a project to get closer to our customer base.

THEM: [Nodding]

YOU: This project has been in the works for some time now, so I've got a pretty good idea of the things we need to accomplish.

THEM: [More nodding]

YOU: First we're interested in improving customer segmentation. This means we'll have to gather information across all of our customer touch points…

THEM: [Jotting down notes]

YOU: …and analyze this raw data. Also, we'd like to automate some field support activities and maybe do something with our call center…

THEM: [Scribbling furiously]

YOU: …So what do you think?

THEM: [Pause]

ROBERT: This sounds like a CRM installation to me…

JANET: …with analytics…

ROBERT: …maybe WAP…

YOU: Huh?

JANET: …and load balancing…

ROBERT: …distributed architecture…

Once again, things seem to have spiraled out of your control, from business subjects you understand and appreciate—"customer base" and "segmentation"—to the arcane technology details required to implement your vision—"CRM," "WAP," and "load balancing."

In our dream house scenario, you (the homeowner) were able to rein in the project by collaborating with the architect and contractor to produce an architectural blueprint. Inexplicably however, most companies don't employ an analogous approach to help you (the executive) visualize scenarios and incorporate domain knowledge in order to overcome a similar dilemma: the business/technology disconnect.

In This Part...

As any researcher will tell you, the first step towards a conclusion is framing the proper question. So that's what *Part I: The Business/ Technology Disconnect* does. Before introducing an approach to solve the disconnect, it first has to demonstrate that the problem itself is big and bad enough to warrant your attention. Part I does this by presenting real-world evidence that shows how the disconnect manifests itself in the enterprise. Then, it makes the jump from problem to solution by tracing the evolution of IT, identifying several emerging challenges, and showing how Business Technology Management, or BTM, can help to overcome these challenges and bridge the business/technology disconnect.

1

Real-World Evidence

WOULD ANY SELF-RESPECTING EXECUTIVE willingly throw millions of dollars at an investment without knowing how it could affect his or her business? The sane answer to this question is "No." But many company leaders make this exact mistake when they blindly allocate money to IT with little concern if it is put to good use or even for the objectives they are trying to meet in the first place. Imagine a pair of children who lob snowballs at each other over a high wooden fence. Neither child can see where their volleys are landing—or even the target that they're trying to hit in the first place—but they keep throwing anyway. Now imagine each snowball costs a million dollars. It's kind of like that.

Ironically, it took one of the most irrational periods in recent history—the New Economy bubble—to return companies to rational thinking about how they invest in IT. After the dust settled from the dotcom collapse, companies surveyed the wreckage to find out what went wrong—and to ensure that it wouldn't go wrong again. Not surprisingly, one of the major problems they discovered was the "business/technology disconnect," a frequent, behind-the-scenes player that's been wreaking mayhem and madness since the earliest days of IT.

Don't just take my word for it, though. The best way to illustrate the true impact of the business/technology disconnect is to look at real-world scenarios. These scenarios stretch from before Amazon.com was a twinkle in Jeff Bezos' eye, to after Enron stock started showing up on eBay as laminated placemats. Throughout each vignette, notice a recurring trend: When companies align their use of technology with sound business objectives, the results are good; but when companies don't, bad things can—and often do—happen.

Enterprise Disconnects and Managing for the Short Term

"One thing that we see over and over is that technology evolution leads to disconnects with business. The obvious reason for this is that business and technology aren't innovated hand-in-hand. A lot of technology is created in a vacuum, simply because it can be done, and without a comprehensive connection as to how it should be used in the business environment.

Look at the personal computer, for example. When the PC first came along some CIOs viewed it as an entry-level system rather than something completely new and disruptive. Eventually, it got in the hands of middle managers and employees, and they led the revolution that molded it into the powerful business tool it is today.

This same story has played itself out with the Internet. After lots of amazing innovation up front—the browser, ubiquitous access to information, global connectivity—executives decided that the Net would be used to sell things. And this sells the Internet short the same way that using the PC as an entry-level mainframe did. The truth is that the Internet—like the PC before it—really provides an opportunity for business transformation.

The thing that's going to drive this transformation is a concept that I call Managing for the Short Term. In the age of connectivity, companies face lots of external demands: from the stock market; from customers; from business partners, etc. To respond to these demands businesses need to be able to turn in a much shorter timeframe than they've had to before, and it is technology and the Internet that's going to enable that.

But most of the technology that we have in place today—CRM, ERP, and so forth—are just the tip of the iceberg; when they are done only by a department or even several departments, they are not really end-to-end.

To successfully manage for the short term, all this technology needs to be connected all the way through the supply chain, from distributors to customers. This is going to drive a new emphasis on alignment within the enterprise."

– **Chuck Martin,** *Author, The Digital Estate, Net Future, and Max E-Marketing In the Net Future; chairman and CEO, Net Future Institute*

Real-World Disconnects and Their Real-World Results

Recent surveys by IT analysts identify the business/technology disconnect as a top CIO concern. This should be no surprise. One group that's always recognized the critical role that the disconnect plays is the practitioners who run up against it every day: CIOs; the project/program management office (PMO); business professionals, including executives, managers, and analysts; and technology professionals, including enterprise architects, developers, and process-focused IT analysts.

There's no more compelling evidence of how seriously these soldiers in the field take the business/technology disconnect than the stories that they tell firsthand. These anecdotes, which run the gamut from engineering systems to enterprise resource planning (ERP), are powerful proof that the disconnect isn't just the stuff of analyst reports and magazine articles; it's real, and it's out there giving business and IT professionals headaches even as you read this.

One more thing before we get to these real-world examples: Until now, our discussion of the disconnect has been relegated to a superficial level. But the whole purpose of this chapter is to help you sink your teeth into what this means in a real business environment. This means fleshing out the definition of the business/technology disconnect a bit more. When I talk about the disconnect, I really mean misalignment between three key areas:

- **Business,** which refers to things like the business objectives, drivers, strategy, and so on
- **Process,** which refers to business processes; the things that the enterprise "does"
- **Technology,** which includes the business applications and underlying systems that companies use to support their processes

The anecdotes that make up the rest of this chapter come from in-depth interviews with respected business and technology leaders who have grappled with the disconnect on a day-to-day basis for much of their careers. Consequently, their real-world examples span beyond any individual technology fad or era. This broad range of experiences gives us a unique look at some specific gaps that exist between business, process, and technology—and also some insight into what type of approach companies should follow to close them.

In Their Own Worlds

Our first example of a real-world disconnect comes from Patrick Flynn, Vice President and CIO of truck manufacturer, PACCAR. Flynn's story, from early in his career, is based on a customs-clearance project that was eventually abandoned by his employer at that time. In many ways, it represents the prototypical example of the disconnect, where each side pursues its own agenda with little regard for how it impacts their counterparts on the opposite side of the fence.

Flynn's customs-clearance system was designed to do real-time confirmation of clearance for a logistics provider. If an item needed to get from Singapore to San Francisco, for example, the system would determine the documentation that was required to pick up and export the item out of Singapore and into the United States:

> It needed to know things like which data elements were required, what would be the sequence of transactions, and how we would know that something had cleared. Plus, it had to handle exceptions and special cases. A government could say, for example, "this is cleared on temporary or preliminary basis" and then say "no we want to hold this one." The basic communications standards were well defined—there's actually a UN standard for customs clearance—but the actual details were flexible; they were left to the participants to nail down.

In an ideal world, these business details would have been signed, sealed, and delivered before Flynn's development team sat down to write the first line of code. As the project progressed further and further along, however, these details remained elusive:

> We knew there was a regulatory change coming that we would be mandated to follow. Then all of a sudden the change was off. And then it was on again—it was a continuous back and forth. As a result, our developers were constantly forced to revise their plans. Sometimes, the change would seem right around the corner, and we'd have to compress our plan and throw out good practices. Other times, you'd sit back and say

"wait a second, now it's going to be six months before we're ready to go" and so we'd sort of back off. There was never a clear definition of what needed to be done and when, and also whether certain features—like supporting these new regulations—were mandatory or optional. And each of these conditions has very different characteristics in terms of how you manage things.

Meanwhile, the development team was making important technology decisions on their own. They decided to build the system using Smalltalk, an object-oriented programming language that was designed for component development. From the start, Flynn remembers, Smalltalk proved to be a mixed blessing: it was great for developing the software (which was why they chose it in the first place), but it was horribly slow in a production environment, where time-sensitive communication was essential:

> We had to communicate with governments, we had to communicate with customs brokerages (to actually have the ability to clear a document you have to hold the broker's license), and we had to communicate with our own internal systems. All these were timing issues that needed to be worked out with the business: when would we be able to say "yes this is clear or not" and so on.

These two decisions—to continually evolve the business requirements and to develop the software using Smalltalk—combined to have a devastating effect upon the project. On the one hand, Flynn's team suffered through dozens of iterations of business requirements as regulatory agencies flip-flopped back and forth. With each change, it got harder and harder for the developers to avoid rewriting code that they'd already finished. On the other hand, Smalltalk couldn't keep up with the strict timing requirements that the business required, and the system always seemed to be operating a step behind. After a significant investment and years of effort, it became obvious that the project would never work, and it was canceled.

The problem with Flynn's project was that business and technology decisions were made independently, with little concern for how each might impact the other. Changes in the business requirements were based solely on shifting regulations, and the ripple effects of those changes upon the code that Flynn's team was developing never entered the equation. Similarly, the decision to develop in Smalltalk was based upon a strictly technical consideration: how good it was for building components. But by coding in Smalltalk, the team created a disconnect between the technology they developed and the strict time requirements that were critical to the business. As a result, business and technology headed in distinctly different directions (see Fig. 1.1). "It was like trying to build a bridge from opposite sides of a canyon," Flynn concludes, "and it never quite met in the middle."

| Figure | 1.1 |

Business and technology decisions in Flynn's project were made independently with no connection to the other

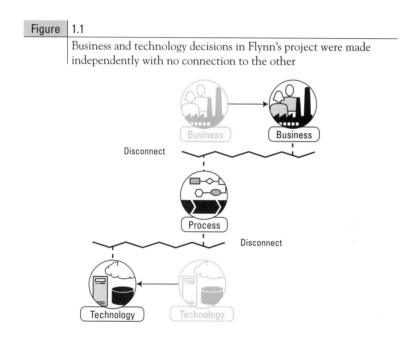

Underestimating Process Changes

This is far from the only way that the business/technology disconnect can reveal itself. Our next example of a real-world disconnect is framed by a common dilemma that IT professionals face: After installing a new enterprise application, they find a gap between the business processes it supports and the processes that are already in place. To bridge this gap, they face a critical choice—to either pay for expensive modifications to the software, or change how the company does business to fit what the technology supports out of the box.

Carl Wilson, Executive Vice President and CIO of Marriott International, Inc., is a strong proponent and successful practitioner of alignment. Marriott, lauded for its progressive alignment initiatives, enjoys the fruits of Wilson's previous experience and lessons learned. Throughout his extensive career in IT, Wilson has witnessed firsthand how disconnects caused by underestimating the impact of process changes can bring about real damage to the business. In this example, he recounts the story of a CEO who wanted better visibility into his human resources (HR) information so that he could assess his company's equal opportunity compliance:

> The CEO started out with what he thought were some pretty basic questions: How many people do we have working at each geographical location? Can we figure out what skills each of our employees has? What training have they received? But when he approached his head of human resources, he found the problem was worse than he imagined. Not only was it impossible to answer these questions, but the HR department couldn't even track straightforward data like the number of people who worked at the entire company.

The CEO quickly kicked off what he expected to be a straightforward project: implement an HR system for the company. But in the end, the disconnect between the new software and the company's established business processes, ended up costing the company millions.

From the start, the project was put on the fast track, and the company hired a large, high-profile consulting firm to implement the system. After a short evaluation period, the consultants recommended three ERP packages from leading vendors.

The consultants were under intense pressure from the executive team to fix the problem as quickly as possible. To save time, they assumed that all HR processes were essentially the same, and brokered a deal with a vendor whose product had been successfully installed a number of times for companies in the same industry. The contract, Wilson remembers, was the standard consultant's contract; there was minimal negotiation, and the company signed right away.

Early on, however, it became apparent that the installation wasn't going according to plan. When the new system came online, employees clung to their familiar business processes and demanded that the software be customized to fit the processes they were used to. The team eventually yielded and undertook a massive customization program. As a result, the project, which was originally budgeted at $4 million, instead ended up taking three years longer than expected and costing $9 million.

Consider what happened in this example: The project started out with the sound business objective of better visibility into HR. But because process changes weren't addressed until after the technology had been designed and implemented, a disconnect cropped up between process and technology (see Fig. 1.2). Modifying this technology to match up with the processes cost millions.

Figure | 1.2

In Wilson's story, a disconnect resulted when process changes weren't addressed until after new technology had been finalized

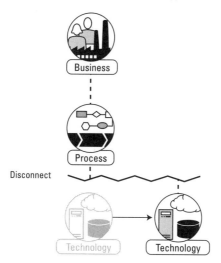

A better solution, of course, would have been to adjust what were essentially low-value HR processes to fit those that the software supported out of the box. But the consultants on the project didn't make the connection between the new software and its affect on existing processes. They never collaborated with the end-users to find out how their processes were carried out today, and never communicated how those processes would have to change. As a result, Wilson says, end-users fought change from day one, even though doing so cost millions in customization:

> Nobody likes change, and they don't want it imposed upon them. So they have to have the benefits clearly demonstrated to them before they'll actually move along and accept any kind of change. So the problem wasn't really the technology. The truth was, ninety percent of the functionality was there. But to make it work they would have had to spend significant time and effort reengineering their processes.

Projects that overlook processes when they make changes to technology do so at their peril. Instead, Wilson argues, companies need to acknowledge that process management is a central component of IT change:

> My early career background was as an industrial engineer, so I'm accustomed to applying the principles of process management. But some companies don't want to invest in the up-front planning that this takes. This is a mistake.

> People in leadership roles who kick these projects off often have a good understanding of what the end result will do and how it will affect them, but a lot of times they don't bother to communicate this to other people to get them involved in the process. As a result, the first time people are brought into a project is when it's being implemented and they're being trained on it. So you end up with a huge backlash and people fight this tooth and nail even though you tell them that eventually it'll benefit them. Until they can see it for themselves, they'll resist embracing new business processes.

Early involvement through process management settles issues up-front instead of forcing people to react later on. If they're brought in early and convinced that the new technology will impact them on a day-to-day basis, they're more willing to accept it, buy into new business processes, and make it work to their advantage.

When you just tell people to stand up and salute the flag they'll do it. But they won't believe it until they get involved and see for themselves the benefits of changing their processes.

What is Really Strategic?

This same struggle for process/technology alignment plays out with a different result in our next vignette. In the previous story, Wilson described how a company elected to customize packaged software to fit their specific business processes. These modifications ended up costing millions and delaying the project for years. The alternative, Wilson noted, was to embrace process management and forgo expensive customization, to leave the software as is, and instead to change the processes to fit what the application delivered out of the box.

Since no custom work is involved, this option immediately sounds appealing. But before you can let an enterprise software vendor dictate exactly how your company does business, you first have to ask a key question: What is really strategic? If the process you're considering changing is crucial to the business model, and a source of competitive advantage, it's probably best to let it drive technology changes. If not, however, the simplest solution may be to leave the software alone, and instead transform the processes accordingly.

Honorio Padron is President and CEO of Business Services at Exelon, an energy giant that was created by the merger of ComEd and PECO. During the merger, Padron tackled a project that seemed straightforward on the surface: implementing an integrated financial system for the newly merged business. But because employees didn't do a good job of evaluating what was really strategic, they almost fell into the same trap that Wilson described—customizing technology with great cost but small benefit.

It's human nature to magnify the importance of the things that take up most of our time and attention. It's no surprise, then, that during his integrated financial system project, Padron found that employees overemphasized the importance of unique business processes:

> In Exelon, you have two energy companies that are identical in what they do. Yet their financial processes had some significant differences that didn't really bring any strategic advantages. And in trying to merge these two types of financial processes, people were trying to come up with a third different way of doing things. Which, again, wouldn't have had any strategic advantages.

Some employees—we'll call them the "customizers,"—pushed for making highly specialized modifications to the ERP package so that it could support a new, third version of financial processes that was a mix of PECO's and ComEd's old ways of doing things. But to Padron, this seemed like the wrong approach: "These are really primitive processes. Unfortunately, even for these primitive processes, the perspective always starts from 'what I want to do' as opposed to 'let me see what the technology brings'."

Padron recognized that Exelon's unique HR processes weren't essential to the business, and eventually steered the team on a course that reflected this conclusion. Instead of making high-cost software customizations to fit low-value processes, he pushed the alternative approach: customize the processes to fit the software out of the box. As a result, Exelon was able to avoid the high cost of modifying their new HR software without any downside to the business.

In Padron's story, the customizers, who pushed for expensive software alterations, did so because their view of what was important was limited only to processes; in other words, there was a disconnect between the processes they had designed and the business objectives for the project (see Fig. 1.3). By not making this connection back to the business (and presumably forward to the technology where they would have figured out the true cost of sticking to their processes), the customizers failed to ask a crucial question: What is really strategic?

Figure **1.3**

Customizers pushed to modify technology to fit custom processes, while Padron elected to standardize low-value processes

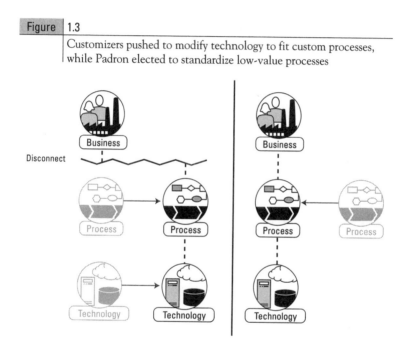

There's often a wrong assessment of what is strategic and what isn't. In my experience the things that are very strategic are also very proprietary in nature, like a Coca-Cola recipe. But beyond these obviously strategic things, what's really important is the ability to implement. It sounds very pragmatic, but it's essential.

This mistake is a common one in IT projects, Padron explains, because of how technology has been put to work in the business environment in the past:

At first we developed code from scratch that automated the processes that we were already doing. So we went from doing things inefficiently to doing things inefficiently but faster. Gradually, we've gotten to saying "now that I've got this tool maybe I can do it a little different." But this requires systemic thinking, and a lot of people have not moved to that level yet, of thinking of it in an integrated fashion.

Exelon's integrated financial system demonstrates this bias. The team took a myopic view that was based on the old paradigm. They approached technology as a tool to automate the processes that they designed in a vacuum. But Padron encouraged a more systemic approach: align business objectives with processes and with the new technology being implemented, and then make trade-offs based on an analysis of the complete, end-to-end picture.

The Synergy of Business and Technology Aligned

These real-world examples should provide notice to companies to sit up straight and take the business/technology disconnect seriously. But remember that so far our examples have only focused on what amounts to one side of the story; all IT projects don't end up being miserable failures, or at best, neutral results. When done right—when business, process, and technology progress hand in hand—they can act as a catalyst that drives some fundamental changes in how companies approach technology. Consider an example from Scott Hayward, Managing Director at JPMorgan Chase and Company and former chief operating officer (COO) of Investment Banking in the Americas at J.P. Morgan.

Industries like investment banking and consulting are notorious for their high employee turnover—especially in response to changing market conditions and the introduction of new and disruptive technologies. As a result, there's a lingering fear among banks and consulting firms that when employees leave they'll take their domain expertise and client relationships—the core of the business—out the door with them. To institutionalize this knowledge so that this information stays put even as employees come and go, firms often turn to call-reporting systems that capture client conversations. Other employees can then access these conversations to brush up on the latest client needs or to help them cross-sell other products and services.

On paper, call reporting seems to be a no-brainer for investment bankers. But in practice, Hayward received a less-than-enthusiastic response:

> Before I got to investment banking and while I was there between 1994 and 1998, I think we probably tried to implement call reporting—something that would capture our conversations with the client—no less than three or four times. Each time, it was just assumed that if we built the system people would use it, even without looking all the way upstream first. But instead, we found limited acceptance.

Despite the complimentary relationship between call-reporting technology and the banker's need to institutionalize client knowledge and relationships, the system went largely unused, and most client information continued to be stored in the same place that it had been before: in the employees' heads. According to Hayward, this disregard stemmed from a failure to modify the processes that the employees were accustomed to:

> The thing people overlooked was that they didn't go through a complete process: What are the objectives of the business? What's the strategy to achieve those objectives? What are the business processes to implement those strategies? And only then: what technologies do you use to enable you in those processes?

But this isn't Hayward's only experience with call reporting. "The other place that I've seen it," he says, "and the only place that I've seen it work, in fact, is where I am now in investment management."

Like before, call reporting was intended to service clients better, so that no matter where a client touched the organization, the employees would know the last conversation they had, what was on the client's mind, and what his or her needs and concerns were. These are crucial considerations anytime you have more than one person interfacing with a client, such as in JPMorgan Chase and Company's client-service model for investment management, which includes three points of contact: client advisors, portfolio managers, and account managers.

The call-reporting system was designed to capture information and share it between each of these groups, so that a client advisor, for example, wouldn't have to pick up the phone and get updates from the portfolio manager and account manager before talking to the client. "Anytime someone met with a prospect they were trying to convert to a client, or anytime they met with an existing client whether it was a telephone call or in-person meeting," Hayward explains, "those things would get captured."

Like in Hayward's previous experience in investment banking, however, there was a risk that despite its promise, the system might go unused. Hayward's team countered this possibility by establishing a system of incentives that encouraged employees to actually modify their business processes and take advantage of the call-reporting tool:

> Basically, people were told that if information wasn't reflected in the call reporting tool, whether it was from the pipeline or new awards we had won, then they wouldn't get credit for it. So the head of sales would say "if I don't see it in the system, then I don't recognize you did it. You get no credit for it. And when we sit down on a quarterly basis and review your progress, you won't get credit for it then either."

> The metrics, then, were deliberately built around not just rolling out the technology, but instead encouraging the end-to-end, business-process-technology change that the project required.

Not surprisingly, the client advisors took to the system and achieved the business advantages the project was intended for in the first place.

Consider how Hayward's successful call-reporting project came to pass. At first, the business recognized an opportunity for innovation. Then, they tasked the IT department to build a new system. But at the same time they made it a priority to stress to the client advisors (with a very big stick) why it was important to use it. So when the system finally arrived, the user base was already on board (see Fig. 1.4).

Figure	1.4

Hayward's call-reporting project maintained alignment between business, process, and technology, with impressive results

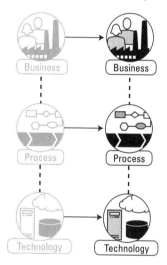

How Alignment Goes Above and Beyond

Compared to some of the horror stories recounted in this chapter, Hayward's call-reporting vignette looks pretty good. In fact, it looks really good. But, in a sense, it only represents a neutral outcome: there wasn't any disconnect, but at the same time, being aligned from business through process through technology hadn't chalked up any pluses beyond what the system was designed to do in the first place.

Hayward's account of this successful call-reporting system, however, doesn't end with just implementing the system and seeing end-users adopt it. As the employees became more familiar with the system and saw firsthand what it could do for them, their attitude towards it changed. Usually, just getting people to take a look at and consider using new features is a battle unto itself. But the most powerful advantage, Hayward concludes, is when you actually get end-users to ask for more functionality instead of needing to have managers cram it down their throats:

> We started to have client advisors or client portfolio managers call the technology team that built the system and the business person who had responsibility for it and say: "Can you build in something so that when I write my call report and put in action steps, it automatically sends a note to the person who's responsible for doing that action step? And as we get closer to the due date of that action step, can it then monitor whether or not it's been completed, and send a reminder when it gets close to the completion date?"

> Now, management didn't ask for that; the end user did. The people who are actually on the front lines asked for that. That's nirvana, in my opinion, when you've designed technology directly into how you do your business.

These ideas from client advisors and portfolio managers got Hayward's management team thinking about some enhancements of their own:

> One of the things that we had been trying to do for a long time was to get the investment management team to cross sell more, so naturally we were looking for information about whether they were doing it and if so, how much (for example, they had specific targets on the number of private equity sales they needed to achieve, the number of real estate sales or conversations they needed to achieve, etc.). Specifically, we wanted to know how much time they were spending on new client acquisition or cross selling as opposed to retention.

All of this stuff is useful for managers, but it's also useful for the users, because then they can say: "you know I spent a lot of time focusing on private equity, and that tells me that the nature of my client base is more focused on private equity. And so, this type of enhancement would help users know the mind of their client better."

What ultimately evolved in this case is really quite remarkable: the project put in motion a cycle of innovation that cross-pollinated ideas across boundaries between business and technology. Managers have been known to gripe that IT specialists with little understanding of the business are given too much control over IT projects. At the same time, CIO's worry that employees with only a limited understanding of technology are asking coders for the impossible. But by aligning business, process, and technology, Hayward's call-reporting project shows that neither of these concerns has to be true. Innovative ideas can come from anywhere, be understood by everybody, and then be put into place with a mutual understanding of opportunities, goals, and responsibilities. But this happens only after a crucial prerequisite has been met: alignment between business, process, and technology.

What To Make of These Stories

These stories are a lot to digest all at once. But even if the particulars of one anecdote vs another still seem a bit overwhelming, there are a couple of key conclusions that can be made.

First, the business/technology disconnect isn't just the stuff of analyst reports and magazine articles. In one form or another, people grapple with the disconnect in every industry from old-line manufacturing to bleeding-edge biotech, and when disconnects crop up between business, process, and technology, it causes serious problems that impact the bottom line. To make this point, I've looked to acknowledged industry leaders—people whose opinions and experiences carry real weight. So when they approach the business technology disconnect soberly and seriously, then you should as well.

Second, and more important, a common undercurrent runs beneath each of these scenarios: companies that employ technology in alignment with sound business objectives succeed, while enterprises whose IT projects have fallen out of line with business objectives fail. This is an important lesson to learn for both business executives and IT leaders: without a dedicated approach to coordinate their efforts, it's impossible to make sure that IT projects will work with—rather than against—the business.

2

Approaching a Solution

THE DISASTER STORIES from the previous chapter should
debunk once and for all the myth that the business/technology
disconnect is just a figment of the imagination for business journalists and industry analysts. Clearly, professionals need a solution
to fix the catastrophic losses, failed projects, and missed deadlines
that the disconnect causes.

But, as any medical researcher would no doubt tell you, recog-
nizing a disease and coming up with a cure are different proposi-
tions entirely. To get from a problem to a solution, you often need
to view the present through the discerning lens of the past. For
BTM, this means understanding IT's evolution from a purely tactical exercise in its earliest days, to a full-fledged strategic partner
with its counterparts in the business. As the function changed,
aligning business and technology—a responsibility that had been

second tier—became progressively more important and introduced new challenges for the IT department. By addressing these challenges the principles, activities, and governance that make up BTM help to align business and technology and to avoid real-world disconnects like those presented in Ch. 1.

BTM and the Office of the CIO

Although the effort to align business and technology needs to include many stakeholders, ultimately, there is one group that should take primary responsibility: the chief information officer and his or her immediate staff, or the office of the CIO. Some companies prefer to give this position a different title—vice president of IS or director of IT, for example. At the end of the day, however, these positions are mostly interchangeable with the CIO in the sense that their primary responsibility is managing the corporate IT department.

IT, like any other major business function, is both highly complex and unique to individual companies and business units. This chapter does not attempt to present an authoritative view on what functions an IT department should include—you could write books and books about the responsibilities of the IT department and still hardly scratch the surface. Instead, what's important to pick up from this chapter is that broad trends describe how the function has evolved (see Fig. 2.1), and emerging challenges for the IT department point to a new approach for solving the disconnect.

The Operational Era

Most early IT departments consisted of a few secluded programmers huddled (figuratively and often literally) around a mainframe system that served the entire enterprise. In keeping with the purely tactical human resources and financial systems that they supported, these primitive departments were considered cost cen-

Figure 2.1

As the IT function has evolved, its business focus has increased dramatically

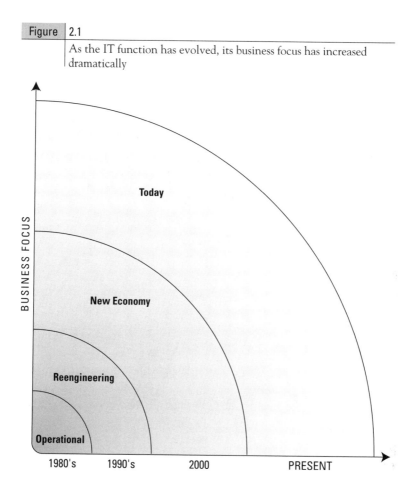

ters that fell under the responsibility of business unit heads or the corporate CFO.

These early IT departments assumed responsibilities such as setting up mainframes, managing early networks of personal computers (PCs), and backing up corporate data. In the end, this was just a supporting role: IT departments either provided back-office support directly, (managing a database of customer information, for example) or developed systems (such as accounting platforms) that were designed to automate back-office functions. These operational tasks didn't give IT much clout with executives, and during the operational era, the department frequently struggled to earn the respect and trust of their peers in the business.

Reengineering

The second phase of IT's evolution happened in response to the explosion of business process reengineering, or BPR, during the early 1990s. Advances in technology like client/server computing encouraged management to envision a world where enterprise software could be used to automate business processes and stream-line operations. In a reflection of the period's challenging business climate, reengineering was used as a pretense for downsizing: Technology, it was reasoned, would either replace workers out-right, or at the least improve their productivity and allow them to assume new responsibilities, which would make extra workers unnecessary.

The IT department evolved in response to BPR to include not only back-office operations, but also deployment of the systems that promised to automate the enterprise. Still, however, the func-tion focused on the technology and let others handle business decisions: Representatives from business units would pass along a description of the systems that they wanted—at times something as simple as a vendor and package—and then the IT department would take over, develop or deploy the system, and hand a fin-ished product back to the business.

These reengineering programs weren't always successful, since having software that was able to execute a process didn't auto-matically make people change their behavior, or guarantee for that matter, that the process embedded in the software was an improvement over its manual predecessor. In any event, IT's inter-action with the business expanded dramatically during this period as they were asked to develop and deploy new systems that would automate business functionality.

The New Economy

When the New Economy burst onto the scene, the IT depart-ment, like all things related to technology, became larger than life. Many companies responded to the astronomical market capitaliza-tion of dotcoms and other startups by creating semi-autonomous "e-business" divisions and giving strategic control over them to the office of the CIO and other senior IT managers. In radical cases, companies elected to actually spin off a dotcom to handle their Internet business, with IT executives as senior managers, and sometimes the CIO as the new company's chief executive.

In either of these cases, both the office of the CIO and IT workers in general found themselves with new, strategic ("e-strategic" perhaps?) accountability. One thing to note here, however, is that these business responsibilities were limited to either the e-business division or the spin-off—they were largely distinct from the business as a whole.

Like many executives, pundits, and analysts caught up in New Economy hype, these newly minted executives frequently failed to reconcile dramatic advances in technology with sound business objectives. As a result, many e-business divisions and spin-offs pursued a strategy that might best be described as technology for technology's sake—where real business objectives took a backseat to IT trends like CRM and e-marketplaces.

Today

Today, of course, mainframe-era IT, reengineering, and the New Economy bubble are all things of the past, and the IT function has changed once again. With the retreat of New Economy excesses, it would be tempting to speculate that the department has relinquished its strategic responsibilities. Instead, however, both the office of the CIO and the IT department in general have been forced to assume even broader business responsibilities. Companies aren't abandoning ambitious technology projects. Instead, they are demanding real, bottom-line results from them. And, more than any other group, it's the office of the CIO and the IT department who are being asked to deliver.

While the specific responsibilities of the IT department can vary from company to company (and even from business unit to business unit in large conglomerates), in general, today's IT department has business responsibilities that touch nearly every aspect of the function: developing and customizing software that improves how the business functions; controlling costs and maximizing efficiency through project management; implementing

The Changing Role of the CIO

"I've interviewed a lot of CIOs over the years, and it's always interesting to see the migration of the profession. I think right now the best CIOs would come in and talk as much about the business equation as they would talk about the IT infrastructure.

What today's CIOs really have to do is get into the minds of the business leaders—the CEO, COO, division heads—and find out what differentiates their product lines, their businesses, from anybody else. What are they hoping to gain in value against their competitors? Or in delivery to their customers? And once the CIO really focuses on the drivers of business success, then they can translate that back into 'how can I build my IT infrastructure to get a better picture of where we're going and where we stand on that strategy?'

Once they see that, then when they go into meetings and start talking about technology investment, they can speak not just in terms of 'this software has a payback of a year', but instead about 'how IT impacts the business drivers and strategic differentiators for the business.' And 'if we put these pieces in place it allows us to do these things that do truly differentiate us.'

And that's a whole different level of discussion than CIOs have had in the past. It's the value that IT is going to deliver to the business, and it's the stepping-stone towards IT being an integral part of the way you pull off a business strategy. That's the mindset that successful CIO's are carrying with them now. So they have as much of an energy to want to learn about the needs of the business as they do about the data centers, hardware, networks, and so on."

– **Jack Mollen,** *senior vice president of Human Resources, EMC Corporation* new hardware and software; managing strategic suppliers (including vendors, consultants, and partners) to maximize the value of the relationship; supporting operations and infrastructure, including the systems that automate crucial components of the business (CRM, supply chain management [SCM], HR platforms, etc.) and the IT infrastructure (servers, networks, PCs, and so on); managing change in the business; and maintaining the crucial corporate data that helps managers throughout the enterprise to make intelligent and informed decisions. Each of these areas is clearly related to the function's traditional technology focus. At the same time, however, each requires a sound mastery of the business which hasn't historically been IT's strongpoint.

Emerging Challenges

Obviously, the increasing business focus that's demanded of the IT department is having a profound effect upon the function. Some of the challenges that the department faced five, ten, and even twenty years ago—such as delivering new technology faster and more efficiently—continue to be crucial components of the job. However, the growing business focus of today's IT department also emphasizes new challenges:

- **Identify opportunities** for business innovation that come from technology, and then coordinate with the rest of the business to hone strategy accordingly
- **Speak the language** of the business to improve IT's credibility amongst business peers
- **Unify services** across multiple, otherwise-distinct business units
- **Mitigate the risk of change** in the face of continuously evolving technology
- **Do more with less** by extending the lifecycle of human and capital assets

Identify Opportunities for Business Innovation

The first challenge facing today's increasingly business-focused IT departments is to monitor technology advances for opportunities that could facilitate business innovation. In effect, this represents the logical evolution of the strategic role for IT executives that emerged during the New Economy. Unlike during the bubble, however, today's executives are expected not only to identify opportunities, but also to coordinate with the business to chart a single, coherent strategy for the corporation.

This process involves communication both from business to technology and vice versa. The business-to-technology dialogue is more straightforward: Important technology decisions—which projects to green light, what standards to set, which vendors should become preferred partners—should always be made with one eye on business impact. To promote this type of exchange, the CIO has to be both a technology visionary and an accomplished business executive.

Communicating from the technology side of the house to help shape business strategy is important as well. One of the major roles for the modern IT department is to interpret emerging technology trends for the business. The CIO needs to be proactive in this regard by taking potential innovations directly to the senior leadership team, communicating the opportunities and pressures, and steering the business strategy appropriately. It's the CIO, in other words, who makes sure that the leadership understands technology, or at least the role that technology should play in transforming the business. To accomplish this, IT needs to be a storyteller who identifies promising technology scenarios; communicates the benefits, risks, and challenges to the business; and then helps to coordinate between business strategy and the technology that supports it.

Speak the Same Language as the Business

The second challenge is to rebuild the faith in technology that was lost with the collapse of the New Economy bubble. One way for IT to reestablish credibility is to speak the same language as the rest of the business: that of profit, loss, return on investment (ROI), and so on. During the mainframe days, when IT was still a tactical exercise, the department was able to pawn this function off to the finance department and the CFO. And during the New Economy, of course, IT was essentially given carte blanche to pursue technology projects with reckless abandon—and little concern for financial metrics.

But now, the collision between IT's continuing strategic relevance and the end of the era of irrational spending demands that projects be justified according to business value and risk—just like any other company initiative. This is important for tactical projects, of course, where costs are justified by direct financial returns. But it's even more essential when the IT department has identified technology trends that it believes will contribute in the future, but that can't yet be reduced to dollars and cents.

In a sense, the IT department's role here is similar to that of the CFO and the finance department. Like the CIO, the CFO is responsible for interpreting complex information (financial data instead of technological advances), and then identifying trends and opportunities that will impact strategy. Unlike the CIO, however, the CFO has automatic credibility to the business by virtue of their financial focus. CIOs need to earn their seat at the table, and the most effective way to do this is to become bilingual: to be able to speak the language of technology to identify opportunities, trends, and threats, but then also to be able to communicate this information to business executives in the language that they expect from their peers.

Unify Services Across Multiple Business Units

The CIO, unlike other business unit heads, doesn't have a specific focus limited to the unit that he or she manages. Some of the tasks for which the IT department is responsible (establishing a development methodology or selecting preferred vendors and implementation partners, for example), do service the department directly. But the vast majority of projects that IT undertakes are designed and deployed for end-users outside the department.

First, and most obviously, there's the complete universe of employees who rely on IT for things like voice mail, PCs, and mobile handheld devices. Then, there are vertically integrated functions that rely on enterprise applications to do their jobs: an

HR administration system for human resources, CRM for the sales force, and so on. And the complete group of "clients" for the IT department extends even beyond the borders of the business to include external consultants who need input for a project, or business partners (like distributors) who want access to internal information (such as inventory levels and available to promise).

In this regard, the CIO's role is somewhat similar to that of the CEO: their sphere of influence includes every part of the business. Dawn Lepore, the former CIO at discount broker Charles Schwab, tells Harvard Business Review that she believes the two positions "do share a number of characteristics. Most unit heads need to have a very focused perspective," she explains. "CIOs must also be focused; additionally, they must be able to consider the business as a whole, as the CEO does."[1]

An important offshoot of this broad responsibility is that IT frequently finds itself brokering a compromise between distinct business units. For example: In order to move from a decentralized IT environment where each business unit supports their own IT functions to a centralized model where the entire enterprise shares certain common services, some units have to sacrifice the individual customization to which they've grown accustomed. Each unit, of course, will lobby for central services that are as close as possible to their previous, homegrown systems. It's the IT department's role to arbitrate between these competing groups and settle on the appropriate trade-offs that are necessary to find common ground.

Mitigate the Risk of Change

The IT department's fourth challenge is to manage functional IT change in the face of technology that, even after the New Economy collapse, continues to evolve at a blistering pace. To manage change, IT first needs to anticipate the impact of making business and technology decisions. This impact is then weighed against potential downside risks to separate smart ventures from reckless gambles.

The idea that IT is closely linked to change management isn't new. Since the middle 1990s when reengineering and process automation were hot topics, one of the IT department's key responsibilities has been to balance the promises of a new technology against the disruption that it might cause in the business. (According to findings in an Emory University study, large-scale failed technology initiatives can depress stock price by as much as 1.75%.[2]) A big lesson that we can learn from ERP and e-commerce disaster stories is to not underestimate the importance of anticipating change to avoid delays, overcome employee inertia, and minimize unforeseen costs. This ability will be crucial today going forward, as technology becomes even more pervasive.

Extend the Life Cycle of Human and Capital Assets

Finally, today's IT department is being asked to tackle more projects than ever before—while simultaneously grappling with shrinking head counts and limited budgets for new hardware, software, and services. The pressure to "do more with less" weighs heavily upon the shoulders of CIOs in both good times and bad. When the value of IT spending is being questioned, allocating resources efficiently is obviously of the utmost importance. But even during good times, CIOs are still asked to do more with less: When IT spending is on an upswing, the market for skilled employees becomes extremely tight, and companies have trouble hiring new resources with in-demand skills.

How BTM Meets These Challenges

These five challenges—identify opportunities for business innovation, speak the same language as the business, unify services across multiple business units, mitigate the risk of change, and do more with less—combine to make the IT function more focused on the business than ever before. Not surprisingly, then, the approaches, tools, and techniques that IT has relied on in the past—development environments, project management, and object modeling, for example—aren't perfectly suited to today's increasing business responsibilities.

To give the office of the CIO and the IT department the ammunition they need to tackle these five challenges, we need a new approach: the principles, activities, and governance that make up BTM. By mapping each of these back to today's challenges, we can see how BTM represents the missing piece of the puzzle that finally helps to close the business/technology disconnect (see Table 2.1).

Table	2.1

Five challenges for IT point to a new approach: the combination of principles, activities, and governance that makes up BTM

	Identify Opportunities for Business Innovation	Speak the Same Language as the Business	Unify Services Across Multiple Business Units	Mitigate the Risk of Change	Extend the Life Cycle of Human and Capital Assets
The Principles of BTM					
Utilize Predictive Modeling	●			●	
Instill Collaborative Decision-Making		●	●		
Reuse Knowledge and Assets			●	●	●
The Activities of BTM					
Business Model Definition	●			●	
Process Optimization	●			●	
Technology Automation	●			●	
Governing with BTM					
Strategic Direction	●	●			
Tactical Control			●	●	●

From Challenges to the Principles of BTM

The principles of BTM represent underlying capabilities that need to be in place before companies can tackle BTM. By themselves, the principles of BTM aren't sufficient to align business and technology. But in order to do business model definition, process optimization, and technology automation—the activities of BTM that do the lion's share of aligning business and technology—companies first need to be able to put three principles to work.

The first principle of BTM, *Utilize Predictive Modeling*, helps companies to construct a blueprint during IT projects so that they can preview change before implementation begins. This, of course, is a powerful mechanism for reducing risk, since potential problems can be identified and avoided up-front, rather than later on, when putting out fires results in costly recoding and abandoned projects. At the same time, models can be powerful props for storytelling—a skill that the IT department needs in order to communicate opportunities for business innovation to a non-technical audience of executives.

The second principle of BTM is to *Instill Collaborative Decision-Making*. Recall that matching technology opportunities with business strategy is an important aspect of the CIO's role. This requires coming to a consensus between the strategy team and the CIO. Without promoting a dialogue to help IT professionals speak the language of the business, companies maintain by default the distinct business and technology strategies that caused such catastrophic harm during the New Economy bubble. Collaborative decision-making is also a crucial skill for coordinating between business units to determine which IT services to centralize and which to delegate to individual units.

Make Knowledge and Assets Reusable is the final principle of BTM. Companies can help to mitigate risks during IT projects by recycling designs and strategies that have worked in the past. Also, reuse can help to promote common enterprise standards for IT, and also to drive otherwise disparate divisions to make use of existing resources (such as applications and hardware) rather than building their own from scratch. Finally, IT managers recognize that reuse enables them to wring the maximum amount of productivity out of their existing resources, allowing them to do more with less in periods of both boom and bust.

From Challenges to the Activities of BTM

The activities of BTM—including *Business Model Definition*, *Process Optimization*, and *Technology Automation*—represent the formal design mechanism for developing a blueprint that aligns business, process, and technology. These tasks help to construct models and create cross-links to check for alignment between the three. During business model definition, teams capture a snapshot of the enterprise in order to capture and communicate strategy. Process optimization, the second activity, identifies and diagrams the processes that are required to support the business model. Finally, during technology automation, the team identifies the applications and systems that will support their business processes. Together, the business, process, and technology models make up an end-to-end enterprise model, or a blueprint for enterprise architecture.

To complete these activities, employees have to make important design decisions, evaluate multiple scenarios, and choose between imperfect solutions. By previewing these decisions in the form of models for business, process, and technology, the team can anticipate problems and reduce the risk of change. At the same time, modeling helps business and IT professionals to discover new uses for technology that can result in business innovation.

From Challenges to the Governance of BTM

Finally, BTM helps to govern both the *Strategic Direction* of and *Tactical Control* over IT. The mechanism that BTM uses to set strategic direction is the IT portfolio, which views projects as a portfolio of investments to be optimized according to both financial and non-financial metrics. By forcing teams to attach metrics to projects, portfolio management helps IT professionals to speak the language of business. And since enterprise models are crucial tools for identifying business opportunities, BTM can also help to synchronize developments in IT with ideas for innovating business strategy.

Governance also helps the CIO to maintain tactical control over IT projects to make sure that they deliver the maximum business value by managing both quality and cost. The tactical control that BTM enables helps both to unify how projects are carried out across multiple business units, and to establish standards and best practices to mitigate the risk that projects will fail. Also, it promotes the reuse of assets across multiple projects in order to extend the life cycle of human and capital assets.

A New Approach

By meeting the challenges that IT departments face in their search for alignment, BTM fills a void that had long been ignored despite its yearly position on top ten lists of CIO concerns; despite its frequent appearance in magazine articles and analyst reports; and despite its first-name familiarity among practitioners in the field. With BTM, however, the office of the CIO and the IT department have a new weapon to wield against the disconnect. And while the IT community would undoubtedly preferred to have come across such a solution a long time ago, in a sense the timing couldn't be better. Today, IT departments are searching desperately for an antidote to the pounding headache left over from their New Economy binge. This disruption has driven IT to reexamine its role in the business, survey the damage that the business/technology disconnect has caused, and ultimately recognize the opportunity for a new approach that aligns business and technology.

The Principles
of BTM

"Important principles may, and must, be inflexible."
– *Abraham Lincoln*

THE DESIGN FOR YOUR IMAGINARY DREAM HOUSE is finally
complete. Over the course of several meetings, you, Janet (the
architect), and Robert (the contractor) have collaborated to
draw up plans for your new home that live up to everybody's
exacting standards. As your last meeting wraps up, you walk
both Janet and Robert to the door, shake each of their hands,
and thank them for a job well-done. Once they have gone, you
return to the kitchen table, where the plans are still spread out.

Even though the three of you spent hours poring through the details of the design—details that fall far outside your own architectural comfort zone—the entire process went off without a hitch. You couldn't possibly hope to understand most of the decisions that Janet and Robert grappled with, but thanks to their expert approach they were still able to tell a simple and concise story about what it will be like to live in the house when it's done, which is exactly what you needed to know to help get the design right. Obviously, this method wasn't just the result of good fortune: Both Janet and Robert are highly trained professionals who have spent years honing their crafts in academic and professional environments.

Only by mastering a set of underlying principles can professionals like Janet and Robert ensure that their approach runs as smoothly as it did in your dream house project. These principles provide the basic building blocks that are necessary for professionals to design buildings that deliver the most value to their clients. Three examples of the underlying principles that are necessary for designing a home are drafting (including subjects like orthographic, axonometric, and oblique drawing systems; dimensioning, and the alphabet of lines), structural engineering (trade math; properties of materials; and designing the skeleton that supports the building, including beams, joints, walls, and so on), and standard blueprint notation (including recognized symbols for plumbing and electricity, as well as architecture and engineering elements in the blueprint).

Without their expertise in areas like these, Janet (the architect) and Robert (the contractor) wouldn't have the tools that they need to bridge the gap between their specialties and your demands as a client. Similarly, Janet (the consultant) and Robert (the CIO) need to adhere to certain principles before they can use BTM to bridge the gap between business and technology. No architect or contractor who expects to get a commission would approach a potential client without an encyclopedic knowledge of drafting, structural engineering, and standard blueprint notation. And no CIO or consultant should expect to align business and technology if they can't apply the three principles of BTM: *Utilize Predictive Modeling, Instill Collaborative Decision-Making, and Make Knowledge and Assets Reusable.*

In This Part...

Part II: The Principles of BTM introduces the principles that provide a solid underpinning for aligning business and technology. The first principle, to utilize predictive modeling, enables companies to preview decisions and designs before beginning costly implementation. At the same time, it helps the team to embrace impact analysis—a technique that replaces myopic decisions with a holistic view of the IT project. The second principle of BTM, instill collaborative decision-making, applies to both vertical collaboration between members of the same project team, and horizontal collaboration, where amorphous "great ideas" are communicated across departmental and project team boundaries. Finally, the last principle, making knowledge and assets reusable, encompasses knowledge management, where companies capture documents and relationships that can be targeted to relevant employees, and create a reusable repository of model designs, which helps to establish standards and minimize rework.

3

Modeling, Collaboration, Reuse

AT A SOMEWHAT ABSTRACT LEVEL, everybody seems to have a pretty good idea of what a principle is: a "theoretical underpinning", or maybe a "guiding purpose", or a "pillar." These amorphous statements are well and good in the abstract. But for the purposes of BTM we need to be more specific: Before you can even think about using the activities of BTM to align business and technology, you first have to embrace three mutually supportive principles of BTM:

- Utilize Predictive Modeling
- Instill Collaborative Decision-Making
- Make Knowledge and Assets Reusable

How the Principles Work Together

The first principle of BTM, *Utilize Predictive Modeling*, is the most important day-to-day task in BTM. In the broadest sense, predictive modeling is a technique that can be applied to any area where underlying details threaten to obscure overall decisions; where real-world scenarios can be decomposed into distinct elements; and where hidden interdependencies between these elements make it difficult to visualize the overall effect of modifying an individual piece of the puzzle.

Once companies start to utilize predictive modeling, the other principles of BTM automatically become important as well. Modeling is an inherently social activity that draws a broad community of contributors, from executives to business managers to process analysts and technology specialists. Their broad base of interests and varying degrees of expertise makes it essential to *Instill Collaborative Decision-Making*, the second principle of BTM. Modelers also need a way to capture and share the intellectual capital that they create. To achieve this, they need to *Make Knowledge and Assets Reusable*, the third and final principle of BTM.

Utilize Predictive Modeling

The core benefit of the first principle of BTM, whether it goes by "modeling" or something else like "design" or "blueprinting," is that it helps to visualize the end goal before beginning costly—and often irreversible—implementation. In the broadest sense, a model is a virtual representation of a real thing. By manipulating this representation, modelers can preview a solution and address design flaws before they manifest themselves in the final product.

There's a widespread and unfortunate misconception that modeling is a highly technical exercise that needs to be tackled by a team of trained specialists. At times, of course, modeling can be found in pocket-protector-friendly environs like nuclear engineering, macroeconomics, or genetics. But this is more a reflection of inherent simplicity than any tendency towards complexity: By helping to simplify design and decision-making, modeling actually clears up complex problems, which is why it shows up in these areas. When observers mistake modeling for a technical, complicated exercise, they're essentially confusing the message (such as modeling a complex chemical reaction) with the messenger (modeling itself).

Some of the most powerful varieties of modeling (such as the spreadsheet example we'll look at in a moment) allow even non-technical users to preview change, or to "predict," before putting new ideas into practice. This, of course, is where the "predictive" in "utilize predictive modeling" comes from. It's also why modeling is such an important part of BTM: It helps to predict the impact of business and IT change by becoming the "aim" in "ready, aim, fire."

BTM puts modeling to work as an innovation infrastructure for IT projects. During the design stage, it functions as a blueprint in which teams can set clear goals and flesh out a solution before actually writing code. In the build, test, and deploy stages, the model acts as a reference point to orient ongoing work and to help guide last-minute modifications in the event that unforeseen challenges and opportunities pop up. By playing these important roles, modeling helps the IT project team pre-empt costly mistakes and improve the quality of the systems that they develop.

BTM's use of modeling isn't just about making incremental improvements to an existing process, however. In addition to relatively modest gains in efficiency, modeling also empowers BTM with other, more dramatic capabilities that can literally reinvent how IT projects approach the "aim" part of "ready, aim, fire." This sounds like a bold claim. However, there is ample precedent from previous modeling revolutions—such as object modeling, computer-aided design/computer-aided manufacturing (CAD/CAM), and especially financial modeling and the spreadsheet—to suggest that modeling can indeed accelerate critical business activities.

Financial Modeling and the Spreadsheet

Before the personal computer revolution, Wall Street analysts performed complex spreadsheet calculations using only a simple calculator. This process was completely inflexible, prone to mistakes, and thoroughly mind-numbing. In order to make changes to a model (whether to vary inputs or correct mistakes), analysts had to rework the entire thing, a process that—needless to say—was inefficient.

In 1978, Harvard Business School student Dan Bricklin recognized an opportunity to automate this tedious process using software and the rapidly maturing PC. He, along with former MIT classmate Bob Frankston, founded Software Arts, Inc., and introduced the VisiCalc spreadsheet to the market. Almost overnight, VisiCalc transformed how financial analysts worked.[1]

The obvious advantage to Bricklin and Frankston's innovation was efficiency. Complex models that once took hours to update could now be modified with a few keystrokes. Not surprisingly, spreadsheets like VisiCalc became the de facto standard for financial modeling, and frustrated business school students and financial analysts clamored all over each other to put the new technology to use. The demand for spreadsheets was so overwhelming, in fact, that it is frequently credited with creating the initial boom market for business PCs.

But the real revolution that the spreadsheet kicked off wasn't just about efficiency and automation. By unburdening analysts from the pedantic work of manual calculations, spreadsheets lowered the marginal cost of evaluating new scenarios from thousands of dollars to almost zero. This, in turn, encouraged experimentation and creativity. The same employee who once spent days perfecting a single model could suddenly produce several alternatives in a single afternoon.

Spreadsheets kicked off an industry-wide movement towards experimentation that revolutionized how analysts—and the financial services industry—worked. By allowing workers to easily create and analyze the impact of multiple scenarios, spreadsheets and predictive modeling encouraged a culture of rapid prototyping and innovation, or impact analysis, that is as applicable for aligning business and technology as it is for the financial world.

From Modeling to Impact Analysis

Impact analysis lets teams alter input factors, create multiple output scenarios, evaluate the end-to-end impact of each, and eventually select and implement the optimal solution. This stands in direct opposition to conventional, linear problem-solving techniques, where decision-makers analyze sub-problems at each logical step along the way, and then assume that the overall impact of their choices is the best one (see Fig. 3.1).

Figure	3.1

Linear problem solving decomposes sub-problems along the way, while impact analysis examines the end-to-end impact of multiple decisions

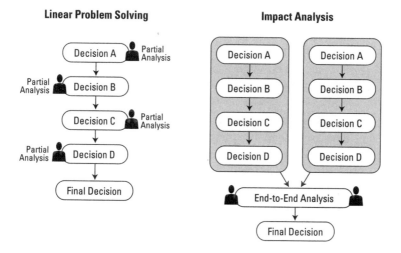

Like modeling in general, impact analysis can be used to address a broad range of activities. For example, it is often used in supply chain planning for advanced, data-driven calculations that optimize a particular function (such as inventory costs) given unique inputs and constraints (such as market demand, logistical restrictions, and manufacturing capabilities). At the other end of the spectrum, impact analysis can address much simpler problems. A good example is Dell Computer's build-to-order website, where potential buyers test multiple PC configurations until they find a good match between the features they want and the cost they can afford to pay. In both of these cases, individuals vary inputs, rules translate these inputs to outputs, and team members compare the impact of multiple scenarios to choose the solution that fits their needs.

In order for impact analysis to work, the scenario being modeled should conform to three guidelines:

- **It should have easily identified inputs, rules, and outputs:** Impact analysis requires employees to define a set of inputs and then link these to outputs using predefined rules. These inputs and outputs are often quantitative (as in the supply chain optimization problem), but they can also be qualitative (such as the PC configuration options). To produce good results, these criteria—the rules that link them—must accurately reflect the real-world problem.

- **It should have multiple configuration options and decision factors:** Problems that contain only a few inputs and outputs aren't suited to impact analysis because the effect of altering inputs is often obvious. When the outputs are less intuitive on the other hand, impact analysis can help decision makers experiment to identify good solutions.

- **The relative cost of implementation to design is high:** Scenarios that are inexpensive to design but difficult to implement are ideally suited to impact analysis. Our ongoing analogy to an architectural blueprint is a case in point here: It's unrealistic for you to contract a builder to build five houses so that you can choose the one you like the most. It's entirely possible, however, that you may choose to commission an architect to draft five blueprints. You can then compare them, choose your favorite, and give it to the contractor to build. This is where the synergy between modeling and impact analysis really comes into play: Predictive modeling is a powerful tool for lowering design costs, and so a crucial driver for impact analysis.

Anticipating Unforeseen Ripple Effects

These three characteristics combine to highlight a point that is crucial to understanding why impact analysis fits well with

BTM. Disconnects between business, process, and technology are often introduced when individual decisions have unforeseen effects on the blueprint as a whole. "Projects lack a holistic view," PACCAR CIO Pat Flynn says, "because we tend to look at it as a linear process: decompose the problem, decompose the problem, decompose the problem, make a decision. But it's very hard to go back and say 'that decision has a set of ripple effects'."

Consider an example: A team of process analysts is working on a project for which they need to diagram the approval process for purchasing non-production goods. Using conventional methods, their actions would be informed by an in-depth analysis of the decision. They would start by gathering as much data as possible: the current approval process; the complete list of approved suppliers, products, and contract types; the organizational hierarchy and current purchasing limits for each employee; the existing technology assets that automate this process; and the supporting systems such as hardware and networks. After pulling all this information together, they would weigh the data, diagram a process flow that best fits the given constraints, and sign off on the decision.

This sounds reasonable at first glance, but it fails to take into account any ripple effects that might spread from this individual decision. Let's say, for instance, that one supplier relied on a legacy order-processing system to interface with our example company's procurement system. Let's also say that when our team reengineered their approval process, they did so in a way that made it incompatible with this legacy application. And finally, let's say that this particular supplier accounted for 40% of all purchases of non-production goods last year. Clearly, this should compel the process analysts to revisit their decision. But without impact analysis they wouldn't find out about the ripple effects until it was too late.

The Perceived of Value of Models and the Whitespace Problem

Before they can get started with modeling and impact analysis, companies need to overcome a couple of obstacles. The most obvious is the common perception that the time it takes to develop a model during the design stage is better spent on implementation. This is due in part to previous experiences with models that were frighteningly inaccessible to all but the most die-hard experts. Since non-specialists (a group that frequently includes managers and other authority figures) couldn't experience their value firsthand, they assumed that the models were a waste of time. The shorthand solution to this concern is to make the modeling environment friendly enough for a broad range of people to pick it up and experiment according to their own level of comfort. A good example of this is a financial model whose inner workings may be exceedingly complex but whose overall purpose is clearly communicated to a non-technical audience.

In extreme cases, however, modeling can be a waste of time. This happens when people get stuck in an endless design loop; By continuously tweaking the model in the quest for a perfect solution, they never get around to actually implementing what they're working on. The way to counter this impulse is by linking a system of real-time monitoring to metrics, goals, and objectives that are established at the beginning of the project. This implies a link to both project and performance management that is crucial to any type of modeling.

The other obstacle that stands in the way of modeling and impact analysis is the gap that exists between multiple models and between models and the real world. These gaps are referred to as "whitespace," and they're familiar culprits in cases where modeling hasn't been successful. Typically, the tools that are available to IT workers to model business, process, and technology are disjointed, and so they tend to exacerbate rather than overcome the whitespace problem. Most are geared either to a particular task (process modeling, object modeling, or knowledge management) or to broad horizontal activities (word processing, drawing, or spreadsheets). A consequence of these disjointed offerings is that companies tend to use multiple tools and environments to develop their models. When changes are made in one environment (say a process diagram) they aren't automatically reflected in other areas (a requirements document or business strategy memo, for example). Without integrated tools, the project team has to proactively anticipate ripple effects to keep their models aligned.

The Advantages of Predictive Modeling

The advantages that modeling provides for BTM are closely analogous to those that spreadsheets deliver in the financial world. By utilizing predictive modeling to align business and technology, enterprises can:

- **Mitigate risk** by forcing teams to flesh out details in the design stage
- **Enable creative impact** analysis by lowering the marginal cost of experimentation
- **Democratize design decisions** by hiding underlying details from non-technical team members
- **Communicate overall design** to promote collaboration

Mitigate Risk

The first of these advantages, mitigating risk, is a key advantage of modeling in general. Initiatives can fail because of any number of unforeseen obstacles: poorly defined business objectives; processes that don't map to application packages; system choices that require heavy customization; even plain, old-fashioned installation failures. By itself, modeling can't guarantee a flawless initiative; but by forcing stakeholders to collaborate and produce an end-to-end design before beginning the actual implementation, it helps work out kinks in the model—where they are far easier to tackle than in the real world.

Mitigating risk is an important factor in any enterprise initiative, and it's a compelling counterbalance to our first concern about predictive modeling—that it isn't worth the time and effort. Implementation mistakes can cost many times more than even the most thorough modeling.

Perform Impact Analysis

Second, predictive modeling helps companies to perform impact analysis. Most enterprise initiatives adhere to a linear planning process, where decisions made early on (the business drivers for the initiative, for example) become cast in stone as the project progresses. This is okay when both the initial guidelines are completely static and the consequences of decisions only affect future decisions.

In IT projects, however, neither of these conditions applies. Early choices such as business drivers can become out-of-date at a moment's notice in response to things like market changes and recent moves by competitors. At the same time, choices made later in the process (such as which application package to select) can affect decisions thought to have been nailed down earlier (such as the process flow that is to be automated). By locking in determinations up front, teams forfeit flexibility that they may need down the road.

Also, linear planning assumes that what's best for any individual decision must be best for the project as a whole. This attitude ignores hidden ripple effects between seemingly unrelated decisions. For example, a consultant choosing an application package may sensibly select the one that fits the most requirements. But this decision assumes that all the requirements are equally important to the initiative. If the consultant chooses a package that leaves out a few crucial requirements, he or she could introduce an inconsistency between the best individual decision (the package that meets the most requirements), and the best overall solution (the system that best supports the overall business goals of the project).

To compound this situation further, ROIs are frequently laced with intangibles such as "improved customer relationships" and "strategic fit with other systems." Managers who have been tasked with making a particular decision in a linear process often feel compelled to invent decision criteria to justify their choices, even if these criteria fail to take into account the project's overall, intangible returns. Eric K. Clemons, a professor at the Wharton School of Business, describes this phenomenon as "the 'concrete' and 'measurable' driving the *significant* out of the analysis."[2]

Impact analysis counters these concerns by letting teams compare end-to-end potential outcomes. Even in cases with intangible returns, the impact analysis technique improves decisions by making it easy to compare the relative value of multiple scenarios, rather than forcing teams to assign allegedly absolute criteria that obscure more important, elusive goals. Seeing end-to-end designs also helps to calm the impulse to enter an endless design loop by encouraging teams to select a final design, move from modeling to implementation, and avoid the temptation to get stuck on an individual decision.

Democratize Design Decisions

The third advantage of predictive modeling is that it hides underlying details from the non-technical audience. By simulating the general behavior of real-world subjects while simultaneously hiding complex details, models encourage even non-technical team members to "play around." This broadens the base of users who can make important design decisions from IT professionals to also include business managers, process analysts, and even senior executives. Collaboration between this variety of stakeholders to leverage business and technical expertise leads to new scenarios and innovative solutions to problems. Michael Schrage, the co-director of the MIT Media Lab's eMarkets Initiative and the author of *Serious Play*, describes how this phenomenon plays out in another modeling discipline, computer-aided design, or CAD:

> Engineering organizations have found that nonengineering managers and marketers want to play with CAD software to test their own product ideas and enhancements. Such "amateur CAD" signifies a growing democratization of design promoted by pervasive and accessible modeling technology. The changing nature of the modeling medium is forcing design professionals to manage the prototyping efforts of design amateurs. The declining cost and rising importance of prototyping is broadening the community of designers.[3]

Communicate Design Details

Finally, models can be compelling communication tools. This can happen in the form of a business unit evaluating an existing enterprise system to see if it could be reused in their division; a development team communicating a proposed project to a manager for approval; or an enterprise architect team communicating interface specifications to an external business partner for integration purposes. This communication is also the key to bridging gaps between distinct models and ultimately to overcoming the white-space problem.

Instill Collaborative Decision-Making

The second principle of BTM is to instill collaborative decision-making. The concept of collaborative decision-making is frequently employed as a catchall that includes everything from face-to-face communication to knowledge management to coordinating partnerships. This scope is too broad for our purposes, of course, so this discussion is limited to the role that collaboration plays in the specific context of BTM: decision-making that is either facilitated by modeling itself or undertaken to support the modeling initiative.

The idea of collaborative decision-making in BTM is a descendent of the broader concept of a virtual workspace, where potentially disparate teams can come together to access a common work environment, post and share supporting information, and communicate in real time to solve problems. For BTM, this virtual workspace equates to a combination of the model itself and three key levels of collaboration:

- **Direct Collaboration** is when people discuss issues in real time using tools like email, instant messaging, and notification services. These discussions are meant to facilitate dialogue between decision makers or to solve a specific problem. For example, an implementation consultant may need to establish which IT standards are in place through a direct question-and-answer session with members of the client team.
- **Model-level Collaboration** happens when more than one team member contributes to any individual model. This occurs quite frequently, such as when analysts require supervision and input from managers, or individual models span multiple skill areas or business units. A good example of model-level collaboration is a supply chain process model, where demand planners, plant managers, and supply plan-

ners come together to diagram an end-to-end flow of how a manufacturer plans and executes their supply chain. Model-level collaboration includes model check-in/check-out, version control, change tracking, and model comparison/merge activities. This level of collaboration can also include aspects of document management to help teams share knowledge that supports their decisions in the model. And it can also act as a gateway to direct collaboration, for example when an inconsistency between two versions of a model is discovered and the team collaborates to determine which version is correct.

- **Alignment-level Collaboration** represents the highest level of collaboration in BTM. It is driven by the necessity to cross whitespaces to align multiple models. Because BTM spans business modeling, process optimization, and technology automation, it by nature includes a variety of stakeholders with unique areas of modeling responsibility. To cross these disciplines, team members often negotiate and come to a shared decision. This may involve a prolonged, robust exchange of information that includes elements of both model-level and direct collaboration. To facilitate back-and-forth exchange, team members utilize a mini-impact analysis of sorts, where each side develops multiple scenarios until an acceptable compromise is reached. A good example of alignment-level collaboration is when analysts from two business units compare process models to establish standards for enterprise processes.

Vertical and Horizontal Collaboration

The three levels of collaboration can occur both vertically (within a single business unit or team) and horizontally (across multiple business units or teams).

Most day-to-day communication within an IT project falls under the aegis of vertical collaboration. Its goal is to improve existing processes by sharing information and expertise. One manifestation of vertical collaboration is communication between team members at different levels of the same business unit, from executives to business unit heads to managers and so on. In the worst cases, top-to-bottom communication between those who set objectives and those responsible for meeting them resembles a version of the children's game, Telephone: The original message is garbled along the way and disconnects crop up between strategy and execution.

Vertical collaboration improves this process by making sure that the directives passed between managers and their reports happen accurately and in real time. For top-down communication this means that changes in strategy or goals are communicated in time to change course, and for bottom-up communication this means that needs and issues are passed back up to executives to make small, corrective changes that don't jeopardize the project as a whole.

However vertical collaboration isn't necessarily limited to members of the same business unit. Another type of vertical collaboration focuses on particular teams or business processes. An example here is product development, when representatives from marketing, sales, and engineering define specifications, share new product designs, and make update requests. The impetus for this collaboration is improved communication and efficiency: The marketing team knows which market niche to exploit, the sales team understands customer needs, and engineers have the technical capability to design new and exciting product offerings. By improving the flow of information between participants, tools that facilitate vertical collaboration in product development can improve speed to market and reduce production errors.

In BTM, vertical collaboration shares important characteristics with both manager-to-report collaboration and process and team-based collaboration such as product development. By encouraging team members to share metrics, project management information, and relevant knowledge bits, collaboration encourages holistic decision-making, and ultimately reduces development time and cost.

While vertical collaboration is all about efficiency, horizontal collaboration is focused on helping to share amorphous "great ideas" that can deliver unique insights that are especially powerful. Vertical collaboration is project and process-based, and includes stakeholders with multiple specialties. Horizontal collaboration is quite the opposite: General trends and opportunities are shared between employees with similar job functions, but who work in different business units or on different projects.

One example of horizontal collaboration could be the interaction between the customer service and product design teams in a consumer products company. Suppose that over time, the customer service team notices that a large number of the calls to their help desk are from users who can't figure out how to use a particular feature of a particular product. After documenting the issues, a service team member contacts the product design team. The two groups collaborate to determine the exact nature of the problem and change future versions of the product to make it more intuitive. In this example, two otherwise disparate teams (customer service and product design) collaborate to share a unique insight (user difficulties with a particular product feature) in a way that was outside the scope of normal processes and regular communication.

The advantages of horizontal and vertical collaboration are predictably unique from one another. In vertical collaboration, the focus is on pervasive integration of well-defined team members and processes in order to share knowledge and improve efficiency. Horizontal collaboration, on the other hand, requires employees to identify and analyze important developments in their own work environment, and then to pass these along through free-form interactions to whomever is most equipped to act upon them. This is the foundation for an integrated organization that recognizes broad trends and shares them across business lines to provide opportunities elsewhere.

T-Shaped Managing

Both vertical and horizontal collaboration are essential components of BTM. Embracing both in tandem requires a management technique that Morten T. Hansen and Bolko von Oetinger describe in the Harvard Business Review as the "T-shaped management" model. In BTM, the vertical component of T-shaped management encompasses most day-to-day work on IT projects, and focuses on individual modeling teams and their managers on up to the office of the CIO and the CxO Suite. But BTM also requires teams to collaborate horizontally to share what Hansen and von Oetinger call "implicit knowledge, the type needed to generate new insights and creative ways of tackling business problems or opportunities."[4] These horizontal interactions could include a marketing manager who identifies a sales trend and passes it along to a product design team, or an IT professional who recognizes an opportunity to reuse an existing ERP system in another department. Figure 3.2 illustrates the roles that vertical and horizontal collaboration play in BTM, and shows some types of information that are commonly exchanged in each:

Figure	3.2

Vertical collaboration encompasses day-to-day work, while horizontal collaboration delivers key insights and opportunities

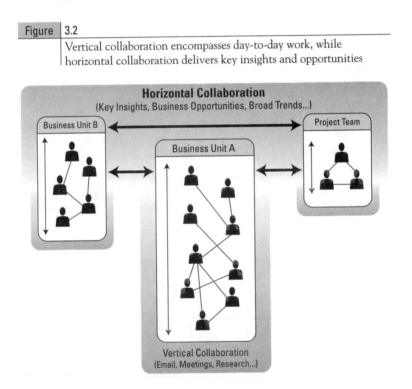

Contextual and Cultural Barriers

Before they can achieve T-shaped management, companies need to overcome both contextual and cultural barriers to collaboration. Contextual barriers are the biggest obstacle that stands in the way of collaborative decision-making. Most collaborative systems, including groupware or virtual workspace applications, don't integrate directly with everyday work environments, so employees are forced to leave their workspace—be it a word processor, spreadsheet, CAD/CAM tool, or even the factory floor—to interface with others. IT analyst IDC describes this phenomenon as a "schism between how people get information and what they can do with it."[5]

For vertical collaboration, the contextualization problem is more practical than anything else: Team members know what to share and with whom, but many times lack the infrastructure to communicate within their familiar business applications. In horizontal collaboration, however, the impetus for collaboration isn't as intuitive. Issues are less likely to be explicitly documented in the first place, and it can be difficult to determine who to collaborate with, as partners come from outside the immediate team or from different business units altogether. This means that not only do employees not know *how* to collaborate, but they also don't know *when* or *with whom* to do so.

People also fail to collaborate because of ingrained cultural and organizational issues. In the simplest case, they fail to recognize either the person with whom they should be collaborating or the need to collaborate at all. A process analyst faced with choosing to modify either a current purchasing process or a new procurement application, for example, might not know that a colleague in another department recently grappled with a similar problem, and so might be a good source of knowledge and advice.

A second, more deep-seated challenge is to overcome the strict concept of ownership that impedes collaboration—especially horizontal collaboration between business units. There are innocent and not-so-innocent reasons why this happens. Sometimes, people simply assume that they should solve their own problems, and consequently miss opportunities to collaborate with peers who may have valuable insight into their dilemma. Other times, cultural barriers get in the way. Information from outside the immediate team may be considered untrustworthy. Or, in other cases, knowledge producers may fall prey to an ingrained tendency to hoard information for their own personal advantage. In organ-

izations where employees compete internally (to acquire customers, for example), this last condition may require a system of
incentives and penalties to encourage open information exchange.

The Advantages of Collaborative Decision-Making

Collaborative decision-making provides a number of important
advantages for BTM. By combining vertical and horizontal
collaboration to employ a T-shaped management model, enterprises can:

- **Achieve** the BTM equivalent of concurrent engineering:
  simultaneous and synchronized business modeling, process
  optimization, and technology automation
- **Maintain** alignment and communication between decisions
  made in disparate environments

Achieve Concurrent Business, Process, and Technology Design

The first advantage of collaborative decision-making is that it
helps companies to achieve the BTM equivalent of concurrent
engineering, where manufacturers collaborate at every stage of
the value chain so that all aspects of product development—from
engineering to marketing to manufacturing design—can be carried out simultaneously. Collaborative decision-making does the
same for IT projects by allowing each activity of BTM—business
model definition, process optimization, and technology automation—to occur simultaneously. When both product design and
BTM occur concurrently, cycle times decrease and critical issues
in quality control are addressed early on in the process.

Maintain Alignment Between Disparate Decisions

The second advantage of collaboration is that it helps team members to make intelligent trade-offs that maintain alignment
between seemingly disparate decisions. When companies employ
multiple tools for each of the three activities of BTM, they invite
disconnects between choices made in separate environments. By
collaborating to unify decision-making across multiple environments, team members can provide visibility into choices that are

made in other areas of the project. For example, an implementation consultant may need to determine why a modification was made to a process in order to balance its relative importance against the changes to the technology infrastructure that it requires. By implementing collaborative decision-making, team members can identify and bridge these whitespace disconnects to maintain alignment across the board.

Make Knowledge and Assets Reusable

The final principle of BTM, to make knowledge and assets reusable, encompasses two concepts that are well-known to both business and technology audiences. The first of these is knowledge management, where companies capture, codify, and communicate knowledge to improve decision-making. The second is a repository that stores templates and previously designed models to encourage project teams to reuse the unique knowledge captured in models.

Knowledge Management

The first component of knowledge and asset reusability is knowledge management—an idea that first rose to prominence nearly a decade ago. Not surprisingly, knowledge management first caught on in businesses where knowledge is a key component of the value proposition: "There's too many terms that have been overused recently," Scott Hayward, a Managing Director at JPMorgan Chase and Company explains, "but knowledge management has already become a reality in industries like financial services and consulting, where knowledge is your main product."

At the simplest level, knowledge management includes three sequential steps:

- **Acquisition:** Enterprise knowledge frequently exists in intangible forms such as individual expertise and shared culture. To disperse this knowledge throughout the corporation it first must be captured in a concrete form such as a document, knowledge bit, or contact information for a subject-matter expert.

- **Interpretation:** Once knowledge has been captured it must be analyzed and codified so that individuals and intelligent systems can use this context to push relevant knowledge to team members.
- **Delivery:** The final step is delivering codified knowledge to the point of decision. This delivery can be either passive (such as documents that reside in a searchable database or team members who wait to be contacted about their specific experiences and recommendations) or active (such as software designed to alert individuals regarding applicable knowledge bits).

This seems to be a simple process, but the hit-or-miss experiences with knowledge management during the last decade betray the danger lurking behind the facade. To avoid the mistakes made in past projects, companies need to appreciate what it is that makes the outwardly simple theory of reusable knowledge anything but simple to implement in real life.

Two pervasive myths are largely responsible for companies' inability to harness the power of shared knowledge. The first is based on the assumption that employees will automatically use an IT-based knowledge management system if it is in place. This misconception stems from the early view that knowledge management was considered purely an IT project. But companies found that building technology to support knowledge management is the easy part—and overcoming cultural and political obstacles to sharing knowledge is much more difficult.

The second myth about knowledge management is that technology will replace face-to-face knowledge transfer. Some early adopters assumed that in the new, virtual office, all interaction would be mediated by IT. The truth is that people are far more likely to share ideas when they're face-to-face with their colleagues, and IT-based knowledge management should be considered a supplement to rather than a replacement for traditional, non-IT-based knowledge exchange.

Two Types of Reusable Knowledge: Documents and Relationships

Knowledge management links people with two types of information: documents (which include pre-built process flows, existing market research, network topologies, and other supporting information); and relationships, (which means referring to subject-matter experts—business unit managers, network architects, and IT team leaders for example—directly).

In keeping with knowledge management's IT-focused history, most of the attention given to reusability centers upon collecting, indexing, and distributing electronic documents. For this to work, of course, knowledge must first be captured and saved in document form and then given context through associations with pre-defined subjects. When employees search for knowledge, they either perform a direct search (in which case context is provided by their search terms), or they browse the subjects until they find something that might apply, and then view the documents that are associated with that subject. This type of knowledge management works best for information that is static, data-driven, and meant to have a long shelf life: metrics, research reports, and basic documentation such as corporate policies, for example.

But sometimes sharing knowledge requires two employees to collaborate directly to adapt their unique experiences to a new context. In these cases, document management systems—the traditional cornerstones of knowledge management—don't work so well. Instead, companies need a mechanism for linking people directly with other team members or experts. When employees look up information, they are directed not to a static document, but instead to the appropriate contact person.

Reusable Asset Repository

The second crucial component of knowledge and asset reusability is a repository that stores models developed during BTM. The concept of a reusable asset repository is closely related to the knowledge management ideal of recycling enterprise knowledge. It differs from knowledge management, however, in that the knowledge being reused is captured in a structured model rather than static documents or contact information for subject-matter experts.

Reusable asset repositories are familiar to component and object developers, who have long used repositories to encourage developers to recycle existing code rather than writing from scratch. Component and object repositories act like a centralized warehouse of pre-developed software that codifies the objects according to the functionality that they implement. Developers search the repository to find a piece of code that does what they need, and reuse it to decrease the development time for their project.

A useful analogy illustrating the advantages of a reusable repository is to the manufacturing innovations realized during the industrial revolution. By using standardized components as building blocks for creating new products, innovative entrepreneurs such as Eli Whitney incited a productivity revolution that led to assembly line manufacturing, the transition from inefficient artisans to moderately skilled line workers, and ultimately to the rise of mass production and inexpensive consumer goods.

Proponents of reusable repositories promise a similar leap forward for BTM: By using pre-built model templates from a repository, team members can concentrate on developing unique project details rather than common, low-value designs. This provides important advantages for companies whose IT projects need to be agile to keep up with multiple acquisitions, fast product cycles, or high employee turnover.

Reuse in Context

As with collaboration, it is necessary to establish context before you can reuse knowledge and assets to give employees not just the right information, but also the right information at the right time. The very idea of reuse as a distinct practice betrays the fundamental problem with most previous initiatives to reuse knowledge and assets. Like knowledge management, reuse isn't just about deploying business applications to save electronic knowledge for later use. Instead, it means enacting a cultural change so that reusing decisions, policies, processes, technology, and standards is indistinguishable from the normal, day-to-day tasks that created this intellectual property in the first place.

One recurring pitfall of stand-alone systems for reuse is the tendency of employees to ignore them altogether. Integrating knowledge directly into the work environment solves this disconnect and increases the likelihood that employees will embrace reusability both as producers and consumers of knowledge. To do this means facing two important challenges: establishing an infrastructure for reuse that integrates directly with other enterprise applications, and defining a methodology for classifying documents that can be linked to enterprise applications to provide the context for determining which knowledge is relevant at any given time.

The Advantages of Reusing Knowledge and Assets

By reusing knowledge and assets within the context of BTM, enterprises can:

- Give decision-makers the right information at the right time
- Minimize rework and improve cycle times
- Establish enterprise standards for processes, systems, and infrastructure to promote best practices
- Reuse existing enterprise applications, hardware, and networks

Give Decision-Makers the Right Information at the Right Time

Knowledge about business and IT initiatives is stored in the form of market research, documentation, vendor profiles, and consulting partner deliverables. By incorporating this information into a knowledge management system, teams can use context to push relevant information directly to the point of decision. This helps team members to access existing enterprise knowledge before making key decisions, and ensures that documents remain up-to-date and relevant as the model is updated or changed altogether.

Minimize Rework and Improve Cycle Times

By saving previously developed models in a reusable asset repository and then making these available as templates for later projects, companies can reduce the amount of time and effort that they spend redoing crucial tasks. This lowers the cycle time required to plan and implement IT projects, and allows individuals to concentrate on high-value decisions in their specific areas of expertise. Even after the dotcom meltdown, valuable IT workers are in short supply, and forcing skilled subject-matter experts to spend time on activities that don't provide a direct benefit to the project is an inefficient allocation of resources. By reusing models from a centralized asset repository, IT workers can concentrate on specific, detailed customization that delivers real value and leverages their unique skill sets.

Establish Enterprise Standards and Best Practices

Oftentimes, enterprise and IT standards are ignored by employees because they are either unaware that the standards exist or they remain unconvinced of the value that they provide. Knowledge and asset reusability addresses this concern in two ways.

First, contextualized knowledge links standards and best practices directly to the model itself. This can be in the form of supporting documents, research reports, or team member experiences. Also, it can link directly to subject-matter experts, such as enterprise architects, who can pass along their accumulated knowledge to those responsible for individual design decisions.

Second, new models based on templates that conform to standards and best practices encourage teams to keep new modeling in line with the design parameters endorsed in the template. To replace an approved networking standard with a renegade design, for example, an IT architect would have to first deliberately remove the approved configuration. This is unlikely, especially in a culture where a standards-based approach is emphasized. Another way to enforce standards is to include models of technology vendors and configurations in the repository. This makes it easier for IT architects to stick with pre-approved configurations than it is to strike out on their own.

Reuse existing physical assets

By recycling models from previous BTM projects, team members are encouraged to reuse the design decisions captured in the model itself. At the same time, however, it is important to note that these previously developed models are virtual representations of the actual business and IT environments. By recycling a portion of a model, then, employees can often recycle its real-world equivalent—strategies, processes, software, and systems, for example.

Consider this scenario: A particular line of business develops a model for a new CRM initiative, installs the software, and rolls out the project in their business unit. When IT workers from another business unit go to reuse this CRM model, they not only benefit from improved decision-making, but by sticking with the model's design decisions, they may be able to reuse a portion of the actual CRM software itself.

By reusing actual enterprise assets rather than just the knowledge and expertise encapsulated in the model itself, companies can reduce the cost of purchasing new hardware, software, and services, and can unify enterprise architecture across multiple lines of business.

From Principles to Specific Activities

The three principles of BTM combine to form a solid foundation for aligning business and technology. Without utilizing predictive modeling, instilling collaborative decision-making, and making knowledge and assets reusable, it's impossible to do BTM. This means that the principles of BTM merit a long and careful look before you dive into your next IT project.

Who Should Lead the Drive to Adopt the Principles of BTM?

"Right now, many corporations don't have a BTM hero who has been tasked with leading the drive towards modeling, collaboration, and reuse. And even where those people exist today, they typically don't have the budget to marshal the resources to do it.

Like any important shift in IT planning, embracing predictive modeling starts with the CIO. He or she may assign somebody else to tackle it, but I think it's got to be very high level. I do think, however, that over the next two or three years you'll see process-focused technology people start to play this role by acting as purveyors of modeling concepts to both sides: to the business side to help them understand what technology can do for them; to the IT group to actually get development done right.

It's these same business process/technology leaders who will be the lynchpins for driving collaboration, and putting the right tools and processes in place to make it happen. And I'd also argue, by the way, that it's these same people that have to start looking at reuse and knowledge management because they're the ones who see things on a cross-functional basis, whether it's cross-departmental, or sometimes even across business partners. I think you really must have a group that is looking after the whole development area on reuse, because reuse starts at the process level: if you can't establish shared processes it's going to be difficult to establish component reuse at a technology level.

People are already arguing 'yes' about alignment, but I think we're at the cusp of where we're going to see this discipline become a critical path, enabling better control of IT spending, better management of projects, better prioritization, and viewing the whole thing as a portfolio. I think that you're going to see a much more coordinated effort. In the past, business/technology alignment has been done more on an ad hoc basis. But today, you need a more architected approach: It needs to be more disciplined, and you need to be able to put different areas to work in pursuit of alignment, including modeling, collaboration, and reuse."

– **Dale Kutnick,** *founder, chairman, and* CEO, META *Group*

Despite this enthusiastic endorsement, however, it's important to remember that the principles of BTM are only one piece of a bigger puzzle. Early on in this chapter we defined the principles as prerequisites for performing the activities of BTM. This is a good way to emphasize the importance of these principles and how they fit with the other pieces of business technology management: It's impossible to do successful BTM without utilizing predictive modeling, instilling collaborative decision-making, and making knowledge and assets reusable. But it's also possible to do these things—to do them well, in fact—and still not make good on the promise of BTM.

The Activities
of BTM

"The great end of life is not knowledge but action."
– *Thomas Henry Huxley*

SEVERAL MONTHS AFTER FIRST HAVING MET with Janet
and Robert to discuss your dream house, you're almost ready to
begin construction. But before the first batch of concrete can
be poured and the first board nailed into place, you need a
mechanism to make sure that the design they've come up with
meets your exacting demands. To earn your confidence (and to
avoid any late-stage misunderstandings that might result in
tearing down a part of the structure to make a change), Janet
and Robert have put together an exhaustive architectural blueprint of your dream house.

Recently, this blueprint has ballooned from a couple of pre-liminary drawings that concentrated on the overall look and feel of the house to a heavy stack of detailed diagrams. Most of the recent drawings focus on details that are beyond your limited grasp of architecture. But you're excited for the house to be done, and so you decide to spend a slow afternoon flipping through the unwieldy drawings and trying to imagine how the section expressed in each might look in the final structure. After just a few minutes, you notice that each of these working diagrams seems not only to focus on a distinct physical area of the house, but also specific subject matter: pipes in some, wires in others, and beams and supports in still others.

In the preceding weeks, Robert, the contractor, hired a team of specialized tradesmen—plumbers, electricians, engineers, and so on—who will handle the day-to-day construction duties. Each of these focused roles needs a set of working drawings that explains the project from their individual point of view. Tony, the plumber, constructs a riser diagram to show how water will get from your well to each of the bathrooms and sinks, for example, while the electrician, Willy, needs to plan circuits, outlets, and switches. The structural engineer, Emily, needs to design beams, trusses, and support.

Obviously, each of the detailed working drawings that you've come across has been constructed with a particular one of these specialists in mind; they represent distinct views, will be com-pleted at different stages, and, generally speaking, don't even include the same building blocks. But at the same time, it's obvi-ous that each working drawing needs to fit seamlessly into an integrated whole. They all refer to the same house, after all, and if Willy were to try and install an electrical socket in the same loca-tion Tony had planned to put a shower and Emily had sited a sup-port beam, it would be a disaster.

The challenge for Robert (the contractor) is to make sure that the design decisions made from each of these three distinct points of view are compatible. Just like it's up to Robert (the CIO) to make sure that decisions from three analogous perspectives—busi-ness, process, and technology—all work together in the design of a single IT project.

Just like for your dream house, Robert (the CIO) puts together a team of subject-matter experts that is responsible for detailed design decisions: Tony, a representative from the business unit, focuses on the business decisions for the project, such as customer segments, partners, and strategies; Willy, a process expert, designs processes to support these business objectives during process automation; and Emily, a systems integrator, outlines the applications and systems that will support these processes. All of this happens during business model definition, process optimization, and technology automation—the three activities of BTM.

In This Part...

It's essential both to recognize that business and IT should be aligned and also to identify the underlying principles that help to accomplish that goal. But without concrete activities that you can perform to determine where you are today, to decide where you need to go, and to define how you should go about getting there, there's no guarantee that alignment will finally become a reality. *Part III: The Activities of BTM* begins by introducing enterprise architecture, which functions as a blueprint for IT projects. Enterprise architecture should be designed using a combination of modeling and impact analysis during the design stage of IT projects. (Just like you shouldn't start drawing up architectural blueprints after you've already dug the foundation, you shouldn't wait to design enterprise architecture until after you're writing code.) Next, it describes the three activities of BTM—*Business Model Definition, Process Optimization, and Technology Automation*—and use a simulated case study to show how they might be put to work in a familiar business environment.

4

The End-to-End Perspective

THE THREE PRINCIPLES OF BTM—utilize predictive modeling, instill collaborative decision-making, and make knowledge and assets reusable—provide an essential foundation for aligning business and technology. Nevertheless, they're more like tools than a finished product: you need them to get the job done, but, in the end, how they're put to work is just as important as what they are. If you're trying to build a birdhouse, for example, you'll need a hammer and nails. But the same hammer and nails can also be used to build a doghouse, a toolshed, or, for that matter, a dilapidated shack.

This same tenet holds true for modeling, collaboration, and reuse. Modeling often shows up in the form of data or object modeling, collaboration in groupware and virtual conferencing, and reuse in document management and repositories of code—all good and useful in their own right, but not necessarily the best approaches for meeting the specific challenges posed by the business/technology disconnect. To deliver on its promise, then, BTM needs to include not just generic principles, but also a blueprint for how to put those principles to work to solve disconnects. This is where the activities of BTM come into play. During business model definition, process optimization, and technology automation, companies leverage modeling, collaboration, and reuse to develop an enterprise architecture that keeps IT projects firmly aligned (see Fig. 4.1).

Figure | 4.1

The principles of BTM combine with the activities of BTM to help companies model enterprise architecture

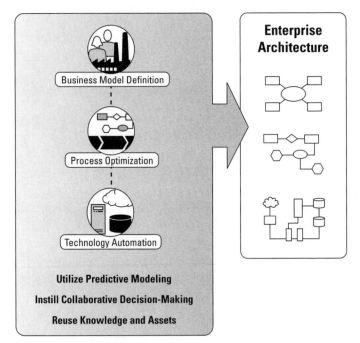

Business model definition, process optimization, and technology automation are by nature specific activities that need to be undertaken by someone somewhere in order to have an effect

upon the enterprise. If you're thinking about practicing BTM, then, a logical question to ask is where and when should all this happen? To answer this question, let's turn back to the real-world disconnects highlighted in Ch. 1. Each of these examples points to specific IT projects that somehow spun off course. This doesn't mean that BTM should be confined to the PMO, however; there are any number of methodologies and guidelines available to help companies manage IT projects that don't focus primarily upon alignment. But projects are the primary mechanism for designing and ultimately changing how IT functions (by installing a network, modifying a business process, or installing a new application, for example), so if we're looking to make changes to close disconnects that have cropped up over time, the IT project is nonetheless the right place to start.

The "Aim" in "Ready, Aim, Fire"

Most project management disciplines divide IT projects into five major stages:
   - **Conceive**, where an initial proposal and cursory description of the project are put forward
   - **Design**, where a detailed plan is developed that lays out what needs to be done, when, and by whom
   - **Build**, where new assets such as processes and systems are assembled
   - **Test**, where the new assets undergo rigorous testing to ensure that they perform as planned
   - **Deploy**, where the new assets and behavioral changes are implemented in the live business environment

Chapter Three, indicated that predictive modeling would help companies go from a "ready, fire" approach to using IT in the business to a "ready, aim, fire" method that "aims" to make sure team members make decisions that keep business, process, and technology aligned. By mapping this crude analogy back to the five stages of IT projects, as in Fig. 4.2, we see some obvious similarities.

Figure	4.2
	By helping to improve the design stage of IT projects, BTM provides the "aim" in "ready, aim, fire"

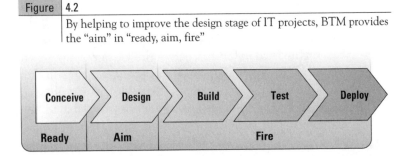

Most importantly, note the connection between aim and design. For BTM to really help companies aim to make better decisions, two assumptions should be true: first, the business/technology disconnect should result primarily from mistakes and oversights during the design stage of IT projects, and second, BTM needs to provide a mechanism to improve this crucial design.

Studies show that the first of these assumptions does indeed hold. In projects of all kinds a huge percentage of the cost is fixed in the design phase, no matter how scrupulously the project team adheres to best practices and careful management during the build, test, and deploy stages (which is where most project management efforts aim to wring value from the initiative). For example, research indicates that although "80% of the money and time invested in supply-chain management information systems is devoted to addressing execution processes…70% of a product's real cost is determined and decided in the early phases of product innovation and design."[1]

The second of these assumptions, that by improving the design of IT projects BTM successfully aligns business and technology, is the focus of this chapter. Each of Ch. 1's real-world disconnects—from Patrick Flynn's customs-clearance system to Carl Wilson's HR initiative to Scott Hayward's call-reporting system—demonstrates that disconnects between three crucial areas—business, process, and technology—are the catalysts for financial, behavioral, and functional disasters. By using modeling to improve the design of these areas before moving on to the costly build, test, and deploy stages, companies can address disconnects before they crop up. And, in fact, the activities of BTM—business model definition, process optimization, and technology automation—help companies to design enterprise architecture, a concrete blueprint that includes these three crucial areas, improves decision-making in their IT projects, and helps bring alignment to IT projects and the enterprise as a whole.

Enterprise Architecture: A Blueprint for Alignment

Enterprise architecture, of course, isn't a new idea that's unique to BTM; many companies already use it today to improve standardization, speed up development, lower the cost of implementing systems, improve quality, and generally govern IT in the enterprise. But BTM is somewhat unique in that it positions enterprise architecture as a blueprint for aligning business and technology.

In general, enterprise architecture is a holistic, end-to-end design that encompasses business architecture (which includes both a big-picture design of the business and the processes that support this design) and technology architecture (which includes the applications that automate business processes, and the underlying systems that support these applications). It's important to note that this definition draws a distinction between how BTM views enterprise architecture and other interpretations of the term:

- **Enterprise Architecture Isn't Just Technology:** Some people assume that enterprise architecture describes only IT assets. By ignoring business architecture altogether, this misconception encourages companies to develop a road map that innovates IT—but with no direct connection to business and process.
- **Business Architecture Isn't Just Processes:** Others make the mistake of interpreting business architecture to mean just the business processes that the company performs. This ignores the big-picture view of the business, and makes it difficult for decision-makers to determine not just what processes exist, but also why these processes are executed the way that they are.

BTM requires a definition for enterprise architecture that is more complete than either of these two misconceptions. To solve the business/technology disconnect, companies need to consider a complete, end-to-end road map that helps them make better decisions about where and how to put IT to work. This road map, pictured in Fig. 4.3, includes both business and technology architectures, and diagrams specifically how each architecture type fits together.

Figure | 4.3

Enterprise architecture includes both business and technology architectures

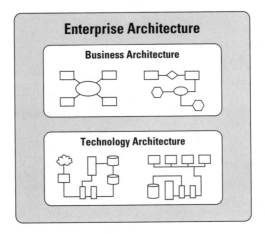

Like an architectural blueprint, enterprise architecture serves as a reference point during later implementation phases, when team members refer back to it to verify important decisions, update the design, and generally determine what they need to do to accomplish the project. But, also like an architectural blueprint, the primary value that enterprise architecture adds isn't just as a reference point for project management; it also helps to prototype solutions during the design stage by identifying how the enterprise is designed today, where the opportunities are for the project to innovate that design, how things will have to change to take advantage of that innovation, and what the final design of the enterprise will look like once the project is implemented.

This helps the project team to evaluate options, make trade-offs, and balance competing agendas. Consider Honorio Padron's example in Ch. 1, where a misunderstanding about the importance of customizing a new financial system almost led to a barrage of unnecessary costs. In this particular case, developing a blueprint of enterprise architecture in the design stage would have revealed the differences between the company's current processes and those supported out of the box, helped to calculate the cost of modifying

Enterprise Architecture and Service Providers

"One of the things that we have suffered from for a number years—and I am sure that this is characteristic of large corporate IT organizations—is that although we have utilized many of the leading consultancies and system integrators, we have actually gained very little in terms of architectural intellectual capital for many projects.

The intellectual capital that these engagements generate is captured in simple documentation form: it may be written documents, it may be diagrammatic, but it is certainly not aligned and not interlinked. So you might have Visio, PowerPoint, or Excel documents that make up the main artifacts for the project. Each document is disconnected, and varies in the structure and detail in which it is defined. So if you've done one project with Accenture and another with PWC Consulting, actually putting those two pieces of an overall enterprise architecture together is a whole new piece of work, basically.

By promoting interlinked models to design enterprise architecture, BTM gives organizations like ours the mechanism we need to work with consulting organizations and actually take the intellectual capital they produce and integrate it into our overall enterprise architecture."

– **Kevin Poulter,** *head of business integration, British American Tobacco; co-founder, Ontology.org* the software, catalogued the strategic objectives for the project, and provided a platform to mediate between the importance of making changes and keeping costs down.

Models Help Predict Enterprise Architecture

Because enterprise architecture needs to be able to design changes before they are actually put into place during the build, test, and deploy stages of a project, it is a prime candidate for predictive modeling. Not surprisingly, then, each of the activities of BTM makes good use of this trait by utilizing business, process, and technology models as important tools for developing enterprise architecture. Together, these three types of models make up a complete enterprise model, which mimics the behavior of end-to-end enterprise architecture.

Like other models in general, enterprise models are composed of four primary building blocks: elements (things), attributes (descriptions of things), relationships (links to other things in the model), and cross-links (links to other things in separate models). Elements within the model can be organized (into parent-child hierarchies, for example), tied together to imply causal relationships, and cross-linked with external elements from other models in order to create concrete connections. This final point is an extremely important one for the purposes of BTM. Any technique that promises to close disconnects between business, process, and technology must clearly rely upon a mechanism to enforce alignment. By cross-linking individual elements in discrete models together, BTM accomplishes this feat, and ensures that the ripple effects of any specific decision are anticipated throughout each modeling environment.

Consider an example: An IT analyst creates an element in a technology model that represents a new software package he or she is installing. Beneath this package, the analyst creates child elements that describe the functional requirements for the package. Each of these functional requirements is then linked back to the individual processes in the process model that it supports. If a change needs to be made to the package down the road, whoever is considering the modifications can trace links back to the processes that would be impacted, and anticipate the full ramifications of the decision before making the final call.

This ability to change models and to dynamically view ripple effects both within an individual model and between multiple business, process, and technology models is the primary reason why conventional drawings aren't sufficient for designing enterprise architecture. In order to simulate the full impact of any individual decision, the design needs to respond dynamically when models are modified. If designing enterprise architecture was an afterthought to IT projects, static drawings would be fine. But because enterprise architecture needs to be developed during the design stage, only predictive models—business, process, and technology models—can get the job done.

The process of designing enterprise architecture and carrying out the activities of BTM begins when the project team identifies an as-is *current enterprise model* (which includes business, process, and technology) that describes the end-to-end architecture as it exists today. Then, the team leverages the capabilities of predictive modeling to develop multiple to-be *enterprise scenario models* (also called patterns), each of which previews potential changes to the architecture. By comparing the current enterprise model and the enterprise scenario models, team members can discover practical opportunities for IT to benefit the company, and ultimately use impact analysis to make better decisions about which opportunities to pursue. Once these opportunities have been identified, the *final enterprise scenario model* becomes the basis for an IT project that implements these changes. After the IT project has been rolled out, the final enterprise scenario model is folded into the current enterprise model to make sure that the changes become part of a new, *updated enterprise model* (see Fig. 4.4).

Notice that before you can follow this sequence of events, you first need to have an accurate, current enterprise model. There are two ways to go about developing this model. The first is to charter a team headed by senior executives to review the current enter-

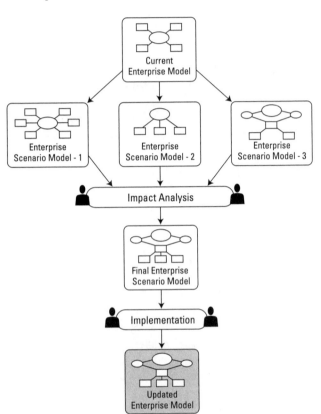

Figure 4.4
During the activities of BTM, companies perform impact analysis
to evaluate multiple scenarios and select the appropriate option
for implementation

prise model (or create it from scratch if necessary) after regular,
but reasonably long intervals (one to three years is typical). These
reviews should be timed to coincide with reviews of corporate
strategy, so that changes in strategy ripple down immediately into
the model. The second method for developing the current enterprise model is by accumulation. As projects finish, final scenario
models are folded into the updated enterprise model, or become
the updated enterprise model altogether if one doesn't yet exist.
Over time, and as projects touch upon different areas of the busi-

ness, the effect will be to flesh out a complete current enterprise model piece by piece.

One final note about the current enterprise model is that it provides a powerful vehicle for capturing and enforcing enterprise standards. Since each enterprise scenario model is patterned after the current enterprise model, design standards such as standard process flows, approved application packages, and technical standards are automatically passed along to each enterprise scenario model, and in turn to the implementation projects that make them a reality. This helps enterprise architects to maintain tactical control over how projects are implemented, a subject that Ch. 8 discusses in more detail.

Introducing The Activities of BTM

Developing and maintaining these models—the current enterprise model, the enterprise scenario models, the final enterprise scenario model, and the updated enterprise model—is the primary purpose of the activities of BTM, which are introduced here, but described in more detail in Ch. 5, 6, and 7:

- **Business Model Definition** helps companies capture and communicate business objectives
- **Process Optimization** helps define and streamline processes to support the business model
- **Technology Automation** helps to select applications and supporting systems to automate selected processes

Business Model Definition

During the first activity of BTM, business model definition, project teams analyze their current business and develop multiple scenarios that describe how technology might be used to improve it. First, they examine the current business model, a big picture that captures a snapshot of the business and communicates strategy, objectives, opportunities, and constraints. Next, they solicit input from relevant subject-matter experts to create a number of alternative business scenario models to accomplish their project's objectives. These scenarios, which form the basis for impact analysis, help to illustrate which aspects of the current business model might be impacted during the course of the project. (Typically, this is a small number, since most projects result in incremental changes to the business rather then a wholesale reinvention of how the company works.) Each of the business scenario models becomes the starting point for a complete enterprise scenario model (including process and technology scenario models developed during process optimization and technology automation) that describes the end-to-end enterprise architecture for the project. After one of the business scenario models has been implemented, it gets folded into an updated business model, which becomes the basis for future episodes of business model definition.

Process Optimization

Process optimization, the second activity of BTM, helps project teams define business processes to support the objectives outlined in each of the business scenario models, associate resources and requirements with individual activities, identify process inefficiencies and redundancies, and enforce standard processes across multiple business units. First, the project team decomposes their current activities into an as-is process model that describes how the enterprise behaves today. Next, they create process scenario models to support each scenario begun during business model definition. Since process optimization provides the link between business and technology, each scenario must take into account both processes that are already automated by existing resources, and processes that are good opportunities for future optimization projects. The team then performs a gap analysis between the current process model and each scenario to help generate specific requirements that drive technology automation later on. Once a final process scenario model has been selected for the current project, the team folds it back into an updated process model to make sure that it remains an up-to-date snapshot of how the company does business.

Technology Automation

During the final activity of BTM, technology automation, project teams identify applications and systems to support the activities selected for automation in each process scenario model; select vendors and implementation partners; establish technology standards, and determine how to integrate the new systems with the company's existing technology architecture. First, the team examines the current technology model, which includes two types of information: software applications that automate business processes; and supporting systems—including hardware, software, networks, and data—that support applications. Next, the team identifies technology scenario models to support each of the scenarios developed during process optimization. They perform a gap analysis for each of these scenarios to determine what applications and systems need to be purchased, developed, or modified. Finally, after the project has settled on and implemented a final technology scenario, it is folded back into an updated technology model.

A System Not a Sequence

So far, we've scrupulously presented the activities of BTM as a series of sequential steps that companies can follow to achieve alignment in their IT projects. There is some merit to this view, since it makes sense to allow sound business objectives to lead the way and be followed by process innovation, and then finally, by technology automation. But, as is often the case, the real business environment isn't always so simple. There are times when the straightforward business-to-process-to-technology sequence breaks down, and changes made in any of these three areas can take the lead. Padron's example from Ch. 1 demonstrates the expediency of sticking to an out-of-the box software application rather than approving extensive modifications. Instead of following the specialized processes employees were used to, Padron allowed technology to lead, and made sure that process and business synced up to maintain alignment. In this sense, the activities of BTM are more of an interconnected system than a sequence: it isn't about doing A, then B, and then C, it's about making sure that all three work together, in concert, to guarantee that IT contributes to bottom-line business objectives.

The Activities of BTM and Enterprise Architecture Make a Better Business Case

By putting predictive modeling to work to create enterprise architecture during the design stage of IT projects, companies can finally put the business/technology disconnect to rest. But, beyond avoiding the types of disaster stories that presented in Ch. 1 (a worthwhile goal on its own, of course), what does this really mean in terms of how companies plan and execute their IT projects?

Recall from earlier on in this chapter that the five stages of project management—conceive, design, build, test, and deploy—roughly correspond with our "ready, aim, fire" analogy, which explains how BTM helps companies "aim" to improve their alignment. This analogy is also useful for representing another key advantage of the activities of BTM. Most IT projects have to pass through a number of approval processes as they move from concept to deployment. One of these approval processes happens after the design, or "aim," stage, when the team develops a business case that tries to justify the money, time, and resources that will be required to make the project a reality. The format for each business case necessarily varies according to the company and specific project, but in general, they include things like the projected business benefit, costs, timeframe, required assets, and so on.

Historically, companies have struggled to develop business cases that end up matching up with what really happens during implementation; cost estimates blow up, timeframes go out the window, and, with alarming frequency, the CIO gets booted out the front door. There are many reasons for this trouble, but the most important is that the conclusions about cost, risk, and other variables that show up in the business case aren't based on any real, significant analysis of underlying design: companies develop business cases in a vacuum, throw them over the fence to IT, and then hope that whatever final solution IT throws back hits close to the mark.

But BTM forces the team to think through an end-to-end design of how the project will impact the business. The educated guesses and approximations of past business cases are firmed up into validated conclusions, and the CIO is empowered to make smart decisions that are traceable back to a concrete source: the enterprise architecture developed during the activities of BTM.

5

Business Model Definition

BUSINESS MODEL DEFINITION, the first activity of BTM, helps to develop multiple business scenarios that describe how the project team might choose to put technology to work. Before describing this crucial activity, however, it's important both to explain what I mean by a business model and to show some of the information that's typically included in one. Then, the chapter dives into more detail about what happens during business model definition, and why some current trends are making it more important than ever before. Next, it presents some vignettes from a simulated case study to illustrate how business model definition happens in a real enterprise environment. Finally, it touches upon who should be responsible for this important first activity of BTM.

What is a Business Model?

Before you can appreciate why business model definition is a crucial activity for BTM, it helps to have a solid understanding of what I mean by a business model. This is especially true since the term is frequently used to describe things that are dramatically different than what I mean in this specific context.

Misconceptions About Business Models

Over time, a business model has come to mean very different things depending on whom you ask. So while you're likely to hear academics, professionals, and journalists use the term both frequently and familiarly, you can't always be sure that one person's "business model" isn't another's "value proposition," "business case," "revenue model," "strategy," and so on. Before explaining what the term means, let me mention two uses that are not related to BTM:

– **The Cocktail Napkin One-Liner:** The first way that "business model" is used mistakenly is when people—journalists, for example—associate it with a convenient one-liner about what a company does. The proverbial business idea scribbled on a cocktail napkin, for example, falls squarely into this camp. Although this gross simplification is too shallow to form an effective basis for business/technology alignment, it does, perhaps inadvertently, echo one of the crucial attributes of a business model in BTM: it represents a big picture of the business.

– **The Financial Model in Disguise:** Ironically, the second way that people misapply the term is almost exactly the opposite of the cocktail napkin mistake: rather than grossly oversimplifying the term, they dive in at a level of complexity that precludes a big-picture view. This happens when a business model is equated with a financial model. Before you can build even the most basic financial model, you have to first make some important assumptions (which industry to compete in, who the customers are, etc.) that preclude the unbiased, big picture that is integral to the business model in BTM.

In the context of BTM, the term business model means something different from both the cocktail napkin one-liner and the financial model in disguise. In our discussion, a business model represents a big picture that captures a snapshot of the enterprise and communicates direction and goals to other stakeholders.

Seeing How the Pieces Fit

"I'm not sure that many executives truly understand what we mean when we say 'business model.' It means more than just the way you operate. Having a strong business model means that you have thought through the way you service the customer, the way you make money, the way you go to market—all these elements and how they fit together.

For many companies, the planning process is still very financially driven instead of being focused on the business model; they tend to take a look at financial performance, projections, and plans, and then try to engineer future financial plans, all within the construct of their current business model. Not many established companies will assess their entire business models in a proactive way—dotcoms will do it because the market has crushed their old business models, but Global 2000 companies tend to start by examining their financial models and not rethinking their business models.

Often in existing companies that have been established for some time, the managers today are typically not the original architects of the current business model. Thus, they may not really understand their own business model or have ever thought about why it's constructed the way it is.

When we in corporate America go through our planning processes, do we really sit back and think through the kind of business we are, how it's put together, and then how to improve it going forward? Too many of us move right into the financial part of the planning process and let that drive everything, as opposed to really rethinking the business model. Without that thorough assessment and by focusing just on financial plans, you tend to find only incremental improvement as opposed to break-through insights about the business model. Not every company needs to dramatically change its business model frequently—that's unnecessary. But you should examine your company's business model regularly and determine your true strengths and weaknesses. Having a well-designed planning process forces your current business leaders and the new generation of leaders coming up to really grapple with these issues and think about how to improve the business every year."

– **Randolph C. Blazer,** *chairman & CEO, KMPG Consulting, Inc.*

What a Business Model Should Be

The best way to visualize how business models add value to BTM is to show—rather than tell—the type of information that an example business model might include. Figure 5.1 presents an example business model that classifies elements into four broad areas:

- **The overall identity of the firm:** The firm's identity might include elements such as brands, the corporate mission, the reputation of the firm in the marketplace, the target market, and general differentiators for the firm. It might also include elements that describe the company's unique culture such as values, office rules, and behavioral expectations.
- **The strategy for the firm:** Elements in this category could describe how the firm translates its mission and values into concrete action. An important component of this role might be the ability to coordinate between multiple business units—each of which presumably needs to play a unique role to help meet common, strategic goals. Strategy might include elements such as goals, a timeframe for achieving those goals, the resources that are required, and custom performance indicators.

- **The internal assets that help the firm to achieve its strategic goals:** Internal assets could include all of the resources that the example firm might muster to pursue its strategy. This might include things like products and services; organizational assets, including the reporting structure, geographic distribution, roles/responsibilities, and individual resources; financial resources; intellectual property; distribution channels; and physical assets such as real estate and machinery.
- **The external business environment in which the firm competes:** Finally, the example business model might also include a category of elements that describes the firm's external business environment, including customers, suppliers, partners, and competitors. In addition, the external environment could include demographics for the market and industry; potential entrants; information about compliance; and general trends that influence the company's position in their market.

Each of these elements maintains textual and numeric attributes (such as metrics, priority, and feasibility) that help give the model the depth of description and interaction that distinguishes it from a simple diagram or drawing. For example, the element labeled "High Value" in Fig. 5.1 could include attributes such as a textual description of who is considered a high-value customer; numerical values that describe the estimated number of customers that fall into this category; and the revenue a customer needs to generate for the company to qualify as a high-value customer. This information provides an important basis for analyzing the model (while managing the portfolio of IT investments that Ch. 8 discusses, for example) and for developing business scenario models. (Different scenarios, for example, could vary according to the revenue required to qualify as a high-value customer.)

Figure 5.1 provides some idea about the type of information that's captured in a business model. But remember, explaining business models by example poses somewhat of a problem. Although it explicitly differentiates a business model from misconceptions like the cocktail napkin one-liner or the financial model in disguise, BTM doesn't limit companies to one empiri-

Figure | 5.1

An example business model that includes four general categories of elements—overall identify, strategy, external business environment, and internal assets

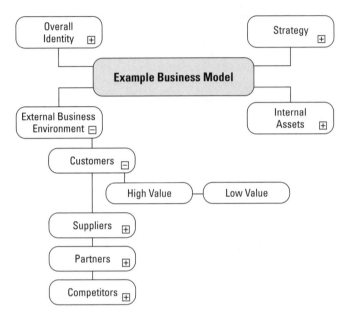

cally correct set of elements to make up the model. So while the categories and elements expressed in Fig. 5.1 provide a pretty good example, they shouldn't be considered a cookie-cutter mold after which every business model should be patterned; each company's unique culture will inevitably produce a unique approach to business modeling, none of which are necessarily "better"—or "worse" for that matter—than any other.

What Varies Within Business Models

Different approaches to business model definition produce specific elements and attributes that are unique to particular companies, business units, or even individual projects. In addition to these differences in content, there are two primary ways in which business models that are developed for BTM differ:

- **The methodology** that is used to define the model
- **The scale** at which the model is developed

Methodology

The first area where business models frequently vary is in the methodology that companies follow to define them. To be effective, the business model must reflect the perspectives, personalities, and priorities that make each company and project unique. This is why there's no one "right" set of elements that defines a business model; anyone who implies that there is underestimates how different companies—and even business units within companies—really are.

In keeping with this spirit of flexibility, this book's discussion of business model definition—and process optimization and technology automation for that matter—doesn't introduce an exact methodology; what works well for Company A's IT project won't always work for Companies B and C. In fact, the unique way that a company goes about defining its business model can be an important source of competitive advantage. But whichever methodology is used should be accessible and familiar to the widest possible audience, so that even non-experts can pick up the business model, understand it, and eventually contribute to it themselves.

Scale

The second area where business models vary is in scale. The scale for a mom-and-pop convenience store is obvious: one store, one business model. But in more complex business environments, the scale at which the business should be viewed isn't always clear-cut. If, for example, you're an IT professional at a huge multinational corporation, is it feasible for you to develop a business model that describes the entire company? Should each line of business have its own model? Or should each business model describe smaller entities like divisions or groups?

The answer to each of these questions is "Yes." Business models can be developed to whatever scale the modelers need to analyze at any given time, from a complete picture of a Fortune 500 conglomerate all the way down to a group of regional salespeople. The purpose that the business model serves, of course, varies according to the model's scale. For example, an enterprise-wide business model can help to break down organizational silos and unify planning across the whole enterprise. A business model scaled to a particular group of employees, on the other hand, can help decision-makers to think through details about how that group functions in order to design IT systems that meet their specific needs.

The way that business models vary according to scale is roughly analogous to strategy—which similarly can be decomposed at any level of the enterprise. The strategy for an individual business unit, for example, might include determining which new products to introduce, how to market them, and so on, while strategy at the corporate level would concentrate on general product lines, markets, and the long-term future direction of the enterprise.

Defining the Business Model In BTM

Having established what business model means in BTM, it makes sense to move on to discuss how companies put business model definition to work helping them develop better business cases for their IT projects. Skipping this crucial activity can lead to damaging oversights. First, developing a business case without first modeling the business makes it difficult to develop and compare alternative business scenarios—a step that is essential for performing impact analysis. Second, business model definition requires planners to think through a complete, big-picture view of the business. Since a picture is worth a thousand words, this view makes it easier for team members to visualize solutions, avoid a myopic focus, and contribute their expertise to the business case. And finally, since most business cases are simply paper documents, they can't be counted on the same way that a business model can to provide the concrete links to process and technology that form the basis for alignment. This last point is especially important because of the unpredictable nature of IT projects. Even the most thought-out initiative invariably faces unforeseen hurdles as it progresses from design to implementation. By giving the IT specialists, who are charged with finding these impromptu solutions, a mechanism for tracing back to the original business model, BTM helps to ensure that even the worst snags are ironed out for the good of the project as a whole.

Business model definition alleviates these concerns by providing a mechanism to perform as-is/to-be gap analysis for the parts of the business that could be affected by the project. The first of BTM's activities involves four general steps: drawing the big picture, understanding the as-is current business model, creating a portfolio of business scenario models that represent possible to-be states for impact analysis, and incorporating changes made by the project into an updated current business model.

Drawing the Big Picture

Since business models represent big-picture snapshots of the business (or business unit, division, or group), realistically they aren't likely to change all that often; established companies don't completely reinvent their business models except in the most extreme cases. Most IT projects, then, find that they're able to leverage an existing current business model rather than develop one from scratch.

There are cases, however, when project teams need to develop a business model before beginning the activities of BTM—after a major change to the business environment such as a merger or acquisition, for example. When this happens, it is essential to include input from as many subject-matter experts as possible. These contributors should work in the model directly to make sure that details aren't lost in the translation, and to increase their own understanding of the business by analyzing other parts of the model. When it isn't feasible to ask subject-matter experts to develop the model directly, the team can gather input for the business model either through surveys and data collection, or by talking to experts face-to-face during a meeting or seminar. No matter how the current business model is developed the first time around, it's important to consider the infamous "80/20 rule": 80% of the benefit comes from 20% of the effort. There's no point in agonizing over every detail in the current business model since its primary purpose is to provide a general starting point for spawning more specific business scenario models.

This highlights an important point about business model definition: The direct benefits that companies derive from modeling the business come from two sources. First, and most obviously, there are the specific elements and attributes that make up each of the models—the end products of business model definition. Second, and of equal importance, is the actual process of researching and defining the model—whether constructing a current business model from scratch or developing scenarios for impact analysis. The deliberate act of creating the model compels decision makers to think through the complete business landscape, and ultimately uncover hidden opportunities for improvement.

Understanding the Current Business Model

The process of creating or updating the current business model is an important one that companies will undoubtedly face from time to time. But it's important to distinguish this endeavor from business model definition as it's typically practiced in most projects. Recall that the purpose of the activities of BTM, (of which business model definition is the first) is to create a series of models that express as-is and to-be versions of the enterprise architecture. Since the as-is enterprise architecture rarely needs to be redefined from scratch, drawing the big picture isn't a part of most IT projects. Instead, business model definition usually begins when the project team sits down, queries their repository of reusable assets, and ensures that they completely understand the current business model.

Understanding the current business model before diving into detailed process and technology solutions improves the process by which companies justify IT projects in two important ways. First, it makes it easier to put a project in the appropriate context, thus freeing team members from the assumption that they need to justify every process, technology asset, and resource on the basis of their current project alone. More importantly, examining the current business model forces even technical experts to view the world from the business's point of view. IT professionals, for example, might learn from the current business model that improving customer service is a priority in the upcoming calendar year. As a result, they might be more likely to suggest that their current project include an audit of the company's call center processes and systems.

Many IT departments have a history of making technology decisions based on myopic, IT-centric justifications (such as the latest technology trends) without anticipating how these decisions may impact the business. By employing the current business model as a reference for IT, experts can help specialists who normally focus on specialized tasks to understand essential business basics. In this regard, the current business model deliberately covers a lot of ground without going into too much detail in any area; the integrated, big-picture view forces the project team to think through how the business works at a high level. They can then base process and technology decisions directly on that understanding.

Creating Business Scenario Models

Once the team understands the current business model, they can begin to create the business scenario models that form the basis for end-to-end impact analysis in BTM. Each scenario represents a viable, to-be alternative for accomplishing the goals set out for the project. For example, a procurement project may require one scenario to describe what it would take to join a public exchange, and another scenario to describe what would be required to develop and host a private exchange for preferred suppliers. By conducting a gap analysis between the current business model and each potential scenario model, the team fleshes out which parts of the current model are relevant to their project. This helps planners to measure the scope of change that each scenario requires, including the people, assets, and internal and external business relationships that will be impacted. Also, the structured and visual nature of models makes it easy for the team to compare these scenarios and eventually combine the best of each.

Incorporating Changes into an Updated Current Business Model

After the project has been successfully implemented, the team folds its final business scenario (or an updated scenario if changes were made before the project was completed) into the current business model, ensuring that upcoming projects have access to the latest, most accurate design of the business. This is similar to roundtrip engineering in software development, which ensures that the actual changes made to the real-world environment (the code in roundtrip engineering and the business in BTM) are reflected in an updated model (the object model in roundtrip engineering or the current business model in BTM). Business model definition, then, helps to bridge the knowledge gaps that traditionally exist between projects, and becomes a vehicle for making sure that the current enterprise architecture remains accessible and up-to-date with a minimum of dedicated maintenance.

Why Business Model Definition?

Three emerging trends illustrate why business model definition is a necessary component for today's IT projects:

- **The continuously evolving technology** environment presents companies with opportunities to innovate the business
- **The formal hierarchies** in the enterprise that were once responsible for discrete components of the business model are breaking down
- **High employee turnover** makes it essential that companies institutionalize knowledge about their business environment

Technology Evolution Drives Continuous Business Innovation

In the past, much of the information captured in the business model had been informally maintained and updated by word-of-mouth and general understanding of the business. Since the pace of business innovation was relatively slow, it was easy to keep track of seemingly routine knowledge such as the customer base, product portfolio, and company vision, and it was assumed that every manager knew this crucial information by heart.

But in the face of one of the enduring legacies from the New Economy—the recognition that technology advances can provide a basis for innovating the business—this familiar paradigm must change. Today's companies have sped up their business planning to keep pace with trends like globalization, deregulation, and especially the torrent of IT breakthroughs that continue to flow out of laboratories and research and development (R&D) departments. To be prepared to capitalize upon the new opportunities offered by tomorrow's technology innovations, enterprises are moving from a paradigm where business priorities are re-evaluated after regular but long intervals, to one of continuous re-examination of the business model. Analyst META Group, in fact, predicts that "30% of CIOs will adopt a shorter planning cycle (no more than three months)," and eventually, "leading global 2000 organizations will [implement] a continuous, dynamic strategic planning process."[1] By codifying the loose-knit information that makes up the business model and providing a central location for storing business designs, business model definition helps companies cope with this perpetually shifting business environment.

Formal Hierarchies Are Breaking Down

The second trend that is driving companies to adopt business model definition is the breakdown of traditional hierarchies within the organization. In the conventional, pyramid-shaped organizational model, IT projects usually addressed only a narrow slice of the business. (The product development team, for example, might have sole responsibility for bringing new products to market and balancing the product portfolio.) This siloed approach meant that members of a particular project team were very familiar with their own area of responsibility, and rarely needed to look beyond the borders of their organizational unit to complete the project.

In many of today's organizations, however, rigid reporting structures have broken down, and IT teams are being asked to develop solutions for a cross-functional audience. In order for these teams to make design decisions to service this broad user base, they need to develop a more complete understanding of the business. At the same time, project teams are frequently staffed with members that come from across the business, including the business unit professionals for whom the project is intended, as well as subject-matter experts ranging from process engineers to enterprise architects to software developers. These diverse teams, regardless of their individual backgrounds, need an accessible, broad-based snapshot of the business around which they can discuss alternatives and make intelligent trade-offs.

High Employee Turnover

The final trend that is driving enterprises to embrace business model definition is the high turnover of employees, especially in the IT department. Before the development of structured business models, crucial knowledge about the business was maintained only in the heads of relevant managers. Since the business was relatively static, these managers could be counted on to educate their reports and make sure that individual decisions complemented overall strategy and objectives.

But in the IT world, turnover runs rampant; specialists with sought-after skill sets are recruited for other projects, consultants walk out the door after their engagement ends, and opportunities in a competitive job market lead employees to pursue new and greener pastures. Information that was once safe with long-time employees might be gone tomorrow. By formally capturing the business model and making it available to new hires or employees with new responsibilities, companies make sure that crucial decisions can be maintained even if the minds that first made them are long gone.

Business Model Definition In Action

The variability in which the activities of BTM can be performed and the breadth of information they cover makes it difficult to capture the essence of business model definition, process optimization, and technology automation without seeing them in action. For this reason, Ch. 5, 6, and 7 each refer to a simulated case that illustrates how the activities of BTM might work in a fictional business environment.

Rauha Communications, a telecommunications company, has kicked off a project intended to roll out CRM in its wireless services division. This initiative, code named Project Alpha, has two strategic objectives: First, the company wants to identify their most valuable customers and cross-sell new data services to them. Second, deregulation has increased competitive pressures on the company, and they want to improve their customer service to minimize the attrition of these high-value customers.

This simulated case provides a series of valuable glimpses into the people and day-to-day tasks that are impacted when a company undertakes the activities of BTM, and, more importantly, into some specific advantages that can follow from doing so. For business model definition, this example illustrates how Rauha Communications goes about defining its current business model, and how stakeholders collaborate with one another and leverage insights provided by the current business model to help build compelling business scenario models for Project Alpha.

Capture An As-Is Current Business Model

Soon after Rauha Communications kicks off Project Alpha, a business analyst staffed on the project meets with the project manager, and is tasked with meeting an important milestone: coordinating between multiple team members and external stakeholders from the business to construct a current business model. This fits well within the business analyst's normal job function, which is to serve as a mediator between the requirements of the business and the capabilities of the IT department.

Normally, Rauha Communications wouldn't be starting from scratch with their as-is state of the business; the project or program management office (PMO) would provide a similar model that could be used as a starting point. But Project Alpha is the wireless services division's first initiative to take advantage of BTM; previous projects relied on unstructured, paper-based analysis of the business. Before Project Alpha can really get underway, then, the business analyst needs to put together a big-picture view of the business to use as a starting point.

Putting this picture together will involve two major tasks. First, the analyst will need to create a general, high-level snapshot of the wireless services division, since this is the functional unit for which the project is intended. The business analyst pulls information from the project charter, the current operating plan for wireless services, and some business cases developed for previous projects to complete this picture. Figure 5.2 illustrates the big-picture view that the business analyst creates.

Figure 5.2

A high-level view of the current business model for Rauha Communications that drills down to reveal the major goals for Project Alpha

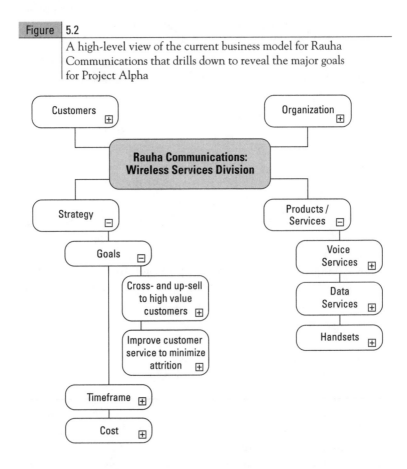

The second task requires the business analyst to define portions of the business model that are relevant to Project Alpha in more detail. This means coordinating in-depth with the business unit, so he reviews the project charter to determine appropriate contacts

from each division. This research yields three names: a marketing manager, a director of sales, and a customer support supervisor. Since these three people will represent the end-user base for the CRM system, it's essential that they be brought into the planning process early on.

Because the marketing, sales, and customer support divisions are all located in the same physical location, the business analyst is able to schedule a morning workshop that includes the three representatives from the business. The workshop begins as the business analyst walks through each of the high-level business model elements that are defined, and asks the marketing manager, director of sales, and customer support supervisor to flesh out the details that relate to Project Alpha. For example, the marketing manager describes each of the product and service offerings, as well as the hardware and distribution partners; the director of sales confirms the specific distribution channels, and refers to a data warehouse of customer information that can be used to identify high-value customers.

By encouraging representatives from disparate parts of the business to collaborate and share information beyond their usual organizational boundaries, the business analyst creates a current business model of the wireless services division that will function as a starting point for Project Alpha. When the next project is kicked off, presumably with different objectives, business model definition will begin with this current, as-is state. Over time, as individual projects flesh out specific areas, the model will become a more accurate and complete picture of the wireless services division.

Develop Business Scenario Models For Impact Analysis

After the current business model is in place, Rauha Communications' project team moves on to developing each of the business scenario models that form the basis for impact analysis. The team collaborates with marketing, sales, and customer support representatives to examine the current business model as a starting point, and to identify areas where technology might be used to improve the business. Once an opportunity has been identified, it is fleshed out as a business scenario model, or potential to-be state.

After examining Project Alpha's current business model, a marketing assistant suggests that the project could help increase revenue if it were timed to coincide with a campaign to cross- and up-sell to existing customers. This prompts a representative of the sales department to point out that the existing data warehouse of customer information could be a powerful tool for segmenting the customer base according to total spend, demographics, and past purchases. The marketing assistant agrees, and adds that segmenting this data would also help her to hone the discount structure and improve margins. This multifaceted analysis of the model leads the team to create a particular business scenario model that promises to increase revenue by cross- and up-selling to existing customers who are identified by a new customer segmentation component (see Fig. 5.3).

Figure 5.3

A high-level view of a business scenario model for Project Alpha that drills down to reveal customer segments

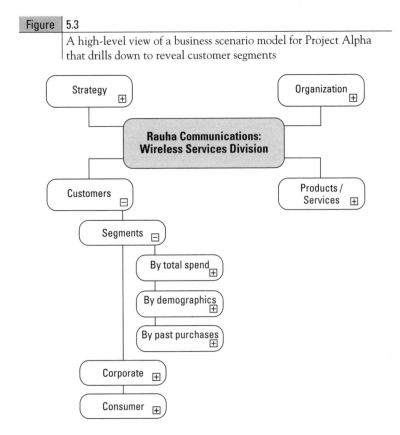

By using the current business model as a vehicle for communication and collaboration between beneficiaries of the project, Rauha Communications' project team helps to ensure that the business scenario models that they build pull together all of the relevant internal and external assets of the enterprise. In this way, the as-is model acts as a vehicle for collaboration between otherwise disparate beneficiaries of the project, who, by contributing their personal expertise, are able to identify drivers for the business scenario model that complements each of their areas of responsibility.

Who is Responsible for Defining the Business Model?

The example of Rauha Communications illustrates a fundamental advantage of business model definition: it encourages communication and coordination between the people who are responsible for justifying IT projects to the business. This group often involves more actors than either of the other two activities of BTM. The primary responsibility for modeling the business falls upon business analysts—members of the IT department who specialize in identifying how the business should put IT to work. These business analysts typically coordinate with representatives from different business units to collect the relevant design information (as illustrated by the inclusion of the marketing manager, director of sales, and customer support supervisor in the example from Rauha Communications). In addition, process experts should contribute to the model as well, since they will eventually be responsible for ensuring that the business processes developed during process automation match up with each business scenario model.

Convincing each of these actors to embrace business model definition is an essential requirement for companies who are looking to adopt BTM. By making this move, they help to close disconnects between IT and the business, breakdown the silos hamper holistic business planning, and end dependency on ple, paper-based strategy documents. But business model definition also provides another important advantage: it helps analysts to decompose abstract ideas about the design of the business into concrete elements. These elements can then be directly linked to the business processes that will be impacted during process optimization—the second activity of BTM.

6

Process Optimization

THE SECOND ACTIVITY OF BTM, process optimization, serves as the critical link between business model definition and technology automation. It is during process optimization that business objectives are translated from the business model into operational processes—a coordinated set of tasks designed to produce a specific outcome. These processes are then broken down (i.e., "decomposed") into sub-processes and activities in order to map functional requirements to the technology that will eventually support them. Our discussion of process optimization begins by describing what goes into a process model. Then, this chapter moves on to discuss some of the primary tasks associated with process optimization and to explain why they are important in the context of BTM's two other models (business and technology). It also revisits the simulated case of Rauha Communications to illustrate how process optimization takes inputs from business model definition and creates outputs for technology automation, before concluding with a discussion of the party responsible for this go-between activity.

What is a Process Model?

At one end of the spectrum, people associate a process model with a simple flow chart. At the other end of the spectrum, people associate it with complex variants such as use cases and discrete event models. BTM's concept of a process model falls somewhere between these two extremes. Process models are highly graphical in nature. They are usually expressed as a diagram in which shapes represent tasks and line connectors represent links or flows. So it is easy to understand why, on the surface, they might resemble common flow charts. In addition to this visual diagram, however, process models also contain a rich set of attributes and depict a complex series of relationships. Attribute information including metrics (average time to process a sales order, for example) can be useful inputs for other activities such as discrete event model simulation, while relationships help to capture process requirements and identify dependencies between people, processes, and technologies. The important distinction to make between a process model and its more simple and complex relatives is that it encapsulates the correct amount of detail for timely, real-world analysis and decision-making, without going to the extreme of empirical unreality.

In general, process models include four categories of items:

- **Process Hierarchies** provide a logical structure that groups processes into levels for easier viewing, understanding, and analysis.
- **Process Definitions and Flows** describe how a company performs operational tasks and indicate both the order in which the tasks are performed and the information that is passed back and forth during the execution of those tasks.

- **Domains and Roles** specify who is responsible in the organization for carrying out particular tasks along with the outright ownership or sharing of responsibility.
- **Metrics and Rules** describe how well a process should perform and indicate how specific conditions dictate the way or timing in which particular tasks are performed.

Process Hierarchies

The depth to which an organization chooses to decompose its processes depends on how work activity is divided among the various horizontal and vertical layers of the organization, and on the extent of the process analysis being conducted. At a minimum, a process hierarchy should include three levels—processes, sub-processes, and activities. The purpose of the hierarchy is to provide a logical structure for drilling down from one process area to the next. This is especially helpful given the complex nature of enterprise processes. A beginning-to-end map of just a single enterprise process—even without depicting any related processes—could easily span the walls of an entire conference room. Organizing process elements into hierarchies makes it easy to group and traverse different levels. For example, the process Invoice and Service Customers could be broken down into the sub-processes Bill the Customer, Provide After-sales Service, and Respond to Customer Inquiries. The Bill the Customer sub-process could be further decomposed into the activities Develop, Deliver, and Maintain Customer Billing, Invoice the Customer, and Respond to Billing Inquiries (see Fig. 6.1).

Classifying processes into a hierarchy also facilitates the identification of appropriate anchor points for cross-links between the process model and business or technology models. This makes it easier to follow decisions from one model to the next to achieve alignment. In the above example, the process, Invoice and Service Customers, could be linked back to the business objective, Make it Easier For Our Customers to Carry Out Transactions With Us, to show how requirements from the business model are inherited into process optimization. Similarly, the activity, Invoice the Customer, could be linked forward to the application functionality, Electronic Bill Presentment, in the technology model to show where specific application and system decisions originate.

An example process hierarchy for the Invoice and Service
Customers process

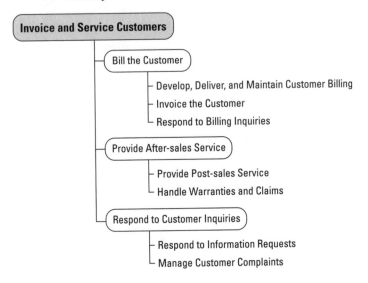

Process Definitions and Flows

The purpose of process definitions and flows is to provide a
detailed understanding of how work is performed from a beginning
to an end point. They describe operational tasks in both graphical
(diagrammatic) and textual terms. Shapes and text identify what
task is being performed and how it happens. While there is no cat-
egorically right or wrong way to describe tasks with shapes, there
are commonly accepted representations. For instance, a rectangle
is often used to represent a process, a diamond to represent a decision, an upside-down quadrilateral to represent a manual operation, a parallelogram to represent data, an ellipse to represent a
termination point, and so on. Text that is associated with each
shape—expressed in clear business terminology instead of technical jargon—provides additional information that explains the task
to a broad audience (see Fig. 6.2).

In general, there are two main types of flows: work flow and
information flow. Work flow refers to the order in which tasks are
performed, and indicates whether tasks are carried out sequen-

tially or in parallel. Information flow shadows work flow and describes how information and decisions travel between tasks. Line connectors graphically tie the tasks together and illustrate the type of relationships (input or output) between them. The combination of process definitions and flows provides insight into the tasks that are manual, automated, out-sourced, or documented; the interdependencies that exist between tasks; and the informational or functional needs of each task.

| Figure | 6.2 |

An example process flow that depicts the billing process for a hypothetical automobile insurer

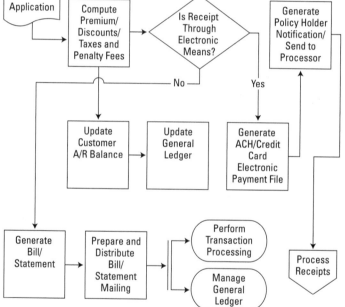

Several notations are available that attempt to standardize how process definitions and flows are depicted, including Rummler-Brache, Integrated DEFinition (IDEF), Entry/Task/Validation/eXit (ETVX), Line of Visibility Engineering Methodology (LOVEM)®, and Role Activity Diagrams (RADs)[1]. These vary according to their application and intended audience. Each has its strengths and weaknesses regarding its balance between uniform representation and the need for practical and flexible use. The decision to adhere or not to a particular notation should be made by each company independently based on the skills of its work force, the scope and objective of its process analysis, and the effort that will be required to enforce compliance.

Domains and Roles

Domains and roles identify the areas of the business and the individuals that are responsible for executing processes. Domains more or less correspond to the enterprise's organizational units. Examples of typical, generic domains include manufacturing, sales, marketing, customer support, finance, and human resource management. Examples of more industry-specific domains are claims processing, store operations, and plant management. Roles (sometimes referred to as actors) indicate who owns tasks at a more granular level—departmental, group, individual, location site, internal, or external. Domains and roles are represented horizontally or vertically as swim lanes that are overlaid on process diagrams to demonstrate how tasks are segregated or shared. Figure 6.3 shows how swim lanes are applied to the previous example of the auto insurance billing process.

The focus on domains and roles sometimes creates confusion between aspects of process optimization and those of organizational design. The primary intent of domains and roles is not to recreate or reengineer the organizational structure of a company. Instead, it is to group similar sets of processes, sub-processes, and activities together in a way that approximates how the business categorizes its operations and to highlight where responsibilities are transferred between organizational entities. This makes it easier to visualize how process changes might impact resource utilization, staffing, training, and cross-functional requirements.

Figure | 6.3

Swim lanes in our example billing process flow indicate who owns each task

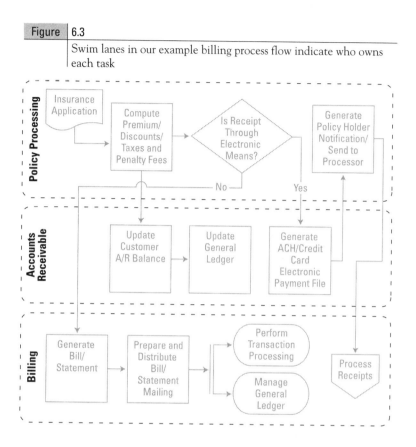

Metrics and Rules

Companies generally apply a combination of performance metrics to their processes. Performance metrics specify how well a company needs to execute certain tasks. They tend to focus on target outputs that are more external in nature, such as meeting customer requirements. These metrics are expressed in terms of frequency, volume, effort level, error rates, cycle time, forecast accuracy, customer satisfaction, and such. For example, a company that wants to decrease return rates for its products might assign an accuracy performance metric to the order fulfillment process. Or, a company following the Six Sigma® methodology might assign a numerical value to the invoice-processing activity to indicate what the statistically valid ideal should be per hour.

The process model also includes rules, designed to act as checks and balances on the execution of a particular process. The business owner of the process (domain, department, group, etc.) determines what rules need to be applied in order to ensure that certain process goals are met. Mostly, these rules are conditional—if condition A is met then do B. Benefits enrollment terms, seasonal pricing schedules, credit checks, inventory replenishment alerts, and purchase-level amount authorizations are typical conditions that might require the application of rules to a process. It is important to note that these are not application logic rules or database triggers that actually automate the process; they do however, guide application and system developers in translating these business principles into programming code.

Metrics and rules are assigned in the process model as attributes. Figure 6.4a demonstrates how metrics are assigned to the sub-process Pick Orders. Figure 6.4b illustrates how rules are assigned to the activity Perform Physical Inventory Count of the Manage Inventory sub-process.

Figure	6.4a

The metric Perfect Order Fulfillment is assigned to the process Pick Orders

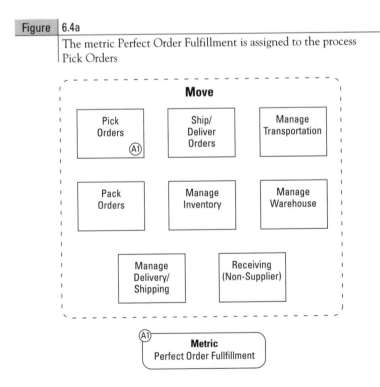

Figure	6.4b

A rule that indicates an alert should be sent to the materials manager if inventory falls below 66% is assigned to the process Perform Physical Inventory Count

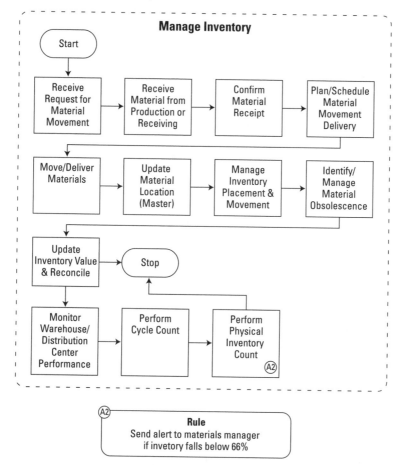

Optimizing Processes in BTM

Before the recent period of "technology for technology's sake," there was an equally irrational time when corporations tackled "process for process's sake." This phase, known as the business process reengineering (BPR) era, called for the radical reinvention of all processes across the enterprise. BPR promised quantum gains in operational efficiency and competitive advantage. However, it often wreaked havoc on organizations, leaving them to wonder what value they received in return for the millions they spent. It's no wonder that now, when you even utter the phrase "process model" some executives and managers go weak in the knees envisioning a return to the "bad old days." So, I want to be clear that when I use the term "process optimization," I do not mean revisiting BPR.

What I do mean by process optimization is the analysis and design of processes to provide a link between the business objectives and the supporting technology for a given IT project. The wholesale revamp of the process environment is not required. Instead, process optimization focuses on improving the specific processes that support each proposed business scenario model. Working from the current process model—which depicts the existing process environment—process analysts and domain experts collaborate to generate to-be models that satisfy the aims of the business scenario models. Next, they perform a gap analysis between the current process model and each to-be model to determine which processes need to be eliminated, streamlined, automated, or out-sourced, and to anticipate the potential impact of these changes on supporting applications and systems.

Drilling down from this high-level view of process optimization, there are four key steps within process optimization: translate business model requirements, assess the value of existing processes, analyze process gaps, and develop functional requirements.

Translate Business Model Requirements

Since the process model acts as a lynchpin between the business and technology models, it is important to first understand the relationship it has with the business model. Each process model takes its cue from to-be business scenario models that describe the objectives of the project, elements of the business that it impacts, and scenarios the organization might pursue. This inherited information is then cross-linked to processes, sub-processes, and activities that can operationalize the business model alternatives. Cross-linking between models enables the process analysts, domain experts, and IT specialists to analyze the repercussions that each business scenario model has on operations, resources, assets, information, and supporting technology.

The benefits of linking particular elements of the business model to those of the process model are twofold. First, by translating what are essentially business model requirements into process terms, it is possible to limit process improvements to those that are practical and achievable. Assumptions made in the business model scenarios (which may be based on superficial process knowledge) need to be validated against the intricate realities captured by the process model. Certain business model requirements may not be feasible given constraints within the existing process environment; nor may they be feasible (or even advisable) after changes are enacted in order to fulfill them. For example, a company may wish to assess the viability of their business objective to lower helpdesk support costs by bringing an out-sourced call center function in-house. By evaluating this business objective against current and alternative process environments, they may discover that it is more cost effective—when considered against the staffing, facilities, training, and systems costs required to support the function internally—to simply renegotiate the current contract and extend helpdesk service to business units not already covered under its terms. This approach to process optimization is iterative; lessons learned in the process optimization phase can be passed backward to business model definition, allowing requirements to be redefined or initiatives terminated if necessary.

The second benefit of linking business model requirements to elements in the process model is traceability. The rationale for certain process optimization changes can be explicitly traced back to the original business requirement driving the change. The resulting audit trail helps teams to communicate to project stakeholders how the organization plans to realize its objectives. Also, it can help the team to educate stakeholders regarding what it will require in order to accomplish specific goals.

Assess the Value of Existing Processes

Assessing the value of existing processes and internal/external participant relationships fulfills a vital step in process optimization. This assessment, which requires analyzing the current process model in the context of business goals, reveals inefficiencies and redundancies; critical interactions and interdependencies between activities; and opportunities for innovation. Because the current process model provides an accurate and realistic view of how work is carried out in practice—including typically undocumented workarounds that equate to hidden tasks or decisions—it can help to uncover bottlenecks, unproductive and counterproductive steps, time delays, hand-offs, and costs. Some activities may be redundant and therefore represent waste that can be excised from the process environment. Others that cross several departmental boundaries may have no identifiable owner and therefore, slip through the cracks. Still others may have outlived the original business rationale that justifies their usefulness. This step is essential for gaining insight into which processes should be eliminated, streamlined, automated, or out-sourced. It also provides the basis for developing to-be process scenario models that describe potential alternatives for operationalizing proposed business model scenarios.

Spending Time on the Future Saves Money

"It's one thing to have a visioning session to discuss 'what we really want to be to our customers,' but it's a whole other thing to say how we actually should bring this off. The future-state touch map is the first step in that sort of actualization of the vision. When you're designing a future state, you're designing it from a vision, and the vision is inherently holistic, because you are looking at your business from the customer's perspective. Once we begin designing processes around that future state, and when we outline the customer interactions around it, we will get a comprehensive, integrated view of our real business.

There are some companies that are extremely self-reflective, constantly examining themselves and paying particular attention to process. For them the kind of visioning that we're talking about—setting up the future state touchmap—is a piece of cake; it might be a perspective they haven't thought of very seriously before, but nevertheless, it's something that's not hard to do. For other companies it can be like picking hens' teeth to generate a touchmap of any kind, because they just don't pay a lot of attention to process. They may be too busy simply making sure that their head remains above the day-to-day financial tidewaters. Done right, however, a future-state touchmap will streamline your interactions, cut out waste, eliminate duplication, and give you a more rational feel for your business, not only cutting out costs but pointing out additional revenue opportunities."

– **Don Peppers,** *best-selling author of the One to One book series, and a founding partner at the management consulting firm Peppers and Rogers Group.*

Analyze Process Gaps

Comparing current process models against process scenario models allows process analysts and domain experts to analyze differences and identify gaps between their existing and desired environments. This analysis is important for understanding the true impact that proposed changes will have on process design, work and information flows, employees that perform the operational tasks, external relationships such as customers and suppliers, and the underlying technology that must be in place to support it all. For example, process analysts and domain experts often need to ascertain which is more beneficial: reengineering a process to match the functional capabilities provided by a particular application package or customizing the package to fit the requirements of the process. In order to make this type of decision they need to be able to consider a wide range of possible implications (see Table 6.1).

What, at first glance, may appear to be a simple either/or decision (reengineer or customize), actually involves making a series of

Table 6.1

Modifying processes can impact the enterprise in a number of areas

Area	Characteristics
Processes	– New, modified, or terminated activities – Automation of manual tasks – Cross-functional/cross-organizational dependencies – Metrics, rules
Organization	– Reassignment, hiring of staff – Training, skills development – Administrative, technical support – Policies, procedures
Information	– Cross-sharing data needs – Data capture, location – Data access, security – Data flow, migration
Relationships	– Physical, electronic interactions – Customer, supplier, partner, service provider, distributor, regulatory interactions
Technology/ Facilities	– Acquire, lease – Build, develop – Enhance, upgrade – Consolidate, retire – Customize

sub-decisions. For instance: If we reengineer Process A what impact will that have on Sub-processes X, Y, and Z? Do we need to require that our suppliers change their processes too? What level of information access is required and does that mean we need to change our security protocol? What is the amount of internal technical support that will be required if we make changes to the vendor's application package? Is this same package already being used by other business units for the same process? By analyzing gaps and determining impacts in this way, process analysts and domain experts can make informed decisions regarding the benefits, risks, requirements, and trade-offs involved in implementing changes. They can also use this same information to solicit buy-in on proposed process scenario models from the project's business and technology stakeholders.

Develop Functional Requirements

During gap analysis, process analysts and domain experts may make the decision to automate specific activities with technology or to enhance how previously deployed business applications function. If this is the case, then the subsequent and final step of process optimization is to develop functional requirements for those activities. Functional requirements describe in non-technical terms the steps and possible rules involved in executing the activity. Take a typical insurance industry sub-process, Review and Approve Claims, for example. The functional requirements for automating select activities of this sub-process may look something like this:

- **Determine claim** type by profile
- **Determine payment** type by profile
- **View claims** status
- **View claims** payment record
- **Route approved** claims for disbursement
- **Single sign-on** to claims environment

Describing functional requirements in this way helps process analysts to communicate how work is performed from the perspective of the end-user. The benefit of this is twofold: first, it helps process analysts to carefully think through how processes are performed, which can prevent them from overlooking critical steps; second, it helps IT professionals understand the needs of the user community from more than a bits or bytes viewpoint when trying to build or deploy supporting technologies. The hand-off between these two domains, which is otherwise difficult, must be as seamless as possible in order to avoid miscommunication or misinterpretation of requirements.

After they are developed and prioritized, functional requirements are cross-linked with application and system requirements defined later in the technology model. Creating linkages between the two types of requirements ensures alignment between process and technology domains. It also provides traceability for process analysts and IT teams to verify that all functional requirements are satisfied.

Why Process Optimization?

Process optimization provides a mechanism to achieve the following challenges and benefits:

- **Integrate processes** across the whitespace that can occur between functions, departments, business units, or companies
- **Achieve business-driven,** rather than function- or component-driven process improvement and change
- **Create a common requirements** vision to mirror shared services across multiple organizational units and achieve continuous improvement
- **Improve visibility** into vendor functionality to understand degree of fit and reduce integration complexities
- **Provide a basis** for simulation or activity-based costing (ABC) process performance improvements

Integrate Processes across Whitespaces

Whitespace, as defined in Ch. 3, is the gap that can occur between strategy and operations, between organizational units, and between perceived or actual behaviors. Whitespace problems can lead to poor operational or financial performance, because responsibilities for tasks fall through the organizational cracks (the old line, "But I thought you took care it!") or because they hide weak or deficient processes. Process optimization helps to identify and eliminate whitespaces.

First, defining and assessing the value of existing processes erases corporate assumptions about how work is performed throughout the organization. Everyone may think that they agree on how processes work in their organization, but few actually possess accurate, detailed process knowledge. Once companies capture the realities of their operational environment with models, they can use them as a basis to detect unknown process breaks and weaknesses. Second, the swim lanes that are overlaid on current process and process scenario models enable process analysts and domain experts to visualize how processes cross back and forth across organizational boundaries. By constructing models in this way, it is possible to highlight who does what activities and when during a process. This is especially critical when processes extend to external parties such as customers and suppliers, increasing the likelihood that the execution or management of particular tasks may be obscured. Third, archived models that serve as templates for future process optimization efforts essentially create an institutional memory that can be recalled to fill in gaps left by employees or contractors who have left the company.

Achieve Business-Driven Process Change

Some companies still use and favor two process modeling techniques designed in the 1980s—the Zachman Framework[2] and the Spewak EAP Model[3]. Given the mercurial nature of today's business and technology environments, there are drawbacks to relying on either. First, they focus on optimizing domain architectures. As a result they are more function- and component-driven than they are business-driven; and they require that a company invest significant time, money, and resources in an exhaustive analysis of enterprise architecture. Traditionally, business stakeholders have had a difficult time justifying the expense of such efforts because of an unclear or lagging return. In contrast, process optimization focuses already scarce resources on analyzing processes and creating improvements that can satisfy immediate or near-term business needs. Business value (not technological prowess) is the aim, and faster proof of concepts can be produced to sell change ideas to management.

Second, both methods were developed during a time in the 1980s when the business environment and enterprise architectures evolved at a slower pace. In complex enterprise scenarios, completing such an endeavor can take up to two years. Nowadays, the rate of business and technological change is blistering, requiring companies to modify their process environments on the average of every six to twelve months. Companies, and therefore project teams, must respond quickly to accommodate unforeseen changes as they ripple throughout the enterprise architecture. Ch. 1 provides evidence of how changes in the business climate can affect the success of a project. Process optimization, which involves the linking of process models to business and technology models, provides teams with the ability to adapt in step as the initiative's business or technology requirements change.

For each of these reasons, the Zachman and Spewak methods are complements to process optimization—they are more practical as stand-alone improvement initiatives or as long-range planning exercises that can supplement the day-to-day design of IT projects.

Create a Common Requirements Vision

The increased sharing of IT services across business units and the need to continually find ways to improve the operational environment has led some companies to create a common requirements vision across multiple process activities. Through modeling activities, process optimization facilitates the discovery and pooling of shared requirements. With this aggregated understanding of functional requirements, companies can streamline activities, avoid redundancies, encourage adoption of process standards, manage change efficiently, and uncover customer service or time-to-market improvements. For example, process analysts may discover that they can increase the efficiency of billing activities and offer customers a single point of contact for invoice inquiries by processing all requests through one system. In another scenario, visibility into previously defined common requirements may lead IT analysts to reuse components, rules, interfaces, and data related to an existing order processing application instead of purchasing a new application. From a change management perspective, process optimization can also help to reveal the magnitude of impact that changes in the technology architecture—such as redesign, replacement, or upgrade—can have on an interdependent processes environment.

Improve Visibility into Vendor Functionality

With the ever-rising complexity and cost of enterprise application integration (EAI) efforts, it is essential that project teams improve their understanding of how vendor offerings map to processes before purchase and implementation. The definitions, flows, and functional requirements encapsulated in the process model help process and IT analysts to evaluate the fit between the two. By examining these elements of the process model and comparing them against the capabilities of the application package, analysts can expose biases, assumptions, and constraints that are not revealed during the typical feature/function checklist review. Let's take the example of a company evaluating a vendor's supply chain package to determine the fit between its automatic load-routing functionality and their transportation management process. The design of the company's Receive and Ship Orders sub-process requires that carriers meet up-to-date contractual requirements prior to receipt and loading of goods. The functional requirement could be Verify Contract Rates Meet Approved Schedule. The process, in effect, demands that the final package account for this condition in its transportation planning module. If the vendor cannot match this requirement with out-of-the-box functionality, this represents a constraint. Analysts will then have to decide if the requirement is non-negotiable, and if so, how they can satisfy the requirement through customization, alternate package selection, or other means.

In the end, process optimization helps project teams make the right judgment call between end-user non-negotiables and application requirements earlier in the evaluation process, resulting in reduced integration costs and improved solution delivery.

Provide Inputs to Simulation and ABC Efforts

Simulation and ABC efforts are extensions of process optimization that attempt to improve how the process itself performs. Simulation is generally practiced during BPR initiatives. It involves conducting animated "what-if" experiments on current process models to reveal bottlenecks or underutilized activities. These experiments (also known as discrete or continuous event simulations) help process engineers measure the effect of changes on variables such as timing, queuing, scheduling, resources, and costs. ABC methods uncover waste or inefficiency by calculating and analyzing cost consumption per activity (e.g., generate purchase order). This differs from traditional accounting methods that track lumped costs per department (e.g., marketing). Once again, current process models provide the basis for analysis, allowing process engineers to associate operating costs and capital charges with the activities represented in the model.

Process Optimization In Action

Let me return to the example of Rauha Communications from Ch. 5. This example shows how process optimization acts as a vital conduit between business model definition and technology automation. First, Rauha Communications' project team will examine their as-is processes to understand how the company currently supports its customers and to uncover inefficiencies, dependencies, and opportunities for improvement. Next, the team will perform a gap analysis for the customer support process to flesh out the functional requirements that will meet the objectives of the business scenario models and ultimately drive technology automation. Finally, process optimization provides the project team with visibility into unforeseen changes so that they can proactively respond as change ripples down from the business model.

Examine the As-Is Process Environment

Taking a cue from the goals outlined in the to-be business scenario model, process analysts assigned to Project Alpha begin to examine the existing process environment to see what changes will be required. The goals outlined in each business scenario model help them to prioritize and to concentrate their efforts on potentially impacted processes. The bulk of their analysis focuses on subprocesses of the Manage Customers process in order to transform customer support operations into a 24-hour solution center. However, the ancillary business goal—to increase revenue by cross- and up-selling to existing customers—prompts them to also look at the high-level Market, Sell, and Manage Store Operations processes. The process analysts enlist the aid of company business professionals who possess detailed knowledge about the processes in question. Because these domain experts are responsible for managing or executing the affected processes, it is essential that the process analysts solicit their guidance and buy-in as they examine and redesign Rauha's process model. Figure 6.5 shows the various domain experts involved in recommending and specifying process improvements.

The cross-functional analysis of as-is processes highlights that Rauha Communications has redundant data capture and storage activities occurring throughout the various functions (customer support, marketing, sales, and retail operations). The project team determines, therefore, that they should streamline the data entry, access, and maintenance activities for the various domains to eliminate this inefficiency.

Figure 6.5

Four domains and four processes that are decomposed during Project Alpha

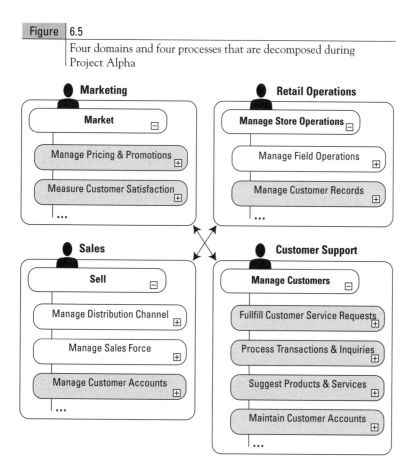

Next, the team decides to use industry best-practice CRM templates to facilitate their design of the to-be process models. This helps the process analysts and domain experts to envision

opportunities to innovate such as self-service Web capabilities, online customer support chat sessions, and targeted Web promotions. Based on this input, the team identifies several new, automated activities that will be necessary to operationally support these recommendations.

The process analysts then redesign aspects of the following processes to accommodate all of the specified improvements: Market (Manage Pricing and Promotions, Measure Customer Satisfaction); Sell (Manage Customer Accounts); Manage Store Operations (Manage Customer Records); and Support Customers (Fulfill Customer Service Requests, Process Transactions & Inquiries, Suggest Products & Services, Maintain Customer Accounts). Through the use of swim lanes, they are also able to pinpoint the interactions and dependencies between functional domains, such as marketing and customer support for integrated cross- and up-selling activities.

Perform Gap Analysis and Determine Requirements

After completing the to-be process scenario models, the project team performs a gap analysis between the desired and existing process environments. The project team calls upon the IT analysts in their company to jointly assess the impact that the proposed changes might have on company operations and technology infrastructure. This helps the team arrive at more accurate conclusions concerning the feasibility, benefit, cost, and risk of pursuing each option. Their analysis reveals that there must be seamless integration between call center and online customer support in order to uphold the business pledge of improving customer service. Otherwise, Rauha Communications runs a high risk of alienating loyal customers that are already accustomed to prompt and reliable service.

Moving forward from the initial functional requirements, the team continues to assess the implications of change and to flesh out requirements that will drive the selection and development of supporting technology. Through this approach, they eliminate unfeasible or out-of-scope requirements and prioritize the remaining requirements. For instance, intelligent routing and a searchable, online solution knowledgebase are identified as non-negotiable items, while online chat is tagged as a low priority, and customer satisfaction surveys that are based on interactive voice response (IVR) technology are dropped entirely. It is also known from business model definition that the marketing manager would like to synchronize promotional campaigns with cross- and up-selling efforts. The IT analyst proposes targeting promotional messages at specific customer segments during any online sessions the target customer conducts at the company's Web site and so this requirement is also added. The team continues along in this fashion, developing the full complement of functional requirements that they anticipate needing at this juncture. From all of those requirements, they identify a few non-negotiable requirements that are key to the initiative's success (see Fig. 6.6):

- **Integrate information** from each touch point and product into a single, unified view of the customer
- **Restrict access** to all online customer support functions according to unique customer identification attributes (e.g. wireless phone number, password)
- **Allow customers** to search the online solution knowledgebase for self-assisted tutorials and installation, usage, and troubleshooting information
- **Provide customers** with the ability to send email and online inquiries to customer support
- **Automatically acknowledge** receipt of inquiry and send acknowledgment to customer via email or wireless device
- **Intelligently route** customer inquiries to the appropriate support representatives based on customer profile, type of request, time zone, and integrated request queuing
- **Display promotional offers** during online customer support session based on customer profile

This collaborative process optimization approach allows Rauha Communications' project team to achieve consensus and buy-in from the company's process owners, while at the same time giving these stakeholders from the business a sense of ownership over the outcome. Allowing process owners to approve or veto process design early on in the process, increases the likelihood that process

| Figure | 6.6 |

A process flow for the Fulfill Customer Service Requests sub-process and some associated functional requirements

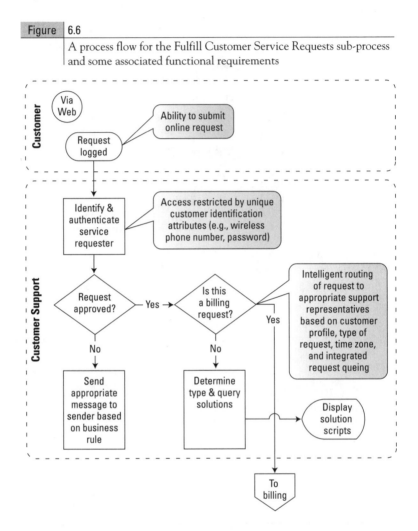

changes will be accepted after they have been implemented. In addition, the development of accurate, prioritized functional requirements in easy-to-understand terms provides software developers and system architects with the essential guidance they need to successfully map technology choices to end-user needs.

Who is Responsible for Optimizing Processes

The Rauha Communications example demonstrates how process optimization fulfills an important role as the critical link between business model definition and technology automation. The primary responsibility for process optimization falls upon process analysts and domain experts who possess detailed, accurate knowledge of how processes work. In some cases, companies will appoint process owners that have overall responsibility for improving particular processes. The discretion of these process owners spans multiple business functions, freeing them from political and process restrictions generally imposed by organizational silos. Together, they model as-is and to-be states of the company's process environment to help the company discover the best way to operationalize business goals. IT analysts should also contribute to the analysis of models, since they will eventually be responsible for applying applications and systems to the business processes that require technology support. In fact, the outputs of process models provide useful inputs to component and class diagrams, data models, sequence diagrams, etc., which make up a part of systems engineering and design.

The principal drivers of process optimization are the goals and objectives inherited from the business model. These drivers keep teams focused on making changes that are in step with espoused management vision and concrete corporate needs. In turn, the results of process optimization drive the set of decisions made during technology automation. By approaching process optimization in this way, companies avoid the costly disconnects that can occur when hand-offs between business, process, and technology are not structured and managed effectively.

7

Technology Automation

THE FINAL ACTIVITY OF BTM is technology automation, where companies design the technology to automate selected processes and ultimately achieve the business goals of the project. In order to appreciate technology automation it is important to have some understanding of the activity's primary tool, the technology model. From there, this chapter moves on to describe how companies should approach technology automation during their IT initiatives, explain some of the advantages that can follow from technology automation, illustrate a simulated case of how Rauha Communications puts technology automation to work, and finally, tell who needs to be responsible in the enterprise for this crucial, third activity of BTM.

What is a Technology Model?

Since modeling is an inherently technical exercise, it's anything but surprising that IT in has become fertile ground for a variety of models. Two of the most popular are object models (which help to develop new software applications) and data models (which describe how data is distributed, communicated, and translated between applications and systems). Although these two types of models (and still others such as network diagrams) can be useful and certainly have an important role to play in the IT department, it's important to recognize that they're not necessarily the best fit for technology automation. This is because many of the important design characteristics that have a profound effect upon whether business and technology are aligned happen at a higher level than that addressed by object and data models. For example, object modeling becomes useful only after a project team has determined what type of software to build, a decision which itself has a profound impact upon alignment and must be dealt with during BTM. Before drilling down to make the detailed decisions that are typical of object and data modeling, IT project teams need a mechanism to address the overall technology environment, make general decisions about the applications and systems that will help meet the project's goals, and get buy-in from their business audience. This device, called the technology model, is the cornerstone of technology automation.

In general, technology models contain two layers:

- **The Applications Layer** includes the business software that directly supports certain processes. Some examples of applications from this layer include customer relationship management, enterprise resource planning, business intelligence, and supply chain management.
- **The Systems Layer** includes the underlying technology that is necessary to implement and support the business software in the applications layer. The systems layer can include servers (e.g., application server, web server, integration server, etc.), software (e.g., browsers, middleware), data (e.g., databases, data warehouses), and networks.

The Applications Layer

The first of these layers, the applications layer, focuses on aspects of the technology architecture that provide direct support for business processes from process automation. The key cross-link between processes and applications is provided by requirements, which can be traced either back to individual activities in the process model or forward to the specific applications in the technology model that support this activity. The act of generating these requirements is shared between process optimization and technology automation, since the process involves give-and-take between each activity. Each application in this layer should also include some crucial attributes that describe it including standards it adheres to, possible vendors, and whether the application exists today or is proposed for the future.

In general, the applications layer serves three important purposes. The first is to help flesh out application functionality, or how requirements are supported by the components that make up each of the applications. One of the major challenges of linking processes to technology is that the two rarely match up one-to-one: a discrete business process may touch multiple applications and vice versa. For example, an insurance agent may directly or indirectly interface with distinct financial, document management, and customer support applications all during the course of processing a claim—which is considered a single, discrete process. This mismatch makes it difficult for line-of-business employees, who tend to view their function in terms of the business processes for which they are responsible, to communicate effectively with IT specialists and developers, whose world view is framed by the distinct applications that they develop and deploy. This disconnect is magnified by today's technology environment, which (because it emphasizes object orientation and distributed computing over monolithic, process-based systems) separates user experience from the application functionality that is split between multiple building blocks of code. Going forward, analysts and researchers predict that Web services (where enterprise applications are broken down into discrete chunks of code that communicate over the Internet using open standards) will become the dominant paradigm for enterprise computing, a development that is sure to exacerbate this challenge even further, and make the cross-links between processes and application functionality, such as those illustrated in Fig. 7.1, even more critical.

Figure | 7.1

Example requirements for the sourcing component of a procurement application in the applications layer

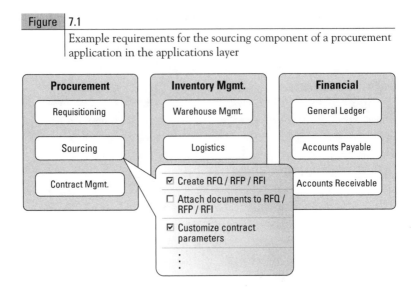

In fact, this trend towards application distribution provides a good segue into the second purpose of the applications layer, which is to help integrate the various systems that make up many technology architectures. Although detailed, nuts-and-bolts integration (such as the data-mapping and translation features provided by EAI software) is too detailed for technology automation, the application layer should provide a mechanism for visualizing where to share information at an application level, and for making sure that new applications are interoperable with existing platforms (see Fig. 7.2). This is especially true during gap analysis, where the project team works to design new applications that need to share crucial data with legacy systems.

Another time when application integration is crucial is when companies need to share information with customers, suppliers, and other entities outside of the enterprise. One of the great promises of the Internet revolution was to make it easier for business partners to electronically share information. But to actually accomplish this, partners need to visualize the information that should flow across company boundaries, and how it integrates with the applications on the other side of the gap. (An example of this inter-enterprise integration is when a sourcing application dispatches a purchase order to a supplier's order-processing platform.)

| Figure | 7.2 |

An example view of application integration between internal platforms and an external business partner

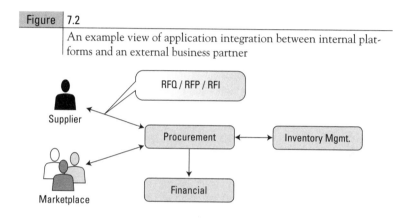

The final purpose of the applications layer is to visualize application flow, or how the applications will behave from the perspective of the end-user. Oftentimes, graphical user interface (GUI) mockups can be important tools here, because they allow users to walk through a simulation of applications, and suggest improvements and changes as they go. In fact, the application flow is most valuable for this very reason: It helps non-technical business representatives (whether they are executives responsible for giving the project a green light or end-users of the platform) visualize how the applications will work before they are irrevocably put into place (see Fig. 7.3).

The Systems Layer

The technology model also includes a systems layer that captures the underlying hardware, software, data, and networks that are necessary for implementing and integrating the applications described in the applications layer. For reinforcement's sake,

Figure | 7.3

An example application flow illustrates a basic GUI mockup for a
buyer logging into a procurement application

Procurement Application Flow

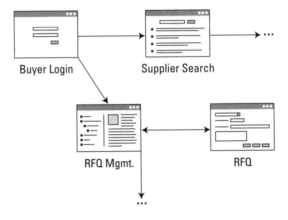

remember that an application refers to business software such as
CRM or ERP that directly supports business processes. A system—
even though it may only be software—differs because it supports
an application or another system. Some common examples of systems include middleware, hardware, networks, and data sources;
some common attributes in the systems layer describe things like
technology standards, configurations, and restrictions.

Within the systems layer, elements can be ordered according to
either logical or physical views. The logical view (of which Fig. 7.4
is an example) partitions the systems into tiers according to the
general function that they provide. While BTM doesn't prescribe

Figure | 7.4

An example logical view of the systems layer that includes five tiers,
including a presentation tier with a browser and PDA

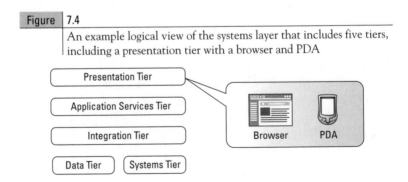

any definitive set, system tiers generally include things like a presentation tier (e.g., Web browsers, PDA's, and dedicated devices through which end-users interface with applications), an integration tier (e.g., middleware, messaging, and enterprise application integration servers that help exchange information between disparate applications), a data tier (e.g., databases, data warehouses, and legacy data), and so on.

The physical view, on the other hand, illustrates how systems are physically distributed between machines that are connected to networks, similar to a network topology (see Fig. 7.5). This perspective is valuable for IT developers, network engineers, and support personnel, who oftentimes are challenged to maintain and upgrade physical systems while making sure that any changes they make don't have unforeseen consequences elsewhere in the technology architecture.

Figure	7.5

A physical view of an example systems tier

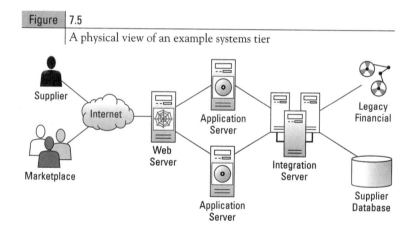

Automating Technology in BTM

So far, this chapter has concentrated on what a technology model is and what types of information are generally captured in one. But to really paint a complete picture of how technology automation helps to align business and technology, this chapter also needs to explain how companies go about automating technology during the activities of BTM.

Technology automation follows the same general pattern as the other activities of BTM: The team starts out by examining the current technology model, which is an as-is snapshot of the applications and systems that exist today. Then they generate technology scenario models that correspond to each of the process scenario models inherited from process optimization. Next, they perform a gap analysis between the current model and each scenario to determine the new applications and systems that are required to pursue each. This analysis results in a final scenario model, which becomes the basis for the full implementation project, and eventually gets rolled into a new, updated technology model.

Within this general framework, however, there are four key tasks that the team responsible for technology automation needs to focus upon: Develop requirements that link processes to applications, design systems to the specifications required by each application, develop technology standards and reuse applications and systems, and select vendors and packages.

Develop Requirements That Link Processes to Applications

Since each of the technology scenario models needs to align with at least one of the process scenario models developed during process optimization, it makes sense that the first major task in technology automation is to develop requirements that cross-link individual applications to processes. This general charge is a specific manifestation of requirements management, a larger process that also encompasses change management, prioritization, and other aspects of development that come into play during both the design and implementation stages of the project.

The cornerstone for alignment between process and technology is the assumption that every application can be traced back to the processes it supports. In some cases, such as an online sales platform that supports the sales process or a call center application that supports customer service requests, this is self-evident. But even applications that don't obviously support individual processes follow this paradigm. For example, it may not be clear at first glance how the information encapsulated in a business intelligence (BI) application—which slices and dices vast quantities of information to identify trends within the business—is a natural fit to automate a process. However, if we consider that decisions are key components of process models, and that BI can be crucial for making informed decisions, we can still create direct cross links between business applications and particular elements in the process model that they support. In other words, even when applications don't "automate" per se, they can still be associated with requirements and in turn, processes, to maintain alignment.

Design Systems to The Specifications Required by Each Application

The second key task that happens during technology automation is the design of supporting systems for each application. Generally speaking, the connection between applications and systems is supplied by specifications, which represent the specific technology conditions that need to be in place in order for the application to run. These specifications, which are often captured as attributes within the model, can take many forms, depending on the specific needs of each application. For example, one enterprise application may require a database that complies with the Java Database Connectivity (JDBC) standard, while another may need a database package from Vendor Bravo, while still another may require a proprietary database that, in turn, requires a particular hardware or software platform on which to run.

At first glance, the specifications that link applications and systems look a lot like the requirements that play a similar role for processes and applications. There is a major distinction, however, that comes from the fact that specifications account for purely technical considerations, while requirements, by virtue of their connection to processes, are more oriented towards business. In addition, specifications differ from requirements in that they can connect applications to systems and also systems to systems. For example, a CRM package that shows up in the applications layer may require a Structured Query Language (SQL) database (a system), which may in turn require a particular operating environment or hardware configuration (also a system).

Develop Technology Standards and Reuse Applications and Systems

Established technology standards commonly show up as specifications that cross-link applications and systems. This points to another of the major tasks that makes up technology automation: Developing technology standards and reusing applications and systems wherever possible. This, of course, is closely related to the general principle of reusing knowledge and assets that Ch. 3 discusses. It makes sense to mention standards and reuse explicitly during this discussion of technology automation, since this is the activity of BTM in which this task plays the most prominent role.

Most IT professionals are familiar with common technology standards such as Extensible Markup Language (XML), Business Process Modeling Language (BPML), or Open Database Connectivity (ODBC). While these are powerful tools for achieving reuse, formal standards such as these aren't the only way that companies can achieve reuse during technology automation. In addition, technology professionals can capture almost any design decision in the form of a standard such as component libraries; packages; technologies for networking and data; and even logical rules and conditions which developers are required to follow. The logical extension of this capability is the establishment of

Standards and Sourcing

"At GE, we have a strong sourcing function that we try to get involved very early, and there are incentives for doing so because they're very good at what they do and they can get incredible leverage with vendors. Traditionally, there's been a tension between technology and sourcing where technology guys want to buy X and the sourcing guys want to buy Y. But we just don't seem to have a lot of those problems because we've streamlined the sourcing process with a couple types of technology standards.

On the one hand, there are some non-negotiable things that we all need to adhere to, and violating them is tantamount eventually to resignation. These are very serious and they're communicated quite well. Typically, they have to do with security or certain core infrastructure functions that are necessary for interaction with systems across the business unit. I'm not going to replace the mail system that I operate with a different mail system, for example, because the Chairman will eventually send email to everybody in the firm and it won't go through and then I'll be in deep trouble. These are kind of easy.

Then there are standards that we say are 'highly recommended', and they're justified either because we have favorable pricing or we have a lot of intellectual assets to go along with that vendor. These standards are wired into sourcing, so when I show up and say I want some random server to run this application, sourcing's initial response may be 'we get this great deal with another vendor because we've standardized on them'. In this case, it's to my advantage to take advantage of the standards. They'll be cheaper in the long run for me because I'll either have more intellectual property at my disposal or more support at a corporate level than I would have if I chose another solution.

So the sourcing and enabling functions that have a vested interest in controlling cost are wired into the decisions for technology standards. You cannot buy a Macintosh; you can buy a Dell and you can have the Dell as long as it's this model loaded with this software and that's what you're going to get. And that's a sourcing and financial decision, not a religious technology decision."

– **Chris Perretta,** *CIO, GE Capital, Card Services*

virtual platforms—complete standard operating environments for which the company's applications can be written. Ever since the beginning of the struggle between centralized and decentralized IT functions, companies have been challenged to set technology standards and to make sure that dispersed teams adhere to them.

By giving centralized enterprise architects a mechanism to capture their standard virtual platforms and disseminate them as templates for far-flung projects, technology automation helps to mediate the struggle between standardization and specialization that tears many IT departments apart.

Select Vendors and Packages

The final task that IT project teams have to tackle during technology automation is the selection of off-the-shelf vendor/package solutions when they elect to buy rather than build application and system functionality. (In fact, the build, buy, or outsource decision itself is a crucial part of technology automation.) BTM doesn't advocate any method for selecting appropriate vendors. Instead, it provides key insights for performing impact analysis to determine the right vendor fit. Since it is rare for even leading vendors to meet every requirement for a project out of the box, the challenge while selecting vendors is fundamentally one of making smart trade-offs between competing priorities, both positive and negative. So, for example, one package may support an inventory management process that is similar to what the project team defined during process optimization, but would require the team to purchase a new application server. Another package might not match the inventory management process all that well, but wouldn't require any new technology purchases to integrate with the existing technology architecture.

Since selecting the best match for vendor/package solutions can mean the difference between on-time, on-budget completion of a project and unmitigated disaster, making smart trade-offs during vendor selection should clearly be a top priority. BTM, by virtue of its interconnected approach to business, process, and technology design helps to promote smart, holistic decision-making about vendors, so that the team responsible for selecting vendors/packages can visualize the end-to-end ramifications of choosing each solution. This is, of course, a specific manifestation of impact analysis, which is described in conjunction with predictive modeling in Ch. 3.

Why Technology Automation?

Technology modeling provides companies with a mechanism for keeping up with five important industry trends:
- **Team members and managers** need to be able to trace individual technology assets back to the processes that they support and ultimately to the business objectives that they are intended to facilitate.
- **IT managers are being asked** to control costs and maximize the value of their investments in technology.
- **More than ever before,** technology specialists need to visualize integration points and improve how technology systems work together.
- **Companies need a single, unified view** of their IT assets, so that they can deploy and enforce standards and develop a technology architecture that is both extensible and durable.
- **The IT department** needs to improve coordination with vendors, including software and hardware manufacturers and service providers.

Technology Decisions Should Trace Back to Business and Process

The first and most important argument in favor of technology automation is that it provides a vehicle for the team to start with each individual IT asset that is proposed for the project, and then trace each asset back to the processes and business objectives that it supports. This is, of course, the primary purpose of all the activities of BTM, but it's a point worth bringing up specifically during our discussion of technology automation because some of the most egregious cases of the business/technology disconnect are spread by the "technology for the sake of technology" misconception. By cross-linking elements in the technology model to corresponding elements in the process and business models, managers can trace back expensive IT decisions (to install an ERP package or purchase a new application server, for example) to the business rationale that is behind them, helping to reign in the notorious fascination that technology specialists often seem to have with the latest and greatest inventions.

Pressure is Increasing to Manage IT Costs

The second trend that is driving companies to examine technology automation is an increased awareness of how IT costs are weighing down the business. Since many of the tangible costs that are involved in a typical project are either the result of specific IT assets (acquiring new or updated packaged solutions, hardware, and networks) or the indirect result of such systems (software development, package implementation, integration, support costs, and so on), a technology model can be a powerful tool for making sure that companies get the most bang for their IT buck.

This is why it is important to link technology models directly with IT asset management, a discipline that aims to catalog financial, contractual, and configuration information about key software and hardware assets. Technology modeling helps companies make intelligent decisions about where to deploy existing assets, what new assets need to be purchased, and what assets have become old or obsolete; it represents an ideal opportunity to make sure that assets are used as efficiently as possible. Companies can achieve this goal by establishing standards in the model that make it easier to develop and integrate new assets, and by identifying existing assets in the technology model that can be reused in upcoming projects. This last point is especially true for legacy systems, which, although they may be a key part of the technology infrastructure, have been in place for so long that the current IT team has never taken the time to catalog their full capabilities. By examining legacy systems during the course of technology modeling, IT project teams often find that they can reuse existing functionality rather than reinventing the wheel with newer technologies.

Research shows that technology models—especially when coupled with business and process models—help companies manage IT costs. In one extreme example, META Group describes how "a consistent mapping of business drivers, the IT capabilities used to enable them, and the underlying IT resources (e.g., infrastructure, applications) enabled IT executives to cut 30,000 worker hours and $135 million from their 2001 IT project list."[1]

Integrating Disperse IT Systems Is More Important Than Ever

Cost management isn't the only reason that standards are important during technology automation. Standards also help to promote unified technology architecture, making it easier to integrate and share data between otherwise isolated systems. Today's IT environment is characterized by the increasing number and complexity of enterprise applications. But, with competing, proprietary vendors jockeying for position within the market, integrating information from each platform remains a huge challenge. Meeting this challenge, in fact, is one of the most important advantages that technology automation provides: By providing a unified view of IT assets it discourages one-off technology architecture decisions that only take into account what is best for the current projects. (This is similar to end-to-end impact analysis which is discussed in Ch. 3, since it helps decision-makers avoid a myopic point-of-view and instead, take the complete, big picture into account at every decision point.)

Technology Architecture Needs to Be Extensible and Agile

Another advantage of technology automation is that the standards captured in the model promote extensibility in the technology architecture. Even after the "dotcom bust," technology innovation continues to progress at a blistering pace, so companies can't afford to lock themselves into a static IT environment. Instead, CIOs need to make sure that their IT investments meet today's latest standards, and also whatever standards tomorrow may hold.

Since predictive modeling is by definition preoccupied with designing the future state of a system, it makes sense that technology modeling would be a prime predictor of upcoming IT change. In the general sense, technology automation helps to promote unified standards and holistic design decisions, which make it easier to modify the technology architecture to reflect changing technologies, business processes, and so on. More specifically, the extensibility enabled by technology automation helps companies to improve the speed and agility with which they can put new technology to work. Ultimately, this lowers the barriers against IT change, and helps companies to focus on low-risk, short-term projects that make incremental changes rather than long-term, high-risk projects that aim to make many major changes all at once. This shift, of course, has impacts that ripple out beyond BTM to include things like culture and the organization.

IT Departments Want Closer Communication and Collaboration With Vendors

The final trend that is driving companies towards technology automation is the increasing importance of interaction and collaboration with technology vendors who provide software, hardware, integration services, and out-sourcing. IT departments make huge financial investments in technology vendors, both in terms of the actual contracts themselves and in related support, implementation, and upgrade costs, so choosing the wrong vendor can add astronomical costs and time delays to almost any IT project.

Technology automation helps to improve how project teams collaborate with vendors to limit the risk of cost and time overruns. In general, technology models make it easier to link requirements to the real software and hardware that supports them. In doing so they provide visibility into how specific packages can (or cannot for that matter) meet the project's ultimate goals. One obvious time when technology models can help to make better decisions is during the vendor selection process; the project team can attach a model to their request for proposal (RFP), and then compare each vendor offering directly to the model to determine the appropriate package. This same interaction can also be facilitated in reverse, when vendors supply potential customers with models that describe how their offerings work off-the-shelf. In addition, technology models can function as an intermediary between the IT department and technology integrators or out-sourcing services. META Group, in fact, predicts that by 2005 over 40% of Global 2000 companies will "promote architectural alignment in sourcing, as early adopter successes become apparent."[2]

Technology Automation In Action

Our simulated case of Rauha Communications and its CRM project in the wireless services division helps to illustrate how technology automation addresses some of these industry trends. First, Rauha Communications uses technology automation to define requirements for a new customer service application in a way that traces back to business and process, and also includes the end-users of the system early on in the project. Next, the company's vendor selection process illustrates how technology automation improves communication between the IT department and third-party vendors and service providers. Finally, Rauha Communications enforces key architectural standards during technology automation, and maintains a unified technology architecture that is both robust and extensible.

Define Requirements for the Customer Service Application

After completing process optimization, the Project Alpha team moves on to technology automation. Their first task is to identify the high-level applications that will be required to achieve the project's goal. After comparing some industry research supplied by an IT analyst firm to the requirements captured in the process model, they identify two major applications: campaign management and customer service (see Fig. 7.6).

Figure	7.6

Project Alpha requires a campaign management and customer service application

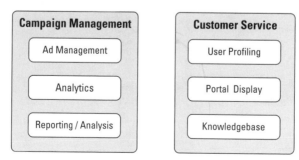

From the start, one of the key objectives of Project Alpha has been to improve service in order to minimize the attrition of high-value customers. The project team determines that to achieve this objective they will need to integrate the customer service experience across two key touch points: their existing call center and the Rauha Communications Web site. This will involve installing and integrating new software, so the Project Alpha technology automation team begins by examining the current state of the wireless services division's technology architecture. Then, they define requirements for the new applications that will be required to achieve their goals.

Technology automation kicks off in Project Alpha when an enterprise architect recommends an existing technology model to use as a starting template. This model, which was developed during a previous IT project, represents an up-to-date snapshot of the company's technology architecture, and specifically the applications that relate to customer service (see Fig. 7.7).

Figure	7.7

Rauha Communications currently employs a legacy call center application and a customer service website that aren't integrated

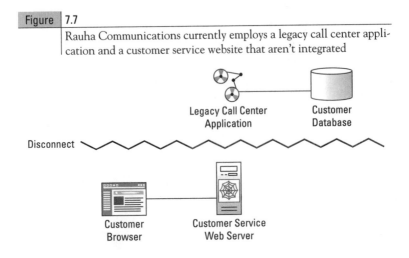

After spending some time examining this model and determining how the current applications help support customer service activity, a team composed of software engineers, customer support representatives, a process analyst, and Rauha Communications' webmaster sits down to perform gap analysis and determine what new systems are required. The customer support representatives begin by reporting that their existing call center application, a legacy system developed some years ago, is both familiar and efficient. The webmaster verifies that Internet support is currently limited to a series of static HTML pages that list and answer some frequently asked questions. Clearly, the team determines, they will need to improve Web support to include a searchable knowledgebase of problems and solutions, and perhaps, as the webmaster suggests, even live chat staffed by support representatives.

This conclusion leads the team to their first major decision: should the project aim to augment the legacy call center application, or should the team look to replace it with a single, integrated CRM platform? In general, they would prefer to reuse the existing, popular system if possible. But since one of the requirements for the project is to integrate information from each touch point and product into a single, unified view of the customer, they recognize that this could be a challenge. The team determines that both are viable options, and decides to create a technology scenario model for each and postpone the decision until they have a better understanding of how both impact the underlying architecture, the related support processes, and ultimately the overall business objectives of Project Alpha.

First, they tackle the scenario where a new CRM system replaces the existing call center application, and develop requirements for the new application. To address concerns early on, avoid buy-in problems, and generally make sure that the requirements service the needs of the customer, they work with the customer support representatives and the process analyst to develop requirements and link them to individual activities in the corresponding process model. Figure 7.8, for example, illustrates how the customer sign-in process depends upon specific requirements that map to user profiling and portal display components within the new Web service application.

The visual nature of the models that are developed during this portion of technology automation helps the end-users, the customer support representatives, visualize how the new systems will

Figure	7.8

Requirements that have been developed for Project Alpha map both to an application flow diagram and also the application that provides the underlying functionality

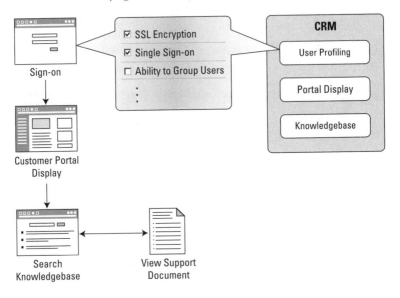

impact them. By getting these people to sign-off on the changes as early as possible, the Project Alpha team helps to mitigate some of the cultural inertia that can weigh IT projects down. In addition to getting sign-off and preparing users for an upcoming change, technology models also help to democratize input into the design. Even though they aren't technical wizards in any sense of the term, the customer support representatives can provide valuable insights into how they do their job and can make sure that detailed requirements make their way into the system before costly coding or implementation begins. For example, after viewing the preliminary model, one of the Rauha Communications' customer support representatives remarks that he would like to be able see every product that the current caller has purchased when taking a support call, since it might help him to pinpoint confusion in bill presentation. This leads the development team to include a new requirement detailing this request, and ultimately improves the utility of the Web service application that gets implemented.

Examine Vendors and Make Intelligent Trade-offs

Eventually, after weighing the full impact of both scenarios, the team responsible for technology automation determines that sharing data between the legacy call center and new Web service applications won't be prohibitively difficult, and decides to pursue that course of action. Since Rauha Communications doesn't have the capability to develop a leading-edge Web-service system in-house, they elect to purchase an off-the-shelf CRM application (which includes a Web services component) and then modify that to achieve the project's objectives. This decision leads to the next phase of technology automation where a purchasing manager, technology architect, and an external consultant collaborate with account representatives and sales engineers from leading CRM software vendors to select an appropriate package and negotiate a contract.

The external consultant, although she is an expert in CRM software solutions, comes into the project with little in-depth understanding of either Rauha Communications or Project Alpha. In order to get up to speed, she sits down with the project team leader who uses each of the business, process, and partially completed technology models to describe the project's objectives and scope, and to visually demonstrate the important decisions leading up to the current vendor selection.

The consultant begins her research; identifies relevant analyst reports, news articles, and product descriptions that pertain to possible vendors; and attaches them directly to the model itself. By contextualizing this information, she helps to make sure that even after her engagement with Rauha Communications ends, the Project Alpha team can trace her decisions back to the supporting evidence. Eventually, the consultant submits RFPs and associated technology models to each vendor. Although this particular vendor selection is concerned only with selecting a CRM application, the package includes business and process models, as well as the systems portion of the technology model. This gives the sales engineers a better understanding of the requirements they are being asked to address, and allows them to generate a more accurate prediction of which requirements their software meets out of the box, and which will require customization. Including the systems side of the technology model serves another important purpose: The new application will need to work with Rauha Communications' current technology architecture, including underlying systems. It is important for the vendor evaluation to consider not just functional requirements that link back to process optimization, but also technology requirements such as event notification and work flow that are mandated by the current systems that make up the company's technology architecture.

After the vendors respond to the RFP, the consultant sits with the rest of the team to determine which package best meets their needs. Predictably, no single package is able to tackle every requirement out of the box, and the team will have to make some trade-offs in order to minimize customization while maximizing the project's business benefit. But since each of the vendors' proposals were generated against the end-to-end models developed for the project, it is relatively easy for the team to evaluate the overall impact of choosing each solution: One of the options, from Vendor Bravo, provides strong search and categorization functionality for its knowledgebase, but doesn't offer online chat. Another, from Vendor Charlie, touts its chat functionality as a differentiator, but is weaker in knowledge retrieval. The consultant is able to trace each of these requirements back to the processes that they support and then from those processes to the original business model, which indicates that the knowledgebase is essential for the project, but that chat is not. As a result, she recommends Vendor Bravo, and helps to assure that the final technology solution delivers upon the project's original objectives.

Establish and Enforce Application and Architecture Standards

Eventually, the project team selects a vendor, completes technology automation, and uses the end-to-end enterprise model to construct a sound business case for moving Project Alpha into implementation. Rauha Communications' CIO and the firm's IT investment committee approve of the design, the project is given the green light, and the new CRM system becomes a key component in the company's wireless services division.

Project Alpha is a success. It is such a success, in fact, that the PMO decides to try and replicate Project Alpha in other business units. Specifically, a program manager wants to establish Vendor Bravo as the standard CRM package throughout the company. The program manager knows from experience that, left to their own devices, far-flung project teams will often forget or ignore standard packages, especially when doing so might benefit them—even at the expense of the enterprise as a whole. But BTM gives him a mechanism to counter this tendency. Recall from earlier in the case that in each of the activities of BTM, the Project Alpha team began with a standard template that it modified to accomplish its own, specific objectives. The program manager recognizes that by placing the models developed during Project Alpha in a central repository and providing them to upcoming CRM projects, he can strongly encourage teams to adopt the standards that he sets, even to the point of reusing the real software and hardware assets already developed for the wireless services division.

BTM, then, provides benefits to Rauha Communications on two levels. First, it gives the team responsible for designing Project Alpha a mechanism to experiment, gain consensus, and validate conclusions before beginning a costly software implementation program. Business model definition helped the Project Alpha team to *capture an as-is current business model* and to *develop business scenario models for impact analysis*. Process optimization enabled them to *examine the as-is process environment*, and *perform gap analysis and determine requirements*. Finally, technology automation helped to *define requirements for the customer service application, examine vendors and make intelligent trade-offs*, and *establish and enforce application and architecture standards*. Ultimately, addressing these concerns in the "aim" rather than "fire" phase saves time, money, and helps to deliver a better end product. But even after these important tasks are accomplished, Rauha Communications continues to derive real business benefits from BTM: By helping the company's program manager and his team to define and enforce standards for enterprise architecture, BTM lowers the cost of and shortens the time that is required to complete similar upcoming projects.

CHAPTER 7

Who is Responsible for Automating Technology?

As our simulated case from Rauha Communications illustrates, technology automation isn't the sole responsibility of developers or even technical employees of any sort. This myopic approach, in fact, is one of the key sources of the business/technology disconnect in the first place. To engender a bigger-picture understanding of technology design, project teams should include end-users and beneficiaries of technology as early on in the project as possible. Technology automation, because of its reliance upon models that democratize user input, makes it possible to include a broader array of input and consultation than ever before. The primary drivers of technology automation are the IT analysts and service providers who are tasked with crafting the high-level technology design for the project. To make sure that this design conforms to centrally administered technology standards and reuses existing IT assets, enterprise architects and the PMO should also play a prominent role. The final group that needs to provide input into the technology automation process is domain experts. This includes business managers and process experts who help to ensure that the new technology will effectively support their own areas of expertise; vendor representatives who help to describe how their offerings can contribute to the success of the project; and, most importantly, the prospective end-users of the systems who, by signing off early on to the design of new applications and systems, minimize the cultural and organizational barriers that stand in the way of the new technology being put to good use.

An End, But Also A Beginning

After completing technology automation, selecting a final scenario model for business, process, and technology, and wrapping up the activities of BTM, the IT project team has an end-to-end design to help them create a better business case and get the funding that they need to move on from the design stage to the build, test, and deploy stages—from "aim" to "fire." However, this doesn't mean that the models produced by business model definition, process optimization, and technology automation become left-over artifacts from a bygone era after the activities of BTM wrap up. In fact, nothing could be further from the truth. At this point, the enterprise model becomes an anchor to which the implementation team refers back to time and again to make sure that what they build matches what the project was designed to do.

As inevitable, unforeseen snags pop up along the way and the implementation team is forced to modify the original design, the enterprise model assumes another important role: communicating between technical implementers and the business and IT executives who commissioned the project in the first place. When the design changes, the implementation team can update the model to reflect their workarounds, and then pass these modifications along to the management team to get a final go-ahead and make sure that everyone stays informed of the progress.

Finally, the business, process, and technology models can provide a useful segue into some of the more nuts-and-bolts disciplines that come to the forefront during implementation. For example, the application functionality, interfaces, and flow that are a crucial part of the technology model can provide a starting point for object modeling, a discipline that helps companies develop applications in-house. And similarly, the IT assets in the model—assets like application software, servers, databases, and networks—can be linked with asset management, which helps to maximize the long-term value of IT resources.

These and other possible examples of how the models developed during the activities of BTM might be put to work elsewhere highlight a crucial point about business model definition, process optimization, and technology automation: their impact is felt throughout the IT department and enterprise as a whole. Naturally, then, governing BTM to ensure that this impact is positive rather than negative will be crucial to its success.

Governing with BTM

"Unless we change our direction, we are likely to
wind up where we are headed."
– *Ancient Chinese proverb*

AFTER MONTHS OF CONSTRUCTION, you finally receive the
call you've been waiting for: It's Robert, and he informs you
that your dream house is almost finished. "Sometime next
week," he says, "we should be all set."

Obviously, you're excited: You've been dreaming about living in a home like this one since you moved into your first
dingy apartment. At the same time, you're surprised to notice
that you don't feel even a pang of nervousness. Even though
your dream house represents a major investment for which
you've been literally saving for your whole life, you're not

worried. From their first sparks of inspiration through the day-to-day grind of construction, Robert and Janet have used the architectural blueprint for the project to keep you appraised of their progress, to communicate design decisions, and to help you visualize the final product. You're thrilled with the blueprint, and so you know there won't be any unpleasant surprises.

This is, of course, a selfish view. Building a house is a major job, and you aren't the only person who has benefited from Janet and Robert's expert approach. Besides the physical structure itself, there are many other ingredients that need to come together to make what is essentially a pile of boards and glass into your dream home.

Just as important as the dimension of each room and the location of the windows, is the neighborhood in which your house will be located and the quaint town that surrounds that. Many of the most desirable towns and cities are extremely careful about maintaining the character and charm that distinguishes them, and your future hometown is no different. New construction has to adhere to strict building codes that regulate everything from your home's height to its setback from the road and the style in which it is built.

All of this falls under the auspices of the local zoning board, which is responsible for approving or rejecting individual requests for new construction in order to maintain the integrity of the town as a whole. The only way for this board to make a determination about whether new construction is up to code is by examining the architectural blueprints. These blueprints capture the design of the house in a format that is accessible and complete; without them the board would have no way to evaluate whether the new construction would compliment or clash with their carefully maintained atmosphere.

Another ingredient that's sure to factor into your satisfaction with the project is its cost. In an ideal world, money would be no object in this project. But for you—as for most of us—sticking to a budget is a must. No one is more important in this effort than your contractor, Robert, who gave you an estimate of what he expected your house to cost up-front, and now needs to make sure to come in on time and under budget.

Like the zoning board's decision, Robert's estimated budget was based directly on the architectural blueprints, which allowed him to calculate the materials he would need and how long it would take to assemble them. Without a blueprint to work from, Robert would have had to pull an estimate for your dream house out of thin air, and then would be left looking like a fool (or worse, a con man) when it came in way under or way over budget.

At the same time, Robert uses the blueprints to help minimize the aggregate cost of all of the houses he's currently building. He does this by improving how he allocates expensive specialists among jobs, and by purchasing materials in bulk and then splitting them up between projects. The blueprints help him to identify which projects will need who and when, and also what materials each has in common.

For both Robert (the contractor) and the town zoning board, the blueprints produced during the design of your dream house are a must. And their corporate-world equivalents are a must as well for Robert (the CIO) and another board—the IT investment committee—which is responsible for managing the IT portfolio, a collection of projects and assets, the integrity and focus of which should be maintained on a case-by-case basis just like in our example. It's also in Robert's (the CIO) best interest to be able to accurately estimate and minimize the cost of getting projects done. In the architecture world, these are known as zoning and cost controls; in BTM, they're called strategic direction and tactical control.

In This Part...

In *Part IV: Governing with BTM*, will show how BTM helps to govern IT by setting strategic direction and maintaining tactical control. The mechanism for managing strategic direction is the IT portfolio. Enterprise models that are developed during BTM provide the basis for analyzing this portfolio and making crucial investment decisions. The enterprise models also help to manage quality by enforcing standards, and costs by reducing maverick purchases and eliminating redundancies and waste. Collectively, these help maintain tactical control.

8

Direction and Control

THERE HAS BEEN AN UNFORTUNATE PERCEPTION for a long time in many companies that IT somehow plays by a different set of rules than the rest of the business. At best, from an upper-level management perspective, it's regarded as an enigma; at worst, it's the proverbial redheaded stepchild. This outlook often diminishes the CIO's credibility with his or her peers, compounding IT's perennial struggle to demonstrate its true value to the business.

To counter the negative perceptions that have traditionally plagued IT, CIOs need a mechanism for speaking the same language as any other senior manager: that of strategic direction and tactical control—or more commonly—governance. First, they need to be able to ask themselves, "Are we doing the rights things?" and then ask, "Are we doing the right things right?"

Being able to answer just these two questions well will better pre-pare CIOs to engage their business counterparts as equals.

While governance is not a new concept for IT, its recognition as a suitable combatant against runaway technology investments has never been stronger. As it relates to the IT function overall, governance encompasses a plethora of management areas and activities—including the management of portfolios, programs, assets, costs, human capital, service providers, etc. Obviously, this entire subject is too broad for this discussion. In keeping with the scope of this chapter, I'll limit the discussion to two primary sub-jects: strategic direction and tactical control.

Strategic Direction

Regardless of whether you primarily view IT as a financial asset or as a product (which is itself is a topic of much philosophical debate) the fact remains that, from the simplest standpoint, *it has intrinsic value* and *it can produce value*. Therefore, its proposed allocation and actual assignment should be governed in the same manner in which you would manage a portfolio of assets or of products: being careful to consider balance, financials, risks, ben-efits, life term, and the like. Many can accept the basis of this argument. What is not well understood, and what this chapter explores further, is how the critical insights necessary to do so effectively can be found in the models generated during the activities of BTM.

The CIO is the Ultimate Portfolio Manager

As the role of the CIO has shifted alongside that of IT, one of the responsibilities that has risen to the forefront is setting the com-pany's strategic direction with regard to technology. To manage this direction, CIOs need to be able to prioritize initiatives, justify decision-making, measure risk versus return, and allocate resources in a way that maximizes their impact upon the business. The fact that this isn't yet standard practice can be readily evidenced through industry surveys:

- 89% of companies are unable to adjust and align their budgets with business needs, other than once or twice a year.
- 66% of IT organizations are not "market-ready." They have no idea of their performance profile in terms of costs or business value generation.
- 89% of companies are flying blind. They have virtually no metrics, except for finance (which is sort of like flying a plane by monitoring the fuel burn rate).[1]

Most CIOs find it challenging to set strategic direction because of three factors. First, it is difficult to gain critical and timely insight into IT. Second, it is necessary to maintain alignment with the business as conditions change or new directions emerge. Finally, the CIO needs a consolidated view of the resources under their purview before they can set direction. Together, these three factors are driving many CIOs to adopt portfolio management techniques for setting strategic direction. In basic terms, this means gaining an aggregated view of IT investments across the enterprise, measuring them against established criteria, and then striking the appropriate balance within the portfolio that best serves the strategic goals of the enterprise.

One overriding concern for portfolio managers is to balance the risk and value in their investments. In one form or another, applying this balance is quite familiar to the CIO's peers from finance, marketing, sales, and product development. If IT is to be managed like the rest of the business, it needs to follow this same path, with the CIO playing the role of the IT portfolio manager. This doesn't mean, however, that IT can be reduced to purely financial metrics. IT is engineering-based; a company can't simply turn their CIO into a financial analyst and expect him or her to manage strictly by a spreadsheet.

Discounted Cash Flow or Cash Cows?

Portfolio management can be an equally important technique whether you choose to consider IT an asset or a product. Companies that ask their CIO to either report directly to the CFO or to function as a fund manager who doesn't shy away from financial accountability probably fall into the asset camp. Chances are that they will gravitate towards portfolio management techniques that are inherited from traditional corporate finance management. This type of portfolio management has roots reaching back to the 1950s with Markowitz's Modern Portfolio Theory and to the 1970s with Black and Scholes' Real Options Valuation.

The product camp, on the other hand, tends to prefer a more market-centric approach to portfolio management that draws upon the Ansoff or Boston Matrix to strategically plot and manage product portfolios along composite dimensions, such as risk and value or growth and share. The inherent risk for this camp is that complex IT investment decisions may not easily reduce to a four-, six-, or nine-quadrant box (see Fig. 8.1, which compares an asset camp technique—discounted cash flow—with a Boston matrix from the product camp).

Figure 8.1

Discounted cash flow (an example of an "asset camp" approach) versus the Boston matrix (a "product camp" approach)

DISCOUNTED CASH FLOW

$$NPV = CF_0 + PV = C_0 + \sum_{t-1}^{T} \frac{CF_t}{(1+r_t)^t}$$

BOSTON MATRIX

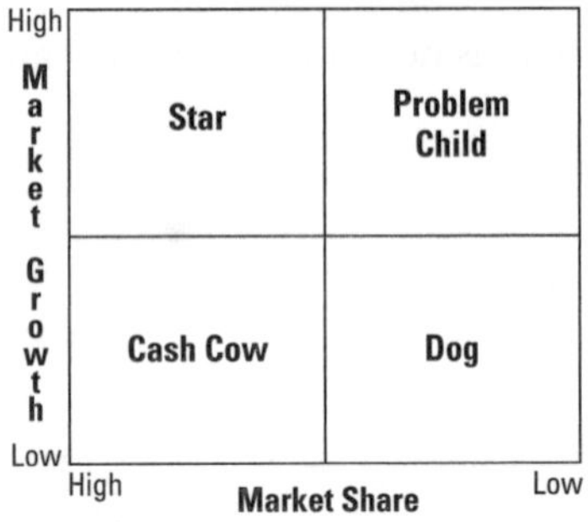

	High Market Share	Low Market Share
High Market Growth	Star	Problem Child
Low Market Growth	Cash Cow	Dog

Regardless of which camp companies fall into, however, the IT portfolio helps them to evaluate the risks and rewards of their investments as an integrated whole. By analyzing parameters including risk, return, capabilities, competitive intensity, market variances, and others, they can measure and understand the assets (or products) for which they're responsible and determine which to pursue, which to abandon, which to invest more heavily in, and which to simply maintain.

The general principle that is driving companies towards IT portfolio management is a simple one. An automotive company wouldn't manufacture a car without first undergoing a comprehensive analysis and design process to determine if the car would sell in a given market, how much it would cost to manufacture, what price it should garner, what features and functionality it should have, how long it would take to produce, what resources would be consumed in its production, where the break-even point would be, how it fits in relation to the rest of the product line, what the relative life cycle and maintenance requirements of the vehicle would be, what competitive or environmental conditions such as new industry regulations would have an impact, and so on. And a corporation shouldn't decide to invest in a particular technology without following the same general rules.

The point of this chapter isn't to carry on an exhaustive discussion of how to use any of the aforementioned methods; there are plenty of websites, articles, papers, and books that cover each, and describe how to apply them from A – Z. Nor is the point to endorse any one vis-à-vis the others. Each organization is different, and so there is no "one-size fits all" answer for managing the IT portfolio. The point that you should take away from this chapter is that, generally speaking, portfolio management of one sort or another provides a mechanism for the CIO to plot strategic direction. As you will see moving forward, it helps companies answer the essential question, "Are we doing the right things?" more accurately.

Not Just Financial Measures

IT has always been subject to financial scrutiny. But much of the analysis has concentrated only on a partial picture, and has resulted in the impression that IT has overspent and under-leveraged its investments. If you are not convinced, just check with any CIO that lost a budget arbitrament (if not a career post) by managing solely by the numbers. This is a mistake. IT portfolio management shouldn't be reduced solely to financial measures. It's simply not as easy as plugging numbers into a spreadsheet and making inferences from that. Just look at where relying on the sacrosanct measure, ROI, has led the industry. For years, IT projects have been subject to approval based upon the merits of expressly quantified ROI. The line of thinking has been that ROI somehow equals project success—work the math, and as long as two plus two equals four, things should turn out right. Unfortunately, countless projects have failed miserably and cost companies millions of dollars (if not shareholder value), despite being justified according to supposedly solid ROI assertions. That's not to say that ROI as a tangible measure is intrinsically flawed and should be discarded altogether. It is an important indicator when formulating IT investment strategies, but it is just one piece of the puzzle. Of equal, if not more importance, are intangible measures.

Intangibles are more qualitative and thus more subjective in nature than tangible measures. Tangibles include operating costs, income, assets, liabilities, profit margins, return on assets, and other measures that lend themselves to being expressed as financial ratios. Intangibles on the other hand, comprise a diverse range of measures, which may include strategic fit, goal alignment, opportunity costs, customer connectivity, competitive threat, return horizons, business impact, process optimization, intellectual capital, skills, and innovation among others.

There are three problems with only relying on tangible measures. First, there is a cultural proclivity to "work the numbers" to make them say what people want them to say. Second, tangible measures are largely reactive, while intangible measures lend themselves to forward-looking views, since they often drive the tangibles. (Intangible measures often contribute directly to productivity, profitability, and ROI, for example.) Finally, many of the benefits that follow from IT projects are hard to define in the direct, financial terms that tangible measures require. For example, a company may notice that after installing a sales force automation platform their revenue increased over previous quarters. But this says nothing about how much of the increase is due to the software and how much is the result of other factors such as a growing market or a new compensation structure for the sales team. What IT is, meaning its life as a capital or physical asset, warrants evaluation with a tangible set of measures. But the majority of what IT actually *does* falls more into the sphere of the intangible.

A good balance of tangible and intangible measures allows IT portfolio managers to anticipate the potential value of technology investments by providing:
- Visibility into future risks and causal relationships
- Safeguards against slippery-slope conclusions
- Counterweights to over-inflated promises and expectations
- Flexible accommodation for rapidly changing environmental influences

By formulating a more holistic picture of the potential value that resides within and that can be generated by the IT portfolio, CIOs can offer their business counterparts more realistic valuations of IT investment returns.

A Single View

One primary advantage of utilizing a portfolio approach is that it provides a single view into diverse IT initiatives that, after the recent wave of decentralization, may be spread across 40 or more business units occupying hundreds of locations. That alone is of tremendous management value for the CIO, whose responsibilities generally span multiple organizational and budgetary silos. Such an aggregated view typically encompasses the following categories, although a different or further stratification can occur depending upon the organization:
- **Infrastructure** (e.g., networks and hardware)
- **Applications** (e.g., commercial off-the-shelf or in-house)
- **Information** (e.g., corporate and customer data)
- **Processes** (e.g., value-chain activities)
- **Human capital** (e.g., skills or experience)
- **Relationships** (e.g., vendors or contractors)

These IT resources are then associated with projects that have specific attributes assigned to them, such as an owner, schedules, milestones, allocated resources, a budget, costs, risk, expected returns, scope, status, priority, and other criteria that can be useful for tracking or applying weighted scores. Projects are further classified into programs (which represent logical groupings of projects) that help portfolio managers utilize a working framework for balancing the portfolio, identifying similar projects to avoid "apple to orange" comparisons, and creating an additional layer of abstraction for the office of the CIO from possibly hundreds of staggered or parallel projects (see Fig. 8.2).

Figure | 8.2

A portfolio can consist of projects and sub-projects that can
be grouped into programs to identify similarities

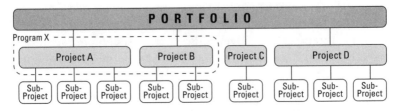

In this manner, CIOs and their extended team are able to view aggregated cross-sections of information about the state of their IT investments for holistic—not stand-alone—decision-making. So, for example, the CIO could use this method to quickly assess all the instances where a particular vendor's solutions were slated for use across the year's remaining projects in order to ultimately strengthen purchasing leverage. Or, they could determine that core infrastructure investments are currently under-funded in relation to the projected increase in demand that will occur as a consequence of adding a new subsidiary business location. Or, they could find out what the distribution of IT spending is across all the departments that IT supports. It may be trite to say that trying to decipher this information otherwise would be like looking for a needle in a haystack, but that is truly the case.

As a best-practice precursor to this type of strategic planning, a baseline assessment of existing IT resources needs to be in place. Recall from the activities of BTM that the very first step is to identify a current enterprise model that describes the organization's as-is state. Since this enterprise model contains the complete set of artifacts enumerated in the categories bulleted above, it helps to construct the portfolio. This baseline assessment is not to be confused with an asset inventory that would be assembled for the purposes of managing an asset's life cycle from procurement to retirement. An inventory, although useful, has limitations in this case. First, the baseline assessment is intended to assess the level of fit between a company's business requirements and its IT investment mix. An asset inventory, by design, will not produce this kind of insight. It would be insensible to base a go/kill decision for a project on a rank list of assets. Second, the asset inventory doesn't take into account the majority of the aforementioned categories, such as processes. The vast store of information that is needed to conduct such an analysis is better derived from the enterprise model, as it describes the allocation of the full range of categories in relation to the business objectives that they support and the critical interdependencies that exist between them.

From the Bottom Up

Analysis is the heart and soul of any portfolio approach; it's where managers make the final call about how to allocate investments in the portfolio. At the same time, analysis is far and away the most difficult step in the process. A common criticism of applying portfolio techniques to IT is that it is done in a vacuum, and so managers aren't necessarily equipped with the underlying data they need in order to effectively evaluate opportunities, threats, and constraints. You can't measure what you don't know about. Consider how effective the practice of CRM, which aggregates data about customers into an overarching view for strategic analysis and action, would be in the absence of sufficient underlying customer data. Customer lifetime value (CLV), which helps companies determine the most profitable customer segments, is one of the most essential metrics in CRM analyses. Without having access to the disparate data that combines to calculate this metric—such as frequency of purchase, amount of customer spend, and cost to acquire and service the customer—it is nearly impossible to assess CLV. The same would be true for conducting effective IT analyses in the absence of any supporting information.

This vacuum is partially attributable to a gap between the IT portfolio and the resident data. The data is either buried in a spreadsheet or project plan or it is locked away in the heads of personnel that perform specialized functions. In any event, this presents a secondary set of complications. The more difficult it is to assemble the required data, the less likely that it will be maintained or even gathered in the first place. The focus then also shifts from the analysis of pertinent data to the collection of it. Charles Popper of The Program on Information Policy Research at Harvard University states it thus:

Relying upon ad hoc, manual methods to collect and process data, with support from standard productivity tools, is certainly possible, but if more effort is expended on data collection and correction, then less time and fewer resources are available for the analysis and decision-making needed to manage the portfolio and its projects.[2]

The final complication is that the greater the distance between data and analysis or the more times information is translated during the course of moving from one point to the next, the greater the likelihood that inaccuracies and misinterpretation will occur.

The models produced during the activities of BTM help to alleviate these data difficulties. Business model definition, process optimization, and technology automation surface the critical underlying data elements that are necessary for applying both tangible and intangible measures to the portfolio. The data elements that are generated as a natural by-product of these activities provide managers with visibility into a wide range of insights that is otherwise missing. These can be insights regarding hidden costs, direct and indirect benefits, requirements (capital, functional, human), process capabilities, mix (customer, supplier, vendor, technology), performance, time-to-market schedules, trade-off implications, standards and quality compliance, feasibility, etc. When funneled up, these insights enable portfolio managers to draw appropriate, non-skewed conclusions in relation to risk and return. That is not to say that it is incumbent upon portfolio managers, be it the CIO or his or her delegate, to sift through the minutiae. Rather, they benefit from the cumulative reasoning that occurs throughout the design activities and have a means to follow the cookie crumb trail of validated assumptions if necessary.

Consider a simplified example: The current year corporate strategy of a large manufacturer entails a directive for increased profit margins via global expansion in a particular market. Executing on this goal requires the development of a series of integrated strategies across the functional domains of the company. From there the decision has been made that product X has the greatest potential for distribution and sales. A central initiative (initiative A) to the business unit's strategy is to connect with key suppliers to reduce the cost of materials. The challenge for the office of the CIO is to set a strategic direction for technology that will achieve that objective given the stated parameters (e.g., budget, time) for initiative A, and to meet it within the context of the company's other running objectives.

The office of the CIO has the IT budget allocated among non-discretionary (maintenance and operations), discretionary (consolidation and upgrade), growth (strategic), and venture (innovation) categories. These categories are likewise broken down into respective projects and programs. Any IT strategy that is devised to meet the objectives of initiative A (along with the associated projects/programs) must be evaluated with respect to its strategic fit with the other categories.

A cross-functional team of business and IT analysts proposes automating regional supplier relationships. But is this the direction that IT should be taking both for the initiative itself and for the portfolio on the whole? The CIO must be sure of this first, before he can sell it to the business unit co-sponsor.

The data that is required to validate this proposal comes from the activities of BTM, since they help to quantify the project's cost, risk, and expected benefits (see Fig. 8.3). The activities validate that automation will lower sourcing costs (business model definition); sourcing and approval processes will have to change while procurement managers, demand planners, and purchasing agents will need to be retrained (process optimization); a new procurement application will need to be purchased; and a consulting partner will need to be contracted to integrate the platform with the legacy financial system and supply chain systems (technology automation).

By using the data derived from these activities, the office of the CIO can make informed assessments of the proposed project's specific risk and value. Next, they can balance criteria like project cost to hedge against unforeseen fiscal constraints, term length to allow the department to address perceived long-term trends without gambling entirely on an untested concept, and scope to mitigate against dramatic changes in the business. The CIO or a member of the PMO can then extend the initial project analysis to determine fit with the overall IT portfolio investment mix. By calculating the tangible and intangible measures derived from the

Figure 8.3

The models produced during the activities of BTM provide the underlying data for analyzing the IT portfolio

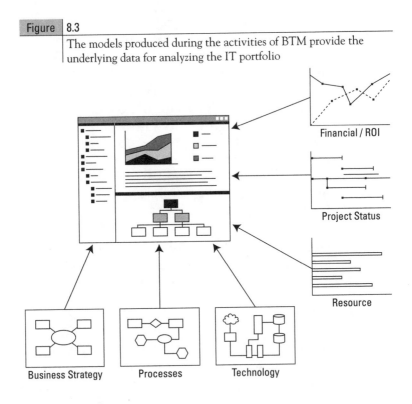

business, process, and technology models, the team is able to demonstrate that their project aligns with corporate objectives and fits within the allocated spend for the IT investment growth category. In this way, the CIO can be assured that IT is doing the right thing and can ultimately demonstrate it to solicit business unit buy-in.

Navigating and Negotiating

Beyond providing the raw data to analyze IT investments, the models produced during the activities of BTM facilitate two additional objectives that relate to strategic direction:

- Monitoring the portfolio to periodically reanalyze risk and value
- Communicating decision-making criteria to other stakeholders

Monitor and Periodically Reanalyze

Even after being given the green light, most project methodologies define gates through which an initiative must pass in order to progress. Gates often coincide with traditional project milestones (such as the selection of a technology vendor), but can also be triggered when total costs exceed a pre-defined amount or in response to ongoing project audits. These are good opportunities for the IT portfolio manager to re-evaluate his or her investment in the project. Assessment should never be a one-time event. Changes in the risk or value of an IT project (and by proxy the whole portfolio) can quickly occur, for example, as the result of a new competitive positioning for the company or a shifting business landscape. Recall from Ch. 1 the continual stream of changes encountered by Patrick Flynn's team in their customs-clearance system project. The decision criteria to stick with the project might have been dramatically different had there been visibility to these shifts in the business climate earlier in the process.

Until this point, the practice of managing by exception—whereby managers take corrective actions based upon proactive notifications of problems—has been traditionally difficult. It requires that key decision-making information about the project remains up-to-date at all times. Generally, standard approaches to project management result in managers receiving lagging updates concerning a project's status. The models developed during business model definition, process optimization, and technology automation can help to overcome this challenge, because they capture an accurate snapshot of progress throughout each step of its design. Decision criteria can be associated with individual elements in the model, and when the model changes, the criteria can be updated in real time to determine if an exception should be highlighted. This helps identify projects early on that are out of variance so that portfolio managers can recalculate their risk and value assessments.

Communicating through Visual Aids

The process of managing the IT portfolio is ultimately about determining the strategic direction in which the IT department is headed. As such, it's the office of the CIO that is the ultimate

ıanager, and the IT department that needs to be respon-
aking sure that investments are aligned with overall
___ ərategy. Keep in mind, however, that the CIO doesn't
have sole budgetary control over every IT expenditure. Projects
may be initiated and ultimately funded by the business units for
whom they are intended, or by an IT investment committee com-
prised of the CIO, line-of-business sponsors, and representatives of
the CFO. This means that senior IT leaders need to work with
other stakeholders from the business to develop business cases
and secure funding. It is far more likely that a line-of-business
sponsor or a financial executive will give the go-ahead if they can
assimilate how the project will serve their aims. Again, the business, process, and technology models developed during BTM can
play a crucial role here. One of the key advantages of modeling
that Ch. 4 discusses was that models are powerful tools for visualization. They can help participants at the negotiating table to
separate the map from the territory and safeguard against funding
determinations that may be shortsighted or that may be driven by
the individual that wields the most power.

MIT professor Peter Senge's seminal work, *The Fifth Discipline*,
addresses how impasses occur between departmental or functional
areas of responsibility owing in part to the fact that people carry
with them ingrained "mental models."[3] People vigorously defend
these models, which contain their hidden beliefs and assumptions. Historically, IT has had considerable difficulty in changing
the mental model that the business holds regarding IT's efficacy.
This leads to perennial conflict when it's time to negotiate, especially if neither side is particularly fluent in the other's language.
With three-quarters of the IT budget traditionally being allocated
to keeping the business up and running, it's always a struggle to
agree on how the remainder of the pie should be divided up to
achieve the organization's goals. This is even more so the case in
times of economic softening when executive decision-makers are
required to take apart budgets and trim excess fat. The outsourcing
craze of the 1980s when IT itself was viewed as excess fat still
sends a shiver down a few CIO's spines.

The models created during the activities of BTM can be used
to eliminate any entrenched biases and objectively demonstrate
how IT plans to align to the business—and how it arrived at its

conclusions. These models represent fact, not fiction. By us. the models as a point of reference in the negotiations, IT can't b. accused of "voodoo economics" and business units can make intelligent concessions according to the dictates of a level playing field. In addition, models, through their visual nature, also provide a common language, allowing an easier exchange of information to occur between the two domains. Traditionally, each domain has had difficulty in understanding the other. Models, however, create a shared language that can reduce the likelihood of misinterpretation between the "bureaucrat" and the "technocrat." At the end of the day, both sides need to come together to prioritize and allocate IT spend in a manner that benefits the corporation as a whole, and models can help foster the rapport and dialogue necessary to do that.

Governance Pop-Quiz

"If you are CIO of a global business, just keeping track of the myriad of IT initiatives across the business units, and aligning these with each other and with corporate goals, is very challenging. You have to make sure that initiatives are consolidated and that you have some sort of perspective going forward, not just looking at the historical performance of the business but looking at the potential future performance. Really, you should be considering how your answers stack up to the following questions:

- **Do you have** a mechanism to communicate in the same language as the CxO community?
- **Can you demonstrate** how you are aligned with the directions the business wants to go?
- **Has your world become** more complex than a spreadsheet can handle?
- **Do you have a good picture** of all your existing resources?
- **Do you know** the relationships and dependencies between the business portfolio and IT assets?

> – **Can you explain** your technology portfolio to
> business management?
> – **Do you know where** new vendor offerings fit and
> may help you?
> – **How do you assess** costs, risks, and the impact of
> changes before you commit to building systems?"
>
> – **Howard Smith,** CTO, CSC *Europe*

Tactical Control

Until this point, the majority of the discussion has focused on how BTM plays a crucial role in helping senior IT leaders govern the strategic direction of their enterprises, answering the question, "Are we doing the right things?" The other half of governance is tactical control: "Are we doing the right things right?" Once strategic direction has been established and communicated, management needs to ensure that it is implemented in a way that produces the intended results. This quandary is reflected in the fact that nearly a third of all IT projects fail or are abandoned before completion. That adds up to a whole lot of waste.

Clearly, there are a multitude of reasons why projects fail. So many so that I wouldn't be able to address how to resolve them all and still do justice to the topic at hand. That said, this section doesn't conduct a "Project Management 101" lesson; nor is it a "Program Management for Dummies" primer. There are a number of resources available in the form of associations, institutes, and published works that offer valuable assistance for the various aspects of the project and program management disciplines. This section does, however, examine the intersection between those disciplines and BTM.

Quality is "Job #1"

For years companies have worked hard to adopt and apply quality management techniques whose goal is to ensure that value-creating activities are conducted in the most efficient and effective manner possible. This formalized practice of mo quality management dates back to the early 1950s and Edwards Deming, Joseph M. Juran, and Armand V. Feigenbaum, whose work, in addition to contributions made by the Japanese (Dr. Kaoru Ishikawa, Dr. Genichi Taguchi, and Shigeo Shingo), resulted in the Total Quality Management (TQM) or Total Quality Control (TQC) methodology. From there, a host of other quality methods have evolved across industries and functions, starting in 1966 with Quality Function Deployment (QFD) in the Japanese automobile industry and culminating more recently in 1988 with Motorola's Six Sigma methodology. (Although, that timeline could be extended out to 1994 with the introduction of QS 9000 by the then big three automakers, Ford, GM, and Daimler-Chrysler.) So if you make use of Pareto and fishbone diagrams today, you can kindly thank Joseph M. Juran and Dr. Kaoru Ishikawa.

The underlying point here is not to advise that a company should run out and embrace a particular quality management methodology—the point is that companies have traditionally invested considerable time, resources, and money into figuring out how they can ensure that they are doing the right things right. Likewise, there should be mechanisms in place that help them institutionalize quality throughout their processes. Typically, companies formalize and/or enforce best practice quality methods by creating standards; however, the difficulty often lies in embedding these standards in respective processes. This is especially true for IT projects.

Much like the manufacturing product development process, IT projects are complex, with a myriad of inputs and outputs involved from the conceive and design stages on through the build, test, and deploy stages. As a consequence, there are a number of opportunities for costly errors or inconsistencies to arise during the project life cycle. In response, project managers at various levels rely on quality management techniques and standards to get the job done right—meaning on time, on budget, and according to business requirements. These may be overarching project management standards such as those endorsed by the

Project Management Institute (PMI) or Six Sigma standards at the business process level; or software engineering standards such as the Capability Maturity Model (CMM); or still others that are proprietary and developed in-house. But how closely such standards are followed depends on the ability of the organization to effectively inject these standards into the daily workings of these projects. The far-flung realm of IT, in combination with the scale and rapidity of the changes that IT is required to enact, make this a formidable task for even the most efficient companies. At any given time in large organizations there are literally hundreds of projects in various stages of deployment, in which there are hundreds of individual resources assigned to thousands of tasks that must comply with prescribed standards. How can even the most proficient project manager know or guarantee that these standards are being adhered to? How can the resources assigned to these projects be notified of these standards beyond traditional managerial oversight?

Once again, the principles and activities of BTM play an integral role—this time in facilitating the institutionalization of standards. First, standards—whether they are component design standards (e.g., Component Object Model [COM]), or engineering methodology standards (e.g., MBase), or vendor-specific standards (e.g., SAP solution map), or another variety—are captured and codified in the business, process, and technology models produced during the activities of BTM (see Fig. 8.4).

Incorporating standards in enterprise models is analogous to encapsulating the detailed information necessary to satisfy high levels of quality compliance in the design specs for multi-phased production of heavy machinery or automobiles. For example, if you are rolling out a large-scale enterprise software package to multiple business units, you'd likely want to make sure that the rollout is standard in each and every instance to reduce risk, contain costs, maintain scope and timetables, and consistently map functional requirements to technology capabilities. In such a scenario, models would serve as the design specs for the IT initiative, enabling project teams to maintain consistent and repeatable levels of quality throughout each rollout. In the automobile manufacturing world, design specs can indicate, for instance, what parts

Figure | 8.4

Standards (such as EJB) that are captured in models are can be rolled up into the portfolio and provide the basis for analysis and decision-making (such as determining what types of projects currently utilize EJB)

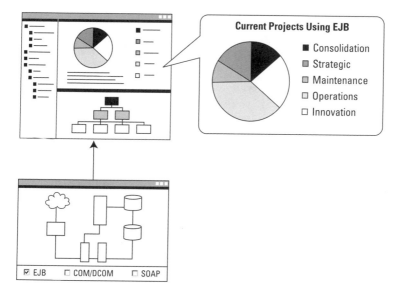

should be used to guarantee that they are QS 9000 standard compliant; in the IT world, models can indicate what systems should be used to conform to data-level security standards. If you fail to build a vehicle with QS 9000 compliant materials, then potentially you've failed to build a car that is safe or meets consumer needs; if you fail to implement systems that conform to given security standards, then potentially you've failed to deliver a system that can get the required data into end-user hands. Design specs—and their BTM-equivalent models—keep designers and implementers in sync with quality standards.

Once standards are defined in the models, they are communicated up-front to the various project team members in the form of element attributes, properties, requirements, process maps, application or system pictographs, and such. Despite the normal management practice of regular meetings or the frequent release of internally documented guidelines, individual working groups often fail to follow universal standards. Project plans, procedural memos or manuals, and meetings help to communicate information about standards, but the ability to reinforce this type of knowledge is better provided by the models themselves. Traditional communication methods tend to fall short as they are more static than models and therefore have a temporal effect. The unique visualization afforded by models, however, substantially increases each project participant's awareness of (and ultimate adherence to) applicable standards at the time it counts most in the process—during design and implementation. By ingraining standards in the models, project participants are exposed to this vital information on a day-to-day basis, resulting in contextual use at the activity level. Simply put, models make information public knowledge, not tribal knowledge.

Finally, by following BTM's principle of reusability, project managers can make certain that even far-flung project teams remain on the same page. They do this by creating and providing access to a repository of models that should be used as governing templates for upcoming projects. In this way, standards are globally propagated across functional and physical geographies, promoting widespread adoption and use. This of course, can be of particular benefit when certain tasks are delegated to external service providers who may be located off-site from the project or whose level of active involvement is irregular. Whether the project participant is internal or external, the use of templates helps project managers increase standards compliance, and by proxy, the derivative return that organizations receive on investment in such methods.

A Dollar Saved Is...

According to best practice approaches, quality management is only one of several sub-disciplines belonging to the overall project management discipline. Likewise, cost management is one of several sub-disciplines belonging to the management of the project procurement process. Procurement management essentially focuses on controlling the acquisition of the products and services that are required to fulfill the objectives of the project. Cost management, in this regard, focuses on controlling costs so that the project is completed within approved budget parameters. Models play an integral role in the institutionalization of standards, so it is easy to understand how they facilitate quality and cost management by:

- **Reducing maverick spending** to safeguard against improper procurement
- **Eliminating redundancies** and waste to reduce or contain costs

Reduce Maverick Spending

The rebuke that IT decision-makers sometimes receive from the business side regarding inappropriate spending often stems from incidents involving maverick purchases. These purchases are maverick in the sense that they involve non-approved vendors or service providers, don't involve competitive solicitations, don't follow stringent vendor-selection criteria, don't incorporate standard contract terms or clauses, and so on. Maverick spending is detrimental in more than a few ways. Some of the most notable include dissolution of corporate purchasing leverage, use of unqualified products and services that quickly wind up consigned to the scrap heap, and unfavorable contract expenses and conditions.

It's not that corporations hold a cavalier attitude toward purchasing or shrug off the responsibility of trying to prevent such instances of squander. Many corporations devote entire departments to formalizing purchasing procedures for the express purpose of combating these errant expenditures. The problem is that they still struggle to universally communicate and enforce these standards. Guidelines and procedures prescribed in a five-inch thick binder have a tendency to get lost in the organizational translation process.

The last section explained how models codify and institutionalize quality and implementation standards. The same is true for corporate purchasing standards. Through the use of models, project participants have immediate visibility and access to these standards at the most critical moment—during vendor evaluation and selection.

To illustrate what I mean, here's a short example: The corporate IT department for a large, multinational conglomerate determines that to save money on integration costs, all CRM projects will be required to install a package from Vendor A. To enforce this standard, the architects create templates that earmark elements pertaining to Vendor A's offering (e.g., functional requirements, specifications, compatible operating systems and hardware, etc.) as the approved vendor. These templates then become a part of the PMO's repository for reuse on similar initiatives. Subsequent use of these templates ensures that when a new CRM project is begun in any of the company's business units, architects don't deviate from the standards and Vendor A remains the selected provider. In this way, the models act as a powerful mechanism for enforcing corporate purchasing standards and preserving spending integrity.

Eliminate Redundancies and Waste

From a cost-management perspective, it is the program manager's responsibility to determine appropriate resource (physical, human) levels, develop cost estimations, allocate budget amounts to tasks, and control changes to cost structures.[4] Bear in mind the scope of the task at hand—hundreds of projects running in parallel with hundreds of physical and human resources involved. The first step in managing this process is to identify and eliminate redundancies between projects. The decentralization of IT, mergers and acquisitions activity, and globalization are just a few of the major factors contributing to the vast amount of redundancy that already exist in many enterprises. New initiatives shouldn't add to the current level of waste; at the same time they should be used as opportunities for right-sizing IT allocation.

Models are valuable tools here because they help to clearly identify elements that are currently shared or have the potential to be shared between projects at the business, process, data, application, system, component, and functional requirement levels. It's shocking, but more than a few organizations don't really know what resources they already have in-house and how they are being utilized. I'm not talking about keyboards and mice here—I'm talking about big-ticket items like rack-optimized servers or enterprise software packages. Models contain dynamic linkages and references between elements that enable architects and managers to gain this critical insight. And, the depth of insight provided by the models goes a long way toward promoting the reuse of functionalities, processes, and technologies that would otherwise go undiscovered. Through models, not only can project managers highlight and excise waste, they can also uncover opportunities to optimize cost-benefit ratios.

The ABCs of Governance

By exercising strict governance over the strategic direction and tactical control of IT projects, CIOs can maximize the business value of their IT investments. A portfolio approach gives senior technology executives, such as the CIO, a mechanism to align investments with overall corporate strategy, and, where possible, exercise familiar, dollars-and-cents control over the somewhat previously inscrutable world of IT. Increasingly, IT is being asked to produce quick wins where the revenue distance (the length between the investment and the revenue producer it supports) is as short as possible. The natural tendency, therefore, is to focus myopically on pure financial indicators such as ROI in lieu of more holistic indicators that incorporate a blend of both tangible and intangible measures. Business and technology decision-makers must resist the temptation to overly emphasize the quantitative at the expense of the qualitative, lest they make inappropriate assumptions regarding risk and value. The underpinning data that portfolio analysts need to draw intelligent conclusions about the status and direction of an IT portfolio is supplied from the bottom-up, through the models that are created during the activities of BTM. In addition, these models help IT managers to reanalyze their investments with respect to current—not outdated—conditions and to communicate more effectively with their business counterparts during the budgetary process.

's principles and activities also ensure that IT project
's maintain the same degree of control, accountability,
al responsibility that is expected of projects in the rest of
the business. In this manner, the CIO can feel confident that the
promises he or she makes when communicating the value of IT to
the business, come true when put into practice.

9

Promise to Practice

EVERY BUSINESS BOOK ASPIRES TO BE actionable in the enterprise, and this one is no exception. But the transition from the written page to the real world can be tricky. In between the covers of a book, ideas stand or fall on their merit alone. But in the real world, these ideas demand that people—employees, customers, partners, whoever—act in certain, specific ways to make them work. As a result, when many people are required to work together in pursuit of a single overarching goal, there's often a conflict between an idea's promise on the page and its practice in the enterprise.

Until now, this book has focused on how companies can align themselves from the perspective of the activities of BTM and from the perspective of strategic direction and tactical control. But to help you bridge the gap between promise and practice and get started with BTM in the real world, there's another perspective that's important as well: That of the people that make up the organization. How should they—with all of their real-world responsibilities and competing priorities—tackle BTM?

So what's the best way to take the ideas in this book and implement them in your own organization? Remember that I've gone out of my way to emphasize that BTM isn't a strict methodology. That's important to mention since methodologies require people to perform specific tasks that may be different from the ones that they currently perform. This puts strain on the organization, and is one of the main reasons that a methodology may succeed in promise but fail in practice: People can't and shouldn't be asked to turn on a dime to accommodate the latest management fad, especially since there's often a lot of knowledge and expertise built into the way things are currently done. But, at the other end of the spectrum, if people don't change their behavior at all how can we expect to do away with the conditions that lead to the disconnect in the first place? This dilemma, in fact, points to a central question whose answer is crucial to understanding how the organization should view BTM: Is it an art or science?

Art Versus Science

The fact that BTM relies upon interconnected models should tip you off that the unspecified genius of an artist isn't consistent enough to solve the disconnect. But, on the other hand, BTM doesn't try to shoehorn very different organizations into the same strict, step-by-step procedure the way a methodology does. The right place to locate BTM on the art/science spectrum is somewhere between the two extremes: It provides just enough structure without checking the individuality that each employee brings to the job. This is why I described BTM as an approach that aligns business and technology rather than a methodology or some amorphous "ten secrets of alignment." The latter relies on too science while the former leans too heavily on art.

A Recipe for BTM

"Is a recipe art or science? It's science to some degree, since it includes measurements, temperatures, and cooking times, but there's also an art to it. If two people followed the same recipe would they come out with exactly the same outcome? A more accurate way to frame the question might be to ask whether it's a bad thing if two people cook the same recipe and the results differ slightly but are equally delicious?

One way to look at BTM is as a recipe which, if internalized by the CIO and senior IT staff, can help to enable the scientific aspects of their responsibilities more efficiently and effectively. But there still is that other, creative side that includes who are you as a person or leader? What are your values? And how well do you communicate the issues and opportunities that emanate from IT to your peers in the business? It's not realistic, in other words, to expect everybody to approach alignment in exactly the same way; we're not little robots or clones. But at the same time you need a recipe, and BTM provides that."

– **Tom Trainer,** *former CIO, Citigroup, Inc.; Eli Lilly & Co.; and Reebok International, Ltd.; chairman of the Executive Committee, enamics, Inc.*

Roles and Responsibilities

So given this balancing act between art and science, what's the best way for the organization to approach BTM? Chapter Two emphasized that it is the office of the CIO that needs to take ultimate responsibility for alignment. This statement is true as far as it goes. But by now it should be clear that the cast of characters that contributes to business model definition, process optimization, and technology automation extends far beyond any one person and his or her immediate staff. In BTM, to make the jump from promise to practice, you should consider the five general roles and responsibilities shown in Fig. 9.1.

| Figure | 9.1

Five roles and responsibilities help BTM make the jump from promise to practice: the CxO suite, the office of the CIO, the project/program management office (PMO), business professionals, and technology professionals

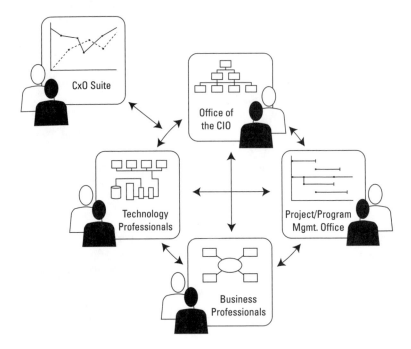

- **The CxO Suite,** including the CEO, CFO, COO, and other business unit heads, which is responsible for understanding the impact that IT has on the business so they can make investment decisions accordingly, achieving general visibility into IT portfolios and projects, and setting the example for how the firm as a whole should view the IT function.
- **The Office of the CIO,** which is responsible for identifying broad opportunities for using technology to innovate the business, managing the IT portfolio, and overseeing risk and general governance of IT.
- **The Project/Program Management Office, or PMO,** which is responsible for controls, prioritization, consolidation, and standards that span individual projects and programs.

- **Business Professionals,** who are responsible for contributing business and process expertise to the activities of BTM, including visualizing and understanding the impact of IT, and for managing operational change.
- **Technology Professionals,** who are responsible for designing applications and systems, coordinating with business professionals to validate IT decisions, implementing the final design, and managing technology change.

CxO Suite

The CxO suite should assume three responsibilities that are related to BTM. First, they need to make smart IT investment decisions by understanding how technology impacts the business. They need this technology acumen for the same reason that the CIO needs to understand the impact of business decisions: to understand IT's transformational capabilities and to allocate funds accordingly. Understanding the impact of IT will help the CxO suite communicate their vision and goals for the company to both their IT colleagues and also to the board of directors—who should be aware of how the CxO suite intends to leverage the company's considerable IT investments to increase shareholder value.

The second responsibility of the CxO suite is to achieve general visibility into IT—to take the general pulse of IT programs and projects, in other words. Without the integrated view of the IT portfolio (supported by business, process, and technology models) that is advocated by BTM, it is difficult for the CxO suite (or any other members of the general business audience, for that matter) to become familiar with the basic workings of IT. Throughout the entire cycle from a project's conception to rollout, the models developed during the activities of BTM improve visibility into IT, which is crucial for collaborating to develop a shared vision with the CIO. In a broader sense, improving visibility into and communication with IT is really the core of BTM, since translating between stakeholders who speak fundamentally different languages—such as the CxO suite and the IT function in general—is a huge part of closing the disconnect.

The final responsibility of the CxO suite is to set an example for how the business should view IT, and create an environment in which the CIO and IT can succeed. Surveys show that 78% of CIOs still earn grades of D– or F with their companies because "they are perceived to be functioning as commodity-based 'order takers'"[1] rather than as strategic partners. To improve this mark, CxOs should include the CIO as an active, visible, and empowered member of the executive team. This may require changing traditional reporting structures and turning over some discretionary powers regarding budget issues. By including the CIO in both short-term and long-term strategic planning sessions, the CxO suite promotes the early integration of technology into the company's goals, and a joint agenda that will reduce risk and increase return.

Behavior and culture also come from the top down, and the organization looks to the CEO to indicate what the company's attitude is towards IT. (This focus could be extended to the entire CxO suite, but it is the CEO who ultimately sets the overarching cultural tone.) Unfortunately, there are still a number of CEOs that either choose to shun this responsibility or are not equipped to respond appropriately. Michael Earl, director of London Business School's Centre for Research in Information Management, and David Feeny, director of The Oxford Institute of Information Management and vice president of Templeton College, group the IT management styles of CEOs into seven archetypes in their Sloan Management Review article, "How To Be a CEO for the Information Age" (see Table 9.1).

Only one archetype, "The Believer," actually combines the right behaviors and attitudes that help companies reap the rewards they expect out of technology. But even today, few CEOs actually qualify for inclusion in this category.[2] Without strong CEO sponsorship of the IT role in their organizations, the CxO suite and companies in general are destined to perpetuate the behaviors and attitudes that thwart alignment and organizational success.

Office of the CIO

The next role that must tackle BTM is the office of the CIO. The CIO, as Ch. 2 discusses, is ultimately responsible for alignment between business and technology. This means that it is essential to make the CIO and his or her office the BTM champion within

Table 9.1

The seven creeds of the CEO: hypocrite, waverer, atheist, zealot, agnostic, monarch, and believer

The Seven Creeds of the CEO	
Archetype	**Attributes**
The Hypocrite	Espouses strategic importance of IT but negates belief through personal action
The Waverer	Reluctantly accepts strategic importance of IT but is not ready to get involved in IT matters
The Atheist	Convinced that IT is of little value and publicly espouses this belief
The Zealot	Convinced IT is strategically important and equally believes he is an IT expert
The Agnostic	Concedes IT is strategically important but needs repeated convincing
The Monarch	Accepts IT is strategically important, appoints the best CIO, and steps back
The Believer	Believes IT enables strategic advantage and demonstrates belief through action

the organization. Typically, it is the office of the CIO who combines high-level strategies and priorities from the CxO suite with emerging technology trends to identify concrete IT programs and projects. The mechanism that the CIO uses to make these crucial decisions is the IT portfolio, which Ch. 8 describes. By managing this portfolio, the office of the CIO can keep tabs on overall investment and risk, and provide a unifying authority for governing IT.

But the CIO's interaction with the CxO suite needs to run the other way as well. The CIO should participate in developing overall corporate strategy by identifying opportunities for IT innovation, and bringing these to the CxO suite. Again, models and the IT portfolio are important mechanisms here, because they help the office of the CIO identify trends, and more importantly, explain trends in everyday terms to their counterparts within the business.

Thinking Like a CEO

"One of the most significant changes in the last five years is because of the rapid proliferation of technology. The CIO definitely emerged at the forefront of the business table and has become the epicenter of the organization. Conversely, CEOs have become extraordinarily more technology savvy because they realize that effective use of technology whether it's insourced or outsourced is going to directly affect the bottom line. And so the role has changed whereby the CIO is now viewed as a strategic business partner. All of the things that a CEO thinks about—acquisitions, divestitures, organic growth—the CIO needs to think about too.

What is required is for the CIO to be much more savvy about where he spends his time, his money, and his efforts. There is virtually no other function in any Global 1000 organization that has a larger capital and expense budget than the CIO. So in reality the CIO ultimately has the largest piece of business, virtually larger than any other stakeholder or executive in a corporation. It's caused the CIO to be much more business oriented, focusing on things like growing the top line, controlling the bottom line, margins, and expenses.

So the CIOs that are not strategic, that are not business partners, that are not aligned—those guys are getting 'sunset-ed' in the marketplace."

– **Paul Daversa,** *president & CEO, Resource Systems Group*

Despite the well-recognized trend in the industry for CIOs to become strategic partners in the business, many companies still leave IT out in the cold when it comes time to set strategies and determine goals. This especially happens when the CIO's subordinate position is institutionalized by unit pricing or charge-back systems, whereby the business pays for IT services. This is the right step if you buy into the argument that IT needs to become a profit center, but it's the wrong approach if you want IT to be accepted as integral to the organization just like other functions such as manufacturing, sales, and marketing.

Project/Program Management Office (PMO)

The next crucial role is that of the project/program management office, or PMO. After the office of the CIO has identified new projects to meet the strategic objectives of the enterprise, they should coordinate with the PMO to monitor, track, prioritize, and retain broad tactical control over these projects. The PMO, which can be organized as either an engaged internal consultancy or a hands-off repository of best practices and general project information, reports either to senior IT executives or to a joint steering committee composed of business and IT leaders. The steering committee is typically assembled in response to a specific initiative, and includes members with a direct stake in that initiative's success. For example, the PMO tasked with a CRM initiative may report to a steering committee that consists of the CIO, vice president of Marketing, the CFO, and senior representatives of the sales and support functions.

As projects move from concept to completion, the PMO periodically re-evaluates them to make sure that they remain on-track to meet their initial promise. Both leading and lagging indicators of the project's performance can trigger these re-evaluations. During each, the enterprise model helps to communicate progress and gives the IT steering committee the information they need to make accurate and timely decisions about the initiative's fate. After a project has been implemented successfully, the PMO rolls up design decisions made during impact analysis into a central repository of best-practice templates and company standards. These design decisions, which are the basis for reuse in BTM, can take the form of standard processes, approved application packages, network and technology configurations, or even complete, end-to-end project designs that can be reused in later initiatives. The PMO also helps to prioritize individual projects and tasks, so that resources in limited supply (whether that means a specialized programmer, network bandwidth, or database storage space) can be allocated intelligently to maximize their benefit to the enterprise. Other key responsibilities of the PMO are to select a project manager, define project methodologies, secure funding, assign resources, and engage service providers for IT projects.

Business Professionals

The fourth and fifth roles that are responsible for BTM—business and technology professionals—collaborate closely to complete the activities of BTM. The process starts with the capture of an as-is enterprise model, continues as companies develop potential to-be scenarios and perform gap analysis between the to-be and as-is states, and concludes when a final to-be scenario is selected and moved along to implementation. Every scenario should include three general areas—business, process, and technology—each of which corresponds directly to one of the activities of BTM: business model definition, process optimization, and technology automation.

Business professionals, of course, are more directly concerned with the first two of these activities, and their expertise and in-depth knowledge of the subject matter should form the basis for developing the business and process models that make up the business architecture. But at the same time, business professionals should be familiar with technology automation so that they can understand the impact of IT and visualize how new and updated applications and systems impact how they do their job.

One final—and often overlooked—responsibility of business professionals is to manage the operational change that is required to take advantage of updates to the technology architecture. For example, a new supply chain management system may require demand planners to adjust how they work. In this case, the business professionals need to make sure that these changes take place (through the use of incentives, training, or creating new positions, for example).

Technology Professionals

The final role that is responsible for BTM is technology professionals, who can be either internal resources from the IT department or external service providers. Technology professionals are responsible primarily for designing and implementing the technology architecture, which includes the applications and systems that are modeled during technology automation. But, at the same time, they need to work with business professionals to validate the impact of IT decisions and make sure that the technology architecture matches back to the company's business needs and objectives.

Technology professionals, including developers, system analysts, and other specialists, are frequently responsible for implementing the final project as well. Once a project receives funding and moves into implementation, the to-be enterprise model developed during the activities of BTM becomes a reference point which helps to make sure that the project stays true to its initial business goals. One other advantage that the enterprise model provides during this stage is that it helps to improve decision-making when the development team faces unexpected but inevitable design changes. In the past, these changes would have been made on a piecemeal basis. But BTM makes it realistic to do end-to-end impact analysis for almost any modification, so that even last-minute technology changes are made with the overall good of the project in mind.

Coordinating Between Roles and Responsibilities

Obviously, these five roles and responsibilities impact a broad range of people (from the executive suite on down to technical developers) and tasks (from overall corporate strategy to detailed design decisions and technology implementation). Coordinating between these people and tasks so that the whole train stays on the tracks is one of the major challenges that every organization faces when working with BTM. In order to put BTM's principles, activities, and governance to work, companies need a formalized management infrastructure to facilitate this coordination between each of the roles and responsibilities.

ι the past, some argued for software solutions like groupware
οrporate portals to play this role, others claimed that all com-
nies needed was a good spate of team-building exercises to
develop the lacking connections, while still others praised balanced scorecards. These are, respectfully, useful communication
mediums, HR techniques, and performance measurement tactics,
but they aren't specifically designed for the range of interactions
between the CxO suite, the office of the CIO, the PMO, business
professionals, and technology professionals that are necessary to
help BTM make the jump from promise to practice. Although
companies appear to recognize that there needs to be some mid-
dleman between each of these players, British American Tobacco's
Kevin Poulter observes that most companies still don't have an
infrastructure dedicated to that goal in the same way that they
have infrastructures for other parts of the business.

> One of the things of which I am a strong proponent is that we
> approach IT as a significant function in the organization that
> needs an infrastructure to automate interactions and decisions
> just the same way as operations or marketing. All of those
> functions have their own systems to support their operations.
> For example, in our business, the marketing function is respon-
> sible for managing a portfolio of brands and operations is
> responsible for managing a portfolio of manufacturing capabili-
> ties. Similarly, IT is responsible for managing a portfolio of
> applications and increasingly so, business services. In a lot of
> major organizations, operations and the marketing portfolios
> are supported quite well by information technology. But find-
> ing organizations that actually support their IT management
> function using IT is somewhat less common. You could almost
> say that the corporate IT department suffers from the "cobbler's
> children have no shoes" syndrome.

Although the overall effort to get BTM to work in the enterprise is shared between the five general roles, the primary responsibility and accountability for putting an infrastructure in place to
facilitate this communication and collaboration resides with the
office of the CIO. Today, most CIOs lack a management infrastructure that is analogous to those that are commonly available to

their business counterparts—CFOs and financial planners have financial modeling and analysis tools, sales and marketing executives rely on sales force automation (SFA) and CRM infrastructures, and manufacturing professionals have SCM at their disposal. These other functions are made more efficient and productive by supporting management infrastructures—after all, I wouldn't refute that just-in-time (JIT) manufacturing is made more feasible because of SCM technologies—so it's logical to demand that IT be supported in equal fashion.

Your Own Unique Contribution

No matter which type of infrastructure you use to coordinate between these roles and responsibilities, you should feel free to add as many of your own contributions as it takes to make BTM work in your organization, just like master chefs might add a secret ingredient or two to give a familiar recipe their own unique flair. For example, since business and technology professionals are primarily charged with carrying out the activities of BTM, one of the things that they have to be able to do is predictive modeling. But in describing these two crucial roles and responsibilities, I don't say anything in particular about how they should go about doing this. Should they develop models using dedicated software, a simple drawing program, or old-fashioned pencil and paper? There isn't any right or wrong answer—this doesn't mean that every choice is equally good, but it does mean that BTM doesn't make the decision for you. Any number of specific approaches could work to meet each of the responsibilities described in this chapter, and each organization's own unique needs should dictate which they choose.

The combination of basic roles and responsibilities with the flexibility of your own unique contribution is the basis for balancing between art and science, and for making BTM make the jump from promise to practice. This balance is one of BTM's primary benefits and at the same time one of the reasons that previous attempts to align business and technology have failed. Translating an idea on paper to a solution in the real world is always complicated, and detailed matrices, frameworks, and methodologies that look brilliant in the classroom often seem rigid and impractical when placed in the context of a real enterprise. But by rejecting a confining, end-to-end procedure for getting started in favor of general roles and responsibilities around which you can fill in the gaps however you see fit, BTM makes it more likely that your IT initiatives will look as good in the real world as they do on paper. And in the end, of course, that's the only thing that matters.

Conclusion

ODAY, TOO MANY IT PROFESSIONALS are overwhelmed or intimidated by the foreign world of business, while many business professionals view IT as a tangle of incomprehensible ones and zeros. As a result, IT remains shrouded from the rest of the business in a way that is unlike any other function. I frequently discuss this persistent struggle to demystify the black-box mentality surrounding technology with my friend and colleague, Tom Trainer. As the former CIO of industry giants such as Citigroup, Eli Lilly, and Reebok, Tom has experienced the struggle firsthand. His remarks on the subject struck me as more befitting of a conclusion for this book than I could ever pen:

> When's the last time you saw a $50 or $75 million marketing campaign where other major functions of the business didn't have top-to-bottom visibility into what was going on? No management team would ever agree to fund a $75 million

Super Bowl ad campaign and then just switch on the TV at halftime and hope they got it right. But that still happens all the time for IT projects with even bigger price tags than that.

Businesses are sick and tired of spending big-time money on technology without getting value. Right or wrong, there's been a long-standing perception, particularly among large companies who spend a large amount of money on IT, that IT is a chronic underachiever that promises the world but reliably fails to deliver. And, unfortunately, there are too many stories that reinforce that perception—stories about ERP initiatives spiraling out of control, about failed supply chain platforms that cause devastating inventory shortages, or about million dollar software that goes unused.

CIOs themselves recognize that the salad days are over and they're going to be scrutinized like never before. They have to act like any other function that has a seat at the CEO's table and describe not only where the money went in plain, understandable terms, but more important, why it went where it did. Generally, other functional managers and the CEOs don't get enough visibility into what's going on in IT. It's not necessary that they understand every single aspect of technology, the bits and bytes and all that. What is necessary is that they are able to understand all the possible impacts (positive and negative) that technology can have on the business.

I find it amazing that the industry hasn't realized before now that something better change when we start spending on IT again. It's like the elephant in the corner—nobody wants to talk about it. Well now people are going to start talking about it a lot more loudly and I think that an approach like BTM, as outlined in this book, is arriving at precisely the right time.

There is absolutely a need for a repeatable infrastructure or set of management capabilities that will help companies close the disconnect between business and technology. It's a capability whose time has come. When the tide's in and companies start spending again, I don't think businesses will be falling over themselves to throw money at IT anymore without a set of capabilities that allows them to get real value out of technology. The combination of principles, activities, and governance that makes up BTM will help them to do just that.

If I have learned one truism over the last 34 years of my career, it is this: Unless something fundamentally different starts to happen, individual enterprises are going to be as they were yesterday and last year and five years before that. And I don't believe there's a single company that can afford that.

APPENDIX

Alignment Maturity Model

IT'S COMMON PRACTICE FOR MOST OF US when we encounter a problem to seek a diagnosis that will tell us the nature, cause, and extent of the difficulty. When we have a medical problem, we go to the doctor knowing that he will examine us and potentially run a series of tests to ascertain what ails us. We do the same thing when we experience car trouble and turn to the mechanic whom we expect will check under the hood or the chassis to properly inspect the vehicle so that he can determine the source of the trouble. And we do the same thing yet again when we encounter computer difficulties, soliciting the analysis of technical support representatives whom we know from experience will run us through a series of probing questions to arrive at the root cause. It shouldn't be hard, therefore, to conclude that in business we should follow the same practice.

If one looks at the statistics and surveys of the top research firms, they indicate that most companies believe they have an alignment problem that needs remedying.[1] These companies have, at the very least, a general sense of the nature of the problem and some undoubtedly may already know the precise root cause. But the majority of companies still don't know the full extent of the problem nor do they agree internally on what the problem is or understand the reason why it has occurred. Ask a dozen different executives and managers from various areas of the organization about their opinion as to whether or not business and technology are aligned, and you are bound to receive a dozen differing responses. It's the influence of mental models, again, that makes it difficult for business and IT leaders to achieve consensus. What these two sides need is a formal mechanism, which will help them objectively diagnose and agree on the level of their alignment.

Getting an Accurate Read

There are various means by which companies can assess their alignment, however, the most comprehensive of these methods is the Strategic Alignment Maturity Model, developed by Dr. Jerry Luftman, Distinguished Service Professor, of the Stevens Institute of Technology. Based on a multi-year research study of Global 2000 companies and his own two decades of practical experience as an IT professional, Luftman created this diagnostic tool to help organizations measure their alignment maturity.[2] According to Luftman:

> It is extremely important to recognize what the business thinks about the relationship as well as what IT thinks about the relationship, and then where they both agree that there are problems/opportunities that should be addressed. Firms must have IT and business executives working together to address these alignment issues because both organizations tend to see the world very differently. So the focus is on finding out where the firm is by formally taking a look at what can be done to make it better. This includes an internal assessment as well as benchmarking against other firms.

The Strategic Alignment Maturity Model is patterned after the Capability Maturity Model (CMM), which was designed by Carnegie Mellon University's Software Engineering Institute to help organizations measure and improve the maturity of their software development processes. In a similar fashion to CMM, but focusing on a much higher level of the company, the alignment assessment includes five levels of maturity. Companies are described from the weakest Level 1—those that lack the processes and relationships needed to attain alignment—to Level 5, the strongest, where IT and other business functions (marketing, finance, R&D, etc) adapt their strategies together using fully developed processes that include external partners and customers. The evaluation criteria between the two are understandably quite different. Dr. Luftman's model focuses on six key criteria essential for the assessment and diagnosis of business/IT alignment: communications, metrics, governance, partnership, technology, and human resources. Each of the criteria is described by a set of attributes, as shown in Fig. A.1.[3]

A team of both business and IT leaders assesses the six criteria and sub components, using the results to converge on an overall assessment level of the firm's maturity. The approach focuses on understanding the alignment maturity and on maximizing alignment enablers and minimizing inhibitors. To help quantify perceptions, the attributes for each criterion are evaluated according to a Likert scale rating method of 1 – 5 (typically expressed as a range from strongly disagree to strongly agree). By examining components of the business/IT relationship through such a framework, both sides can objectively assess and then mutually agree upon their level of alignment maturity. Business and IT leaders can then use the diagnostic results of the assessment to better understand what areas require improvement and why.

Regularly Scheduled Check-up

How often a company assesses its business/technology alignment depends on the individual nature of the organization. Certainly, it uld be impractical to stop and assess the level of alignment maturity before the start or end of every project. However, the assessment frequency could occur on an annual schedule, or could even match the company's strategic planning cycles. It may be necessary to conduct alignment checks on a more frequent basis when there is a significant degree of misalignment and then the company could shift to longer intervals between checks once the highest level of alignment maturity has been attained. Anytime corrective steps are determined and agreed upon pursuant to an assessment, these should be mapped against current/planned strategies, organizational/operational capabilities, and environmental conditions so that actions are not formulated and executed in a vacuum. Alignment is not a one-time or isolated event—it should be part and parcel of the company's strategy and operations.

Figure	A.1

Dr. Jerry Luftman's Strategic Alignment Maturity Model measures alignment according to six criteria: communications, metrics, governance, partnership, technology, and human resources.

	LEVEL 1 Initial/Ad Hoc Process	**LEVEL 2** Committed Process
COMMUNICATION		
Understanding of Business by IT	IT management lacks understanding	Limited understanding by IT management
Understanding of IT by Business	Managers lack understanding	Limited understanding by managers
Organizational Learning	Casual conversation and meetings	Newsletters, reports, group email
Style and Ease of Access	Business to IT only; formal	One-way, somewhat informal
Leveraging Intellectual Assets	Ad hoc	Some structured sharing emerging
IT/Business Liaison Staff	None or use only as needed	Primary IT/Business link
METRICS		
IT Metrics	Technical only	Technical, cost; metrics rarely reviewed
Business Metrics	IT investments measured rarely, if ever	Cost/unit; rarely reviewed
Link Between IT and Business Metrics	Value of IT investments rarely measured	Business, IT metrics not linked
Service Level Agreements	Use sporadically	With units for technology performance
Benchmarking	Seldom or never	Sometimes benchmark informally
Formally Assess IT Investments	Don't assess	Only when there's a problem
Continuous Improvement Practices	None	Few; effectiveness not measured

LEVEL 3 Established Focused Process	LEVEL 4 Improved/Managed Process	LEVEL 5 Optimized Process
Good understanding by IT management	Understanding encouraged among IT staff	Understanding required of all IT staff
Good understanding by managers	Understanding encouraged among staff	Understanding required of staff
Training, departmental meetings	Formal methods sponsored by senior management	Learning monitored for effectiveness
Two-way, formal	Two-way, somewhat informal	Two-way, informal and flexible
Structured around key processes	Formal sharing at all levels	Formal sharing with partners
Facilitate knowledge transfer	Facilitate relationship-building	Build relationship with partners
Review, act on technical, ROI metrics	Also measure effectiveness	Also measure business opportunities, HR, partners
Review, act on ROI, cost	Also measure customer value	Balanced scorecard, includes partners
Business, IT metrics becoming linked	Formally linked; reviewed and acted upon	Balanced scorecard, includes partners
With units; becoming enterprise-wide	Enterprise-wide	Includes partners
May benchmark formally, seldom act	Routinely benchmark, usually act	Routinely benchmark, act, and measure results
Becoming a routine occurrence	Routinely assess and act on findings	Routinely assess, act, and measure results
Few, starting to measure effectiveness	Many, frequently measure effectiveness	Practices and measures well-established

Figure | A.1 (*continued*)

	LEVEL 1 Initial/Ad Hoc Process	**LEVEL 2** Committed Process
GOVERNANCE		
Formal Business Strategy Planning	Not done, or done as needed	At unit functional level; slight IT input
Formal IT Strategy Planning	Not done, or done as needed	At unit level; slight business input
Organization Structure	Centralized or decentralized	Centralized or decentralized; some co-location
Reporting Relationship	CIO reports to CFO	CIO reports to CFO
How IT is Budgeted	Cost center; spending is unpredictable	Cost center by unit
Rationale for IT Spending	Reduce costs	Productivity, efficiency
Senior-level IT Steering Committee(s)	Don't have	Meet informally as needed
How Projects are Prioritized	React to business or IT need	Determined by IT function
PARTNERSHIP		
Business Perception of IT	Cost of doing business	Becoming an asset
IT's Role in Strategic Business Planning	Not involved	Enables business processes
Shared Risks and Rewards	IT takes all the risks, receives no rewards	IT takes most risks with little reward
Managing the IT/Business Relationship	IT/Business relationship isn't managed	Managed on ad hoc basis
Relationship/Trust Style	Conflict and mistrust	Transactional relationship
Business Sponsors/Champions	Usually none	Often have a senior IT sponsor/champion

LEVEL 3	LEVEL 4	LEVEL 5
Established Focused Process	Improved/Managed Process	Optimized Process
Some IT input and cross-functional planning	At unit and enterprise, with IT	With IT and partners
Some business input and cross-functional planning	At unit and enterprise, with business	With partners
Centralized, decentralized or federal	Federal	Federal
CIO reports to COO	CIO reports to COO or CEO	CIO reports to CEO
Some projects treated as investments	IT treated as investment	Profit center
Also a process enabler	Process driver, strategy enabler	Competitive advantage, profit
Formal committees meet regularly	Proven to be effective	Also includes external partners
Determined by business function	Mutually determined	Partners' priorities are considered
Enables future business activity	Drives future business activity	Partner with business in creating value
Drives business processes	Enables or drives business strategy	IT/Business adapt quickly to change
IT/Business start sharing risks, rewards	Risks, rewards always shared	Managers are given incentive to take risks
Processes exist but not always followed	Processes exist and complied with	Processes are continuously improved
IT becoming a valued service provider	Long-term partnership	Partner, trusted vendor of IT services
IT and business sponsor/champion at unit level	Business sponsor/champion at corporate level	CEO is the business sponsor/champion

| Figure | A.1 (continued) |

	LEVEL 1 Initial/Ad Hoc Process	**LEVEL 2** Committed Process
TECHNOLOGY		
Primary Systems	Traditional office support	Transaction oriented
Standards	None or not enforced	Defined, enforced at functional level
Architectural Integration	Not well integrated	Within unit
How IT Infrastructure is Perceived	A utility; run at a minimum cost	Becoming driven by business strategy
HUMAN RESOURCES		
Innovative, Entrepreneurial Environment	Discouraged	Somewhat encouraged at unit level
Key IT HR Decision Maker(s)	Top business and IT management at corporate level	Same, with emerging functional influence
Change Readiness	Tend to resist change	Change readiness programs emerging
Career-Crossover Opportunities	Job transfers rarely occur	Occasionally occur within unit
Cross-Functional Training and Job Rotation	No opportunities	Decided by units
Social Interaction	Minimal IT/Business interaction	Strictly a business-only relationship
Attract and Retain Top Talent	No retention program; poor recruiting	IT hiring focused on technical skills

LEVEL 3	LEVEL 4	LEVEL 5
Established Focused Process	Improved/Managed Process	Optimized Process
Business process enabler	Business process driver	Business strategy enabler/driver
Emerging coordination across functions	Defined, enforced across functions	Also coordinated with partners
Integrated across functions	Begins to be integrated with partners	Integrated with partners
Driven by business strategy	Beginning to help business respond to change	Enables fast response to changing market
Strongly encouraged at unit level	Also at corporate level	Also with partners
Top business and unit management; IT advises	Top business and IT management across firm	Top management across firm and partners
Programs in place at functional level	Programs in place at corporate level	Also proactive and anticipate change
Regularly occur for unit management	Regularly occur at all unit levels	Also at corporate level
Formal programs run by all units	Also across enterprise	Also with partners
Trust and confidence is starting	Trust and confidence achieved	Attained with customers and partners
Technology and business focus; retention program	Formal program for hiring and retaining	Effective program for hiring and retaining

References

Chapter Two

1 Lepore, Dawn. "Are CIO's Obsolete?" *HSB Working Knowledge*, October 23, 2000. [Online: http://hbsworkingknowledge.hbs.edu/item.jhtml?id =1748&t=operations&sid=1749&pid=0]

2 Poe, Jonathan. "The Negative Impact of Failed IT Initiatives." *META Group* Research Note section, February 1, 2002. [Online: http://www.metagroup.com/metabits/mbDl0509.html]

Chapter Three

1 Jacobs, Peter K. "A Class Inspiration Returns to HBS." *HBS Working Knowledge*, January 18, 2000. [Online: http://hbsworkingknowledge.hbs. edu/pubitem.jhtml?id=1271&sid=-1&t=topic%3Dentrepreneurship]

2 The Wharton School of the University of Pennsylvania. "Measuring Returns on IT Investments: Some Tools and Techniques." From the Managing Technology section of the *Knowledge@Wharton* newsletter. [Online: http://knowledge.wharton.upenn.edu/articles.cfm?catid=14& articleid=396&homepage=yes]

3 Schrage, Michael. An excerpt from his book, *Serious Play: How the World's Best Companies Simulate to Innovate* (Harvard Business School Press, 2000). In "Playing for Keeps." *CIO.com*, June 15, 2000. [Online: http://www.cio.com/archive/061500_new.html]

4 Hansen, Morten T. and Bolko von Oetinger. *Introducing T-Shaped Managers: Knowledge Management's Next Generation* (Harvard Business School of Publishing). From the Product Overview page of the *Harvard Business Review* Web site, March 01, 2001. [Online: http://www.hbsp. harvard.edu/products/hbr/mar01/R0103G.html]

5 Mahowald, Robert. "From ICE Age To Contextual Collaboration." From the Analyst Corner section of *CIO.com*, June 29, 2001. [Online: http://www.cio.com/analyst/062901_idc.html]

Chapter Four

1 Bairstow, Lynne. "Collaboration." *e-com*, June 2001. [Online: https://www.e-commag.com/]

Chapter Five

1 Passori, Al. "Value at Stake: Making the IT Investment Portfolio Lean and Well Done." META *Group* Research Note section, Executive Directions, Delta 186, September 7, 2001. [Online: http://www.meta group.com/cgi-bin/inetcgi/search/displayArticle.jsp?oid=26355]

Chapter Six

1 For more information on the LOVEM notation, refer to Soper, Paulette. *Business Process Reengineering and Beyond*. IBM International Technical Support Organization. December 18, 1995. Information regarding other process definitions can be found in the following report: Bristow, David J. et al. *Process Definition Guidebook*. Lockheed Martin Federal Systems Report, May 12, 1997.

2 Zachman, John A. *Concepts of The Framework for Enterprise Architecture: Background, Description, and Utility* (Zachman International: 1996).

3 Spewak, Dr. Steven H. and Hill, Stephen C. *Enterprise Architecture Planning: Developing a Blueprint for Data, Applications, and Technology* (John Wiley & Sons: September, 1993).

Chapter Seven

1 Lynn, Doug. "Can't Plan (Course of Action) Without a Map." *META Group* Research Note section, Executive Directions, Delta 250, November 15, 2001. [Online: http://www.metagroup.com/cgi-bin/ inetcgi/search/displayArticle.jsp?oid=27581]

2 Handler, Robert. "Leveraging Architecture to Mitigate Issues and Risks With Outsourcing (Revisited)." *META Group* Research Note section, Executive Directions, Delta 131, August 27, 2001. [Online: http://www.metagroup.com/cgi-bin/inetcgi/search/display Article.jsp?oid=26152]

Chapter Eight

1 Rubin, Dr. Howard. "Doing The ROIght Stuff," *InformationWeek*, August 6, 2001. [Online: http://www.informationweek.com/story/ IWK20010802S0012]

2 Popper, Charles. "A Holistic Framework for IT Governance." From the Program on Information Resources Policy, Harvard University, February 2000. [Online: http://www.pirp.harvard.edu/publications/pdf-blurb .asp?id=417]

3 Jones, Larry. "System Thinking and Managing Behavior," From the Articles section of The Performance Management Homepage Web site. [Online: http://www.p-management.com/articles/9911.htm]

4 Project Management Institute. *PMBOK® Guide* (Newtown Square, PA: 2000), pg. 190.

Chapter Nine

1 Passori, Al. "CIOs Must Redouble Efforts to Make the Grade." *META Group* Research Note section, February 7, 2002. [Online: http://www. metagroup.com/metabits/mbDl0513.html]

2 Earl, Michael, and David Feeny. "How To Be a CEO for the Information Age." MIT Sloan Management Review, Winter 2000, Volume 41, Number 2.

Appendix

1 Alignment between business and technology has been cited for several years as a primary executive concern, typically ranking in the top third of most studies. These studies include the Computer Sciences Corporation. "14th Annual Survey of IS Management Issues," January 2001; Duffy, Jan. "IT/Business Alignment: Delivering Results." IDC Research Note section,

December 31, 2001; Poe, Jonathan. "Top CIO Issues for 2001." *META Group* Research Note section; Executive Directions, May 17, 2001; and Rosser, Bill and Carrie Smith. "Aligning Business and IT Strategies." Gartner Research Report, September, 9, 1996.

2 The Conference Board (TCB) and Society for Information Management (SIM) are presently working with Dr. Luftman on a major research initiative involving the Strategic Alignment Maturity Model. The study is designed to produce benchmarking results and best practices that address the business/IT relationship. To date, Dr. Luftman's research shows evidence that on the average most organizations only rank at a Level 2 in terms of alignment maturity. Dr. Luftman also serves as Chief Knowledge Officer for enamics, Inc.

3 The Strategic Alignment Maturity Model is also reproduced in "Diagnosing Your Organization." *CIO Insight* Whiteboard, November 1, 2001. [Online: http://common.ziffdavisinternet.com/download/0/1278/0107whiteboard_screen.pdf]

Additional Reading

Brown, Carol V. and V. Sambamurthy *Repositioning the IT Organization to Enable Business Transformation* (Pinnaflex Educational Resources: 1999).

Burke, Brian. "Enterprise Business Architecture: Defining High-Level Business Processes." *META Group* Research Note section, August 1, 2001. [Online: http://www.metagroup.com/cgi-bin/inetcgi/search/displayArticle.jsp?oid=26038]

Collins, Jim. "Aligning Action and Values." *Leader to Leader*, No 1. Summer 1996.

Davenport, Tom and Laurence Prusak. *Working Knowledge: How Organizations Manage What They Know* (Harvard Business School Press: October 1997).

Federal Architecture Working Group (FAWG). "A *Practical Guide to Federal Enterprise Architecture*." Version 1.0 produced for the Chief Information Officer Council, February 2001.

Gerrard, Michael and Barbara Gomolski. "Driving IT Planning with Business Strategy." Gartner Group Report, October 13, 2001.

Mahoney, J. "The Office of the CIO: What Is It and Why Do You Need One?" Gartner Group Research Note, June 14, 2001.

Meyers, Paul S. "*The Theory and Practice of Organizational Change*" (Ernst & Young Center for Business Innovation: 1994).

Pickering, Chris. "Cultural Barriers to Business-IT Alignment." Cutter Consortium Interview, 1999.

Sauer, Christopher and Philip W. Yetton. *Steps to the Future: Fresh Thinking on the Management of IT-Based Organizational Transformation* (Jossey-Bass: May 1997).

Schrage, Michael. *Serious Play: How the World's Best Companies Simulate to Innovate* (Harvard Business School Press: December 1999).

Senge, Peter. *The Fifth Discipline: The Art and Practice of the Learning Organization* (Currency/Doubleday: October 1994).

Strassmann, Paul A. "The Hocus-Pocus of Reengineering." *Across the Board*, June 1994.

Thorp, John. *The Information Paradox: Realizing the Business Benefits of Information Technology* (McGraw-Hill: February 1999).

United States General Accounting Office (GAO). "*Maximizing the Success of Chief Information Officers: Learning from Leading Organizations.*" March 2000.

Vitale, Michael and Peter Weill. *Place to Space: Migrating to Ebusiness Models* (Harvard Business School Press: May 2001).

Weill, Peter and Marianne Broadbent. *Leveraging the New Infrastructure: How Market Leaders Capitalize on Information Technology* (Harvard Business School Press: June 1998).

Contributors

Industry Contributors

Randolph C. Blazer is Chairman and Chief Executive Officer of KPMG Consulting, one of the world's largest consulting and systems integration firms. Under Mr. Blazer's leadership, KPMG Consulting launched the second largest IPO of NASDAQ's history, had 18 consecutive quarters of double-digit growth (1997-2001), increased revenues from $800 million to nearly $3 billion, and institutionalized a "Client for Life" culture resulting in a 96% retention rate of KPMG Consulting's top clients.

Paul Daversa is President and CEO of Resource Systems Group, one of the most sought-after executive search firms for enterprise software and broadband communications by the venture community and the companies they back, as well as by Fortune 500 organizations. Mr. Daversa, who personally architected the firm's strategy to support GE's globally acclaimed e-Business executive search campaign, is frequently sourced by major national news media on job market trends and conditions.

Patrick F. Flynn, Vice President and Chief Information Officer of truck manufacturer PACCAR Inc., is a manufacturing and service industry veteran who has implemented global client-server architectures and software process improvements. He is responsible for the design and implementation of award-winning electronic commerce products, and is a sought-after speaker on enhancing multi-tier supply chain networks using electronic commerce.

Scott Hayward is Managing Director at JP Morgan Chase & Company, where his 14-year career with the company has spanned strategy, operations, sales, service and technology. He heads client service and marketing for the Americas in the investment management business, was previously Chief Operating Officer of the Americas in the investment banking division, and spearheaded several reengineering efforts in swaps, private banking, human resources, and finance.

Dale Kutnick, Chairman, CEO and Research Director of META Group, is a recognized authority in all phases of the IT industry and is sourced extensively by the business and industry trade press. Mr. Kutnick, whose analysis spans two decades, co-directs all of META Group's research and analytic activities, and contributes to the company's Executive Directions program, which prepares customized research for CIOs.

Dr. Jerry Luftman is Executive Director and Distinguished Service Professor for the graduate Information Systems programs at the Stevens Institute of Technology. Dr. Luftman, whose 22-year career with IBM included CIO, is best known for his Strategic Alignment Maturity Model, which was developed from over ten years of research and testing with Fortune 500 companies and is the basis of a benchmarking study sponsored by The Conference Board and the Society for Information Management.

***

Chuck Martin is Chairman and CEO of the NFI Research, a U.S.-based research firm exploring the future of electronic business (E-business) and the Internet. Mr. Martin helped shape the Internet landscape through his work as a corporate Internet strategist for a variety of industries and businesses, as author of the best-selling books *Managing for the Short Term, The Digital Estate, Net Future*, and *Max-e-Marketing in the Net Future*, and as a journalist for several high-profile print and electronic media.

***

Jack Mollen is Senior Vice President of Human Resources at EMC Corporation, where he is responsible for all global human resources for EMC's 24,000 employees. His extensive HR experience includes senior management positions at Citigroup, where he managed the HR operations for 90,000 employees in 100 countries for the merged global operations and technology organizations of CitiCorp and Travelers, and at Harris Corporation, where he also had responsibility for information systems, engineering services, merger and acquisitions, facilities, and quality.

***

Honorio J. Padron is President, Business Services, Exelon, where Unicom's merger with PECO Energy brought to bear Mr. Padron's experience as both a business executive and an information technology executive. Throughout his career, he has served as Executive Vice President of Process Engineering and CIO at CompUSA and has held several executive management positions at companies such as PepsiCo, Flagstar and Burger King Corporation.

Don Peppers, founder and partner of the management consulting group, Peppers and Rogers Group, is co-author, with Martha Rogers, Ph.D., of several highly acclaimed business books on customer relationship management (CRM), including *The One to One Future*, *Enterprise One to One*, *The One to One Fieldbook* (co-authored with Bob Dorf), *The One to One Manager*, and *One to One B2B*. Mr. Peppers has delivered countless keynote addresses, workshops and consulting projects for clients on six continents.

Chris Perretta is Senior Vice President and Chief Information Officer for GE Capital Card Services, which provides private financial services to North America retailers and their private and commercial customers. Mr. Perretta also served as Chief Technology Officer for GE Capital, and previously spent 13 years with Andersen Consulting in its New York, France and UK consultancy practices.

Kevin Poulter is Head of Business Integration at British American Tobacco, where his responsibility for the company's overall business technology portfolio spans application architecture and integration strategy to B2B integration and information management. Before joining British American Tobacco, he was Chief Technology Officer at Computer Science Corporation, co-founded Ontology.org, and participated in several e-business standards initiatives, such as ebXML, eCo and ICE.

Howard Smith is Chief Technology Officer for Computer Science Corporation's European Group and co-chair of the Business Process Management Initiative. As co-founder of BPMI.org he has contributed to the development andadoption of Business Process Modeling Language (BPML). Previously, as CSC's director of e-business strategy, he co-founded Ontology.org and through his involvement as an invited expert to CommerceNet's eCo Framework Project, created the seminal ideas which led to many of today's well known XML standards for B2B e-commerce.

Tom Trainer is a recognized, 34-year industry veteran who spearheaded major IT efforts for the likes of Eli Lilly and Company, Reebok International, and Joseph E. Seagram and Sons, and was most recently Executive Vice President and CIO of Citigroup. Mr. Trainer has lectured extensively internationally on the role of information technology in the consumer packaged goods, pharmaceuticals and electronics industries. He currently serves as Chairman of the Executive Committee of enamics, Inc.

Carl Wilson is Executive Vice President and CIO of Marriott International, Inc., where he has global accountability for all business information technology resources. His extensive career in information technology spans the hospitality, paper, retail and food and beverage industries, has made him a favorite source among business and industry media, and a repeat honoree of such distinguished industry titles as CIO 100 and InformationWeek 500.

Special Contributors

Ryan J. Sheehan is a Senior Research Analyst at enamics, Inc. His responsibilities include developing leading industry analysis for the company's knowledgebase and advising enamics' clients during their alignment initiatives. Previously, Mr. Sheehan was a contributor to *e-Enterprise*. He holds a Bachelor of Arts degree in Computer Science from Dartmouth College.

Christine D. Aruza is Vice President, Marketing of enamics, Inc. She is responsible for the company's corporate and product marketing programs. Ms. Aruza has spent the majority of her career helping F500 multinationals succeed in their efforts to better align information technology with corporate goals. She holds a B.A. degree in Liberal Arts & Sciences, graduating magna cum laude from the University of Florida.

The *Financial Times* delivers
a world of business news.

Use the Risk-Free Trial Voucher below!

To stay ahead in today's business world you need to be well-informed on a daily basis. And not just on the national level. You need a news source that closely monitors the entire world of business, and then delivers it in a concise, quick-read format.

With the *Financial Times* you get the major stories from every region of the world. Reports found nowhere else. You get business, management, politics, economics, technology and more.

Now you can try the *Financial Times* for 4 weeks, absolutely risk free. And better yet, if you wish to continue receiving the *Financial Times* you'll get great savings off the regular subscription rate. Just use the voucher below.

8 reasons why you should read the Financial Times for 4 weeks RISK-FREE!

To help you stay current with significant
developments in the world economy ...
and to assist you to make informed business
decisions — the Financial Times brings you:

❶ Fast, meaningful overviews of international affairs ... plus daily briefings on major world news.

❷ Perceptive coverage of economic, business, financial and political developments with special focus on emerging markets.

❸ More international business news than any other publication.

❹ Sophisticated financial analysis and commentary on world market activity plus stock quotes from over 30 countries.

❺ Reports on international companies and a section on global investing.

❻ Specialized pages on management, marketing, advertising and technological innovations from all parts of the world.

❼ Highly valued single-topic special reports (over 200 annually) on countries, industries, investment opportunities, technology and more.

❽ The Saturday Weekend FT section — a globetrotter's guide to leisure-time activities around the world: the arts, fine dining, travel, sports and more.

For Special Offer See Over

FT FINANCIAL TIMES
World business newspaper

The Rescue and Romance
Popular Novels Before World War I

The Rescue and Romance
Popular Novels Before World War I

Diana Reep

Bowling Green State University Popular Press
Bowling Green, Ohio 43403

Library of Congress Catalog Card No.: 82-061169

ISBN: 0-87972-211-8 Clothbound
      0-87972-212-6 Paperback

To my father, Howard Reep

Contents

Preface

My study of the rescue motif in popular American novels before World War I focusses on the rescue convention as part of the romantic plot of the novels. The rescue as a structured convention which controls the movement of the romantic plot appears in all types of popular novels. It appears in domestic novels, in gothics, in dime novels, in historical romances and in westerns. It is used by writers as disparate as Edward Ellis and Susan Warner. It is present at the introduction of the novel as a genre and continues to appear in popular novels of this day.

For this study I used some fifty novels. I am indebted to the works of Alice Payne Hackett, James D. Hart and Frank Luther Mott for the titles of bestselling novels or titles by consistently popular writers before World War I. I was concerned less about the total sales of the novels than about whether the books easily fit the definition of popular works or are the works of writers who sold well over a long period of time. The early American novels that I have used were surpassed on sales lists by British novels of the time. But I have examined these novels, written before Cooper's main work, because they are part of the development of the American popular novel.

Chapter I

The Rescue

In 1853 Nathaniel Hawthorne received $144.09 in royalties for *Mosses From an Old Manse*. Also in 1853 Henry David Thoreau learned from his publisher that his *Week on the Concord and Merrimack Rivers* had sold only 219 copies since its 1849 publication. These figures, however, were not indicative of a terrible slump in the American publishing business. In that same year, Susan Warner got $4,500 for six months' sales of *The Wide, Wide World*. And Fanny Fern sold 70,000 copies of *Fern Leaves from Fanny's Portfolio.*

The next year, a novel about a poor orphan girl who is befriended by a kindly lamplighter and later taken into the home of a warm-hearted blind woman, where, years later, she is discovered by her long lost father (now wealthy) sold 40,000 copies within the first eight weeks of publication.[1] *The Lamplighter* is one of the reasons Hawthorne exploded with his well-known comment about the "damned mob of scribbling women":

> What is the mystery of these innumerable editions of the 'Lamplighter' and other books neither better nor worse?—worse they could not be and better they need not be, when they sell by the 100,000.[2]

Actually, Hawthorne's competition was not just a few scribbling women. Many women found writing popular novels a good way to make money, but so did many men. Hawthorne's competition was a sizeable group of writers who apparently knew precisely what the public wanted to buy. Sylvanius T. Cobb, for example, wrote 122 novels from 1850 to 1873—they all sold very well. Timothy Shay Arthur's *Ten Nights in a Barroom: and What I Saw There* (1854) sold 100,000 copies a year for twenty years. George Lippard and E.Z.C. Judson (Ned Buntline) wrote lurid novels about vice in the cities—and had great success. E.D.E.N. Southworth (the "Queen" of the domestic novel) sold 200,000 copies of her first novel,

Retribution (1847) and wrote sixty-one more novels, all successful.[3] What really frustrated Hawthorne was the question of what made this fiction so enormously popular.

This same question has interested critics such as John Cawelti, Russel Nye, James Hart, Frank Luther Mott and Ray Browne, all of whom have explored aspects of popular fiction. These critics have frequently defined popular art through negatives. It is not serious; it is not complicated; it is not ambiguous. Abraham Kaplan, writing in *Journal of Aesthetics,* comments that popular art is simple in the sense of being easy to understand:

> It contrasts with art in the markedly lesser demands that it makes for creative endeavor on the part of its audience. An artistic form, like a life form, is a creation, and like the living thing again, one which demands a cooperative effort, in this case between artist and audience. We cannot look to popular art for a fresh vision.[4]

Kaplan's rather caustic view of popular art focusses on the lack of aesthetic value and ignores what other critics have found to be the special value of popular art and, in particular, popular literature. That is, popular literature reflects the beliefs of the society that reads it. James D. Hart, in *The Popular Book,* comments that "In some way or another, the popular author is always the one who expresses the people's minds and paraphrases what they consider their private feelings."[5] Russel Nye has also emphasized that popular art confirms experiences rather than exploring new ones:

> For this reason, popular art has been an unusually sensitive and accurate reflector of the attitudes and concerns of the society for which it is produced. Because of its lesser quality, aesthetically, than elite art, historians and critics have tended to neglect it as a means of access to an era's—and a society's—values and ideas.[6]

It is in the reflection of the values and ideas of a society that popular literature is valuable, and the study of those beliefs contained in popular literature should deepen our understanding of the public that bought those books. While it is not safe to assume that each reader agrees with everything in the book, it does seem safe to assume that a bestseller reflects a general view of the world held by most of its readers. The formulas and conventions of popular fiction provide the keys to

an understanding of the social mores of the readers.

Popular formulas have produced, for example, the western, the domestic novel and the historical romance. What these formulas have in common is the goal of escape and entertainment for the reader. They stress intensity of experience, ranging from the desperate sword fight to the agony of the heroine as she watches her fiance flirt with another woman. Through these charged incidents, the reader is momentarily freed from the drab limitations of reality. The intensity of existence, which comes to most of us in isolated moments, is multiplied and heightened in the popular novel so that within a short time the reader vicariously experiences a range of emotions that is possible to experience in no other way.

The conventions used in the formulas change as the contemporary scene changes. The blonde of the twentieth century no longer carries the same connotations as the blonde of the nineteenth century. Often though, what changes is not so much the convention as the contemporary description. For example, an extremely popular figure in nineteenth century fiction was the poor orphan. Literature now does not have many poor orphans, but it does have the young runaway. Our term for the character has changed, but he is still the young person on his own in a hostile world. Popular fiction before World War I frequently included the poor orphan, the awkward spinster, the chaste maiden, the dark brooding man, the grieving widow, the seducer, etc. Readers could be comfortable with all these characters because they were familiar and fulfilled conventional expectations.

Just as the characters in popular fiction are familiar, so too are certain events. The gunfight remains a staple of the western. The decline into alcoholism or drugs, followed by a religious conversion that saves the sinner was enormously popular in nineteenth century melodramas. The raging thunderstorm, flickering lights and strange noises have always given readers of horror stories a familiar shiver. Most familiar of all is the rescue, which is important in most popular formulas.

The study of a convention as popular as the rescue should reveal some of the basic beliefs of a society that avidly accepted the convention. John Cawelti suggests that as a culture

becomes more diverse, the function of articulating and affirming cultural values, once the province of religious ritual, is taken over by the popular arts.[7]

Cawelti also acknowledges the arguments that we cannot adequately substantiate deep symbolic interpretations of a culture's inner motives and needs by examining formula fiction. Admitting the problem of an absolutely reliable analysis of the function of formulas, Cawelti says,

> I am convinced that the Freudian insight that recurrent myths and stories embody a kind of collective dreaming process is essentially correct and has an important application on the cultural as well as the universal level, that is, that the idea of a collective dream applies to formula as well as to myth.... My argument, then, is that formula stories... are structures of narrative conventions which carry out a variety of cultural functions in a unified way.[8]

The nineteenth century in America saw increasing diversity in American life. The opening of the West, the flood of immigration, the movement to the city, the surge in industrialization all created multiple societies and, therefore, multiple cultures within the expanding American society. Popular fiction provided a synthesis of these diverse values and beliefs and offered a way for millions of Americans to subscribe to uniform goals and standards. Writers found that the rescue provided a good base on which to build characters and plots that satisfied readers and reflected their values. The rescue also satisfies the essential requirement for popular work—entertainment.

The rescue is exciting. Whether the rescue comes early or late in the novel, no matter which character rescues which character, the reader gets a jolting, vicarious thrill that is much more intense than the satisfaction he gets when the heroine marries the hero or justice triumphs. William Dean Howells once wrote to Edith Wharton, "What the American public always wants is a tragedy with a happy ending."[9] The rescue convention presents potential tragedy and then averts it, thus precisely supplying what Howells said people wanted.

The rescue also embodies the American ideal of action. When Chad Buford in *The Little Shepherd of Kingdom Come* (1903) rides a desperate sixty miles to prevent Dan Dean from

being shot as a guerilla, he makes a decision and acts on it.[10] The rescue is an active event, not an accident, not a fortuitous stroke of luck. The American ideal of the self-made man clearly stresses individual initiative and action. The rescue requiring decision and action fits that ideal.

Most important, the rescue is one of life's main events. It ranks with birth, death and marriage. Because of a rescue, a life may be saved, disaster averted, a dilemma solved. In popular fiction, which stresses the intensity of experience, the rescue is crucial. It involves a peak of excitement because of the very fact that it is a change in direction, a thwarting of fate, a crucial moment, a second chance, a major turning point. All the finest human qualities are involved—heroism, disregard for oneself, brotherhood, justice and (most important) the tingling acceptance of risk. There is risk in rescue for both parties, risk beyond physical danger. When events are abruptly altered, the question that arises is whether the rescue was good or bad. Should anyone try to change fate?

When the rescue is used with the romantic plot, it controls the progress and development of the romance. The convention dictates absolute standards of behavior for men and women and reinforces the accepted, traditional roles and relationships of the sexes. The convention in some instances sets the structure of the novel and in others acts as the only possible way to resolve the dilemmas of the romantic plot.

In order to examine the rescue convention, we must clearly define it. The rescue is a voluntary act on the part of the rescuer, who is neither forced to act nor paid to act. Although the idea of reward is implicit in the rescue convention, the rescuer does not act for the reward. The situations in which the rescuers act may vary to a considerable degree, and the extent of danger to the rescued party may vary, but these two limits—that the rescuer is neither forced nor paid to act—are always applicable. The elaborate escape plot is not a true rescue. In the escape situation, one character may aid another and seem to rescue, but if the second character takes a very active part in his own escape by killing guards, forcing locks, using something given to him, the situation is not a true rescue.

In the novels of the nineteenth century, there are two conventional situations where the woman is often said to have rescued the man. One is the conversion of the male to active

Christianity, away from his evil ways. Although the woman may be quite active in converting the man, there is a strong element of "Christian duty" in the situation, and we might well be dealing with another sort of convention—the conversion to Christianity.

The other conventional plot situation is that of the woman nursing the man back to health after an illness or injury. Although in the novels, the man frequently exclaims that the woman has saved his life, the situation is really part of the woman's normal duties. In domestic novels, nursing someone back to health is almost akin to running an efficient kitchen, and the situation does not fit clearly enough as an active decision on the part of the rescuer.

Another situation that is not quite a rescue is the timely confession which either frees someone or improves his status. The confession may, in fact, save someone from a terrible fate, but the act is subject to the pressures of conscience or, perhaps, the pressures of other characters. So the confessing character cannot be said to have rescued freely.

Since a rescue should be voluntary and not obligatory, the situation where an orphan is taken in by an appointed guardian is not a true rescue. The appointed guardian is not voluntary and often that very fact leads to the plot convention of the rejected orphan in a hostile home.

Series fiction using a continuing hero does not include the kind of rescues relative to this study. This kind of fiction usually spotlights a super-hero who constantly engages in daring exploits. The writer of series fiction has a definite need for continuous peaks of excitement. To examine the rescue and its implications, we must consider it in those cases where it is an option, chosen by the writer because it functioned in some particular way to support a theme or moral view.

Rescues may be divided into several types depending upon which character is rescuing and which character is being rescued. Some rescues occur simply because a character is so good that he literally rescues whenever a need arises. The heroes of both *Uncle Tom's Cabin* (1852) and *Ben-Hur* (1880) rescue members of the oppressing group when they themselves are slaves. Uncle Tom jumps into the Mississippi to rescue little Eva St. Clare; Ben-Hur saves the Roman Tribune Arrius when their ship sinks. Ishmael Worth in *Self-Raised* (1876) rescues

nearly everyone in the novel, including the pasengers and crew of a sinking ocean liner.

Characters frequently prove their nobility by rescuing enemies or rivals in love. Horatio Alger's hero Grant Colburn (*Digging for Gold, a Story of California,* 1891) rescues the villain Dionysius Silverthorn from Indians; Gertrude in *The Lamplighter* (1854) saves Isabel from drowning even though Isabel appears to have won the love of Gertrude's sweetheart.

The types of rescues strongly connected with romance in popular novels before 1916, however, are the rescue of a child, the rescue from physical danger of a female by a male, the rescue from a dilemma of a female by a male, and the rescue of a male by a female. These four support and, in fact, dictate the structure of the romantic story in the novels as well as define acceptable male and female roles.

The rescue of a child was an extremely popular convention in the domestic novel, but it also was used in novels of adventure. It appears with fair regularity throughout the period from 1800 to 1916. It was apparently so popular that novelists writing books about social issues often used part of the pattern to catch the reader's attention. The rescue of a child established the structure of the romantic plot in the novel. It also provided the opportunity for the rescued child to develop the acceptable standards and values of society and grow up to be a respectable and successful adult.

The rescue from physical danger of a female by a male is unquestionably the most popular rescue pattern. The form of the rescue does not alter much over the years. Women scream and men save them. The later novels, however, sometimes present a broader situation, allowing the male to rescue someone close to the female and obtain the same results as if the female were rescued. The structure of this rescue and the fact that it changes so little offers an interesting area for exploration of the American view of male and female roles.

Appearing in fiction after the Civil War is the male rescue of a female from a dilemma. The dilemma is used primarily in the domestic novel, and its position in the structure of the plot differs from the position of the physical rescue. The dilemma rescue also differs from the physical rescue in the kind of man doing the rescuing, in what is being proved, and in the emphasis in the results of the rescue. The dilemma rescue, like

the physical rescue, reflects society's views of male and female roles, and also apparently reflects the changing position of women after the Civil War.

The fourth romantic rescue is the rescue of a man by a woman. This act is the least consistent of the four, but it may well be the most interesting. The rescue by a female divides into two patterns, depending upon whether the woman is white or Indian. The Indian woman rescues quite efficiently and quite consistently. The white woman rescues in a variety of situations which do not form a clear pattern. Often she rescues in a far less dangerous situation than the Indian, and there are strangely mixed results. The fact that writers who used formulas consistently had difficulty using the rescue convention as it applied to females rescuing males rather clearly reflects the idea that women rescuing men was considered unnatural. Women were expected to nurse men back to health or convert them to the true faith, but beyond these clearly defined situations, the rules were murky.

Beginning with the earliest novels, popular writers claimed a moral or didactic purpose for their work. The introduction to *Malaeska; The Indian Wife of the White Hunter* (1860), the first dime novel, contains the following:

> It is chosen as the initial volume of the Dime Novel series, from the chaste characters of its delineations, from the interest which attaches to its fine picture of border life and Indian adventure, and from the real romance of its incidents. It is American in all its features, pure in its tone, elevating in its sentiments.... it is hoped to reach all... to instill a pure and elevating sentiment in the hearts and minds of the people.[11]

This lofty description of purpose is typical of that usually given for popular fiction. In fact, of course, the novels were written and published to make money. And at the same time, the readers were not reading for edification. They read for entertainment. They read, as Kaplan emphasizes, to see a world "not as it is, nor even as it might be, but as we would have it."[12] The rescue convention in the romantic plots shows us what kind of romantic world those readers wanted to have.

Chapter II

The Rescue of a Child

The appealing child in want or in danger has always represented a guaranteed means of getting a sentimental reaction from any audience. Therefore it is not surprising that writers of popular novels frequently used the convention of the rescue of a child. Since the convention usually was placed at the beginning of the novel, readers were caught immediately by the pathetic situation of a helpless child in trouble.

In its most conventional form, the rescue of a child controls the course of the novel. For the purposes of this study, we will consider a child as age fifteen or under. At age fifteen, the relative helplessness of an individual becomes less clear since in the nineteenth century it was possible for boys to earn a living and for girls to marry at that age. The rescue situation opens the novel as the child (almost always an orphan) is found in a serious danger or dilemma. The danger may be imminent death, or a cruel stepparent/aunt/guardian, or the total absence of a guiding and protective adult. Since the child is not old enough to function independently in an adult world, the rescue is crucial, in an immediate sense, in providing care and support and, in the future sense, in allowing the child to grow into a productive person.

The rescue moves the child from the immediate danger and from whatever social environment he is in. The new environment is often, but not always, in a better social class. However, the new situation always offers safety and an opportunity to reach adulthood.

In its full pattern the rescue, by putting the child into a new atmosphere, also puts him in immediate contact with his future loved one. Frequently, the future romance is signaled to the reader by the immediate affection the two children develop for each other. Readers knowing the pattern, as most of them surely did, could be confident that the novel would provide a satisfactory romantic situation.

The rescued child is going to be the main character of the

novel, and usually most of the novel concerns his adult life, its trials and tribulations, and, of course, romance. The rescue situation in the opening generates the reader's immediate concern in the welfare of the child. Once this concern is established, the reader will naturally wish to continue learning about the adventures of the hero or heroine.

The usual pattern for the rescue of a child, then, is to provide instant sentimental appeal as the novel opens by showing a helpless child in difficulty. The rescue itself moves the child to a significantly improved social environment and puts him in contact with his future loved one. Once the child is established as the main character, the novel concentrates on his adult life. The last major element in the pattern is that eventually the child pays back the debt incurred by his rescue. The repayment may take a variety of forms, but it is always an affirmation of the rightness of the rescue of this child so many pages back.

Augusta Evans Wilson's novel *Beulah* (1859) illustrates the full pattern of the convention of the rescue of a child. The novel opens with thirteen-year-old Beulah Benton and her younger sister, Lilly, in an orphanage. Since Lilly is the pretty one, she is adopted. Beulah is sent out as a nursemaid to a family interested in cheap labor. Things get worse for Beulah. The couple that adopted Lilly refuses to let Beulah see her sister, who dies shortly thereafter of scarlet fever. Beulah is now alone, friendless, and in a situation that would condemn her to a life of menial labor.

At this crucial point in the story, Dr. Guy Hartwell sees poor Beulah's tear-streaked, homely little face bending over her sister's coffin. (Wilson spends a great deal of time telling us how homely Beulah is, probably to emphasize how altruistic the coming rescue must be.) Dr. Hartwell, although he has been introduced as a cold, unfriendly man, is quick to offer refuge. "Beulah, come home with me. Be my child; my daughter."[1] Beulah rejects rescue. "No. You too would hate me for my ugliness. Let me hide it in the grave with Lilly. They cannot separate us there" (p. 44). Dr. Hartwell, a man not used to being refused, takes more positive action by lifting her into his carriage and taking her to his spacious mansion. "I am glad I have you safe under my own roof, where no more cruel injustice can assail you" (p. 45). Beulah has been rescued. She is given

an education and all the material advantages.

She does, however, refuse to be adopted formally and continually remarks upon the debt she owes to Hartwell. Completing her education, she gets a teaching job. This independent action upsets Hartwell, who wants her to live an idle life. "Relinquish the idea of teaching. Let me present you to society as my adopted child. Thus you can requite the debt" (p. 148). Children are not rescued in popular fiction to live idle lives, however, and Beulah refuses his request. "God knows I am grateful.... Oh, that it were in my power to prove to you my gratitude" (p. 148). The obligation of the child to repay his rescue is very strong in the convention, but few novels discuss the necessary payment as endlessly as *Beulah* does.

The bulk of the novel is concerned with Beulah's adult life. Very independent, she goes from teaching to writing and becomes moderately successful. This career development is amid a stream of domestic complications, insults from society about her humble origin, and romantic crises involving Beulah and a wide circle of friends.

Finally, however, the rescue must be repaid. Hartwell comes to see Beulah where she is living in the modest cottage that she has paid for with her earnings from writing. He proposes marriage, but Beulah refuses. After four more years of career and domestic crises, however, she realizes where her heart is. When Hartwell proposes again, she accepts. Now, after all the talk of the debt, Hartwell wants to be loved for himself. "Beulah, do you cling to me because you love me? or because you pity me? or because you are grateful to me for past love and kindness?" (p. 432). "Because you are my all," she answers. Beulah repays her rescuer by making him happy in marriage. Furthermore, her rescue when she was a child did put her in immediate contact with the future loved one, just as the pattern dictates.

Beulah was very successful, selling 30,000 copies within four years.[2] Wilson knew enough to keep a good pattern going and used the rescue of a child for her next book, *St. Elmo* (1867), one of the all-time best sellers in American fiction. Her heroine in this book is Edna Earl, who achieves greater personal success than Beulah did, has a stronger interest in religion, and is prettier. These are the only major differences between the books as Wilson once more used the rescue of a child to

structure the novel.

In *St. Elmo* twelve-year-old Edna Earl (an orphan) lives with her grandfather and his second wife. Within a few pages, both old people die, and Edna is left alone. She sets out for Columbus, Georgia, where she has heard that children can get work in factories. There is a train wreck:

> She was held fast between timbers, one of which seemed to have fallen across her feet and crushed them, as she was unable to move them, and was conscious of a horrible sensation of numbness; one arm, too, was pinioned at her side."[3]

Edna sustains a broken foot and dislocated shoulder. Her pet dog is killed in the wreck, leaving her completely alone and friendless. At this low point in her life, the widow Mrs. Murray comes along and takes her in:

> "What splendid eyes she has! Poor little thing! Of course you will come and prescribe for her, and I will see that she is carefully nursed until she is quite well again" (p. 33).

Edna is so charming that Mrs. Murray makes the arrangement permanent, and Edna is rescued from an uncertain fate:

> "Child, will you trust your future and your education to me? I do not mean that I will teach you—oh! no—but I will have you thoroughly educated, so that when you are grown you can support yourself by teaching. I have no daughter.... I shall prove a good friend and protector till you are eighteen, and capable of providing for yourself" (p. 38).

Edna has been taken from friendless poverty to the estate of a wealthy woman. Her environment has clearly improved.

Following the pattern, Edna shortly meets Mrs. Murray's son, St. Elmo, who is the dark, brooding, dangerous hero so popular in fiction:

> ...the fair, chiseled lineaments were blotted by dissipation, and blackened and distorted by the baleful fires of a fierce, passionate nature, and a restless, powerful, and unhallowed intellect...the ungovernable flames of sin had reduced him... (p. 40).

Just the sort of man to be reformed by love! But first Edna has to grow up. She studies diligently and becomes a religious

scholar and world famous author, turning down proposals from virtually every male in the book. She prays continually for St. Elmo, until he at last leaves his life of total dissipation and becomes a minister. "Can you be a minister's wife, and aid him as only you can? Oh, my darling, my darling! I never expect to be worthy of you. But you can make me less unworthy" (p. 486). In reforming and then marrying St.Elmo, Edna thoroughly repays Mrs. Murray's rescue of her from that train wreck.

The novel that excited Hawthorne's frustration, Maria Cummins' *The Lamplighter* (1854), also was structured around the rescue of a child. The novel begins by introducing the ragged and unloved eight-year-old orphan Gertrude. Gertrude, whose only joy is her pet kitten, lives with a woman who beats her and becomes enraged when she discovers the kitten:

> Gerty heard a sudden splash and a piercing cry. Nan had flung the poor creature into a large vessel of steaming hot water.... The little animal struggled and writhed an instant, then died in torture.[4]

Gertrude throws a stick at Nan and, in turn, is thrown out of the house to wander the streets alone. Fortunately, she is rescued.

The kindly lamplighter, Trueman Flint, takes her into his home. Gertrude's original social level was so low that even a humble lamplighter's home is an elevation of status. Her new home is also far superior to the old one in warmth and happiness. Young Willie Sullivan lives in the same building, so Gertrude meets her future love very quickly.

Gertrude grows into a fine young woman. However, the lamplighter dies by the time she is grown, and she cannot truly repay the rescue to him in an active way although she has made his life very happy. She also rescues someone else later in the novel, thus affirming the importance of her own rescue. In many novels, bringing happiness and contentment to the rescuer's life is an important part of the repayment made by the child.

An earlier example of the rescue of a child in American popular fiction occurs in Jessee Holman's *The Prisoners of Niagara or Errors of Education* (1810). This novel opens with the hero, a colonial rebel, held prisoner in a British fort. But Holman quickly flashes back to show the hero at eighteen

months being stolen from his Indian captors by William Evermont, a trapper. Since in popular fiction anything is better than being held by Indians, young William (named after his rescuer) has been rescued from a terrible fate and transferred to a better environment. The trapper deposits the child with a farm family and moves on. Unfortunately, the family turns out to be cruel to the child, and by age five he needs another rescue. Playing in the woods with his puppy, he sees a well-dressed gentleman ride by. Getting directly to the point, Williams says to the man, "I want a better father. Will you be my father?"[5] The gentleman agrees "with the fondest look" our hero has ever seen (p. 46). The gentleman promises to come back in the morning and get him. This rescue occurs none too soon since that night William's puppy is killed by the nasty boy in his adopted family, and William runs away.

Holman rushes along the rest of the pattern by having a five-year-old William jump into the Potomac the next morning and rescue two-year-old Zerelda Engleton:

> Young as I was, the hope of assisting a suffering being, overcome [sic] the idea of danger so natural to the infant mind, and I flew in an instant to the place from whence the noise preceded (p. 48).

Zerelda, it turns out, is the niece of Major Hayland, who (not very surprisingly) is the gentleman who had said he would be William's father. So, William repays his own rescue immediately and comes in contact with his future loved one. His social class is markedly improved—he is now in the American class of landed gentry who mingle with British aristocracy. The rest of the novel catalogues his growing up, his education, and his sexual and military adventures. In the end, he marries Zerelda after Holman has used another rescue convention, the rescue from physical danger of a female by a male, to settle the romance.

Although the whole pattern of the rescue of a child is present in this early novel, it is not as clearly or successfully controlled as in the mid-century novels of Wilson and Cummins. Holman has to have his child rescued twice. An eighteen-month-old baby might need rescuing, but he does not have the endearing personality that a five-year-old can have. The first rescue, therefore, is wasted effort in terms of

effectively snaring the reader's sentimental interest when measured next to the second rescue.

The second major structural problem Holman has is in putting the repayment of the rescue immediately after the rescue itself. The repayment placed at the end of a novel gives a finished look to the plot, a rounding off of events, and it affirms the innate worth of the hero and the original rescue. Wilson and Cummins both build to the repayment situation while Holman wastes its dramatic and conclusive effect by putting it in the beginning of the novel.

Another novelist in the first half of the nineteenth century made ineffective use of the convention in his novel *Wyoming, a Tale* (1845). Caleb Wright tells a story of pioneers in northern Pennsylvania. In a brief flashback, he reveals that Colonel Dinning's daughter, Ruth, was adopted by the childless colonel when an old Indian woman literally left the three-year-old girl on the doorstep.[6] The colonel is wealthy, and, again, anything is better than living with the Indians, so Ruth is certainly rescued. Wright, however, wastes the possible interest generated by such an episode when he simply has one of the characters relate the story. He also fails to introduce Ruth's future love until she is ten years old—the kind of gap most novelists using the convention did not allow. Moreover, Ruth is not the main character of the book. She is not, in fact, very important except that she eventually marries the hero. She never does anything specific to repay her rescue, except that she brings a good deal of happiness to the colonel.

From these early weak uses of the convention, we can see that the domestic novelists of the mid-century probably were responsible for developing the rescue of a child so that it controlled the movement of a novel. Once this pattern was established in a successful way, the rescue of a child was used over and over by popular novelists.

It was used even by a writer like Hamlin Garland whose reputation rests on his realistic portrayal of Midwestern frontier farm life. Garland's *A Little Norsk or Ol' Pap's Flaxen* (1892) is built on the rescue of a child. On a cold winter day on the plains of Dakota territory, partners Anson Wood and Bert Gearheart take in a five-year-old orphan from a neighboring farm. Her father has been lost in a blizzard, and her mother has frozen to death in their cabin.[7] Obviously, little Flaxen is in a

dangerous situation, and when the two partners take her in, she is moved to a place of safety. There is no rise in social level as in the earlier novels. Since no one claims her, Flaxen grows up with the two men, goes to school, and at the age of fifteen marries a young man from a nearby town. She has repaid Anson by filling his life with the happiness of fatherhood and then grandfatherhood. After Flaxen marries, Bert realizes that he has fallen in love with her, and he goes west to forget her.

Her husband turns out to be a scoundrel and a thief. Fortunately, he is soon killed in an accident. Flaxen and Anson live quite happily for a time. Then Bert returns. He asks Anson, "Say, it seems pretty well understood that you're her father— but where do I come in?" (p. 156). Anson tells him that he "ought to be her husband," and everything is settled, apparently to the satisfaction of all parties. Both men have been repaid for their original rescue of Flaxen. This slight novel by Garland is structured almost entirely around the pattern of the rescue of a child. Aside from some realistic details of daily life, the novel contains only the plot elements comprising the convention.

Another rescue of a child in Dakota territory takes place in William Lillibridge's *Ben Blair, The Story of a Plainsman* (1905). Eight-year-old Ben Blair watches his drunken father set fire to the house in which Ben's mother has just died. While the fire rages, Ben huddles under the house, hoping the flames won't reach him. After the flames subside, Ben crawls out and looks at "the charred, unrecognizable corpse of his mother."[8] Wealthy rancher Rankin comes along after seeing the flames from his ranch and helps Ben bury his mother. Then Rankin takes him home and raises him. In true laconic western style, Rankin answers a brief "yes" when Ben asks him, "Am I to—to stay with you?" (p. 42). Ben is now living on a prosperous ranch and is under the guidance of a man who can properly serve as a model for manhood. Within two days of his rescue, Ben visits a neighboring ranch and meets five-year-old Florence Baker, his future love.

Ben's repayment of his rescue is in the western tradition. He hunts down and captures Rankin's killer—Ben's father who has reappeared after all these years. Ben then has to defend Tom Blair from an angry lynch mob in town. His repayment continues when he discovers papers in Rankin's

safe which clearly indicate that Rankin was really Ben's father. Because Rankin obviously did not want the facts known while he lived, Ben decides to preserve his secret. He destroys the papers and decides never to tell anyone. This repayment of the original rescue follows the code of honor stressed in the western formula. Ben keeps his rescuer's secret, hunts down his killer, and then defends the killer from a lynch mob, supporting the code of justice Rankin had taught him. He wins his love, Florence, on the last page of the novel.

In contrast to the western novel of action, a bestseller that has almost no action and is concerned almost entirely with a portrayal of the homely virtues is Irving Bacheller's *Eben Holden* (1900), which sold 250,000 copies.[9] The title character is the rescuer here. The story opens with Eben carrying six-year-old Willie on his back in a basket. Willie's entire family drowned while on a picnic, and Eben, a penniless farmhand, takes the boy away rather than letting him be sent to the county home. Willie feels "very warm and cozy wrapped in the big shawl."[10] Here the improvement in environment is in the fact that Eben offers personal attention and caring in contrast to the impersonal county home. Bacheller, in fact, has lowered Willie's social level by moving him from the position of a son of a prosperous farmer to the companion of an itinerant farm worker. But this variation in the general pattern is clearly connected to Bacheller's purpose in the novel of presenting the virtues inherent in the New England rural people.

Eben takes work at the farm of David Brower where Willie meets Hope Brower, "a barefooted little girl a bit older than I, with red cheeks and blue eyes and long curly hair, that shone like gold in the sunlight" (p. 70). Bacheller is less concerned than some other writers with the repayment element of the convention. Because Bacheller is emphasizing goodness as a way of life and as its own reward, Willie repays his rescue by growing up to be a good and successful man. In the world of this novel, such a development is ample repayment.

An equally successful regional novel is John Fox, Jr.'s *The Little Shepherd of Kingdom Come* (1903), set in Kentucky. This novel has sold over a million and a quarter copies over the years, and thirty years after publication was one of the books in highest demand in libraries.[11] Like Jessee Holman in 1810, Fox has his child rescued twice. But unlike Holman, Fox

employs one of the most highly developed rescue plots to control the structure of his novel. Both of the rescues are connected to later events, and they are also connected to other types of rescues.

The novel opens with the young orphan Chad wandering the mountains of Kentucky with his dog. The Turner family takes him in, in the casual way of the mountain people by giving him supper and a bed and then just expecting him to stay. In spite of the casual attitude of the family, Chad definitely is being rescued. In this mountain society, such a rescue is natural. "Already the house was full of children and dependents, but no word passed between old Joel and the old mother, for no word was necessary" (p. 27). Although Chad is not surrounded with wealth, he is surrounded with a large, caring family. He also meets Melissa Turner with tangled yellow hair and large, solemn eyes. Melissa is also adopted. She will be prominent later in the novel as a female rescuing a male.

Chad lives happily in the mountains for a year. On a visit to Lexington, he hurts his foot, gets left behind by his party, and becomes lost and hungry. Major Calvin Buford passes by in his carriage. And the second rescue is underway. Chad gets a ride, a meal and goes to a horse auction with the Major. By the end of the day, Major Buford takes him home and asks him, "Wouldn't you like to stay here in the Bluegrass now and go to school?" (p. 90). Chad says he thinks he probably would and everything is settled. By this rescue Chad is elevated to living in a fine town house with the leading citizen of Lexington. His life now promises education, culture and opportunity. The Major's neighbor is General Dean, who has a daughter, Margaret, a little girl with "dancing black eyes" (p. 98). Chad has been in his new home only one day when he meets the girl he is to love. Margaret will figure later in the novel in the rescue of a female by a male.

Having carefully constructed two totally satisfactory rescues for his child, Fox moves the action of the novel back and forth between the mountains and the town. Chad grows up well educated, honest, thoughtful and courageous. But he joins the Union side in the Civil War and thereby wounds both the Turner family and Major Buford, all of whom are loyal to the South. This division of families in the war is one of Fox's major

themes. There is no question that Chad is a fine adult, but he cannot truly repay his rescues because of his betrayal of the rescuer's political beliefs. Bitter feeling results as he goes to war. When the war is over, Margaret tells him that the major forgave him before he died. On a visit back to the hills, Chad sees Mother Turner, who "broke down and threw her arms around him and cried" (p. 313). It is because of the impossibility of repaying those childhood rescues and particularly the impossibility of repaying Melissa, who has rescued him, that Chad does not allow himself to accept the offered happiness with Margaret at the end of the novel. He heads west "starting his life ever afresh, with his old capital, a strong body and a stout heart" (p. 336).

Fox's balancing of three rescue conventions in the novel testifies to his control over the patterns. His two rescues of Chad reflect the two essential ways to improve a child's environment. The rescue by Major Buford brings Chad the opportunity for wealth and education. The rescue by the Turner family gives Chad a loving, supportive home.

Fox's sophisticated balancing of rescue patterns did not necessarily reflect a major shift in popular fiction. The original standard pattern continued to sell. Jean Webster's *Daddy-Long-Legs* (1912) introduces seventeen-year-old Jerusha Abbott, the oldest orphan in the orphanage. Jerusha is plucked from the orphanage and sent off to college by an anonymous trustee of the orphanage who is described as cold and odd.[12] The only condition of the college education as explained by the matron is that Jerusha must write to the trustee every month and report her progress:

> "That is—you are not to thank him for the money; he doesn't care to have that mentioned, but you are to write a letter telling of your progress in your studies and the details of your daily life" (p. 14).

Mrs. Lippert stresses that these letters are the only payment required.

Jerusha writes faithfully while she completes her education, and she continues to write to her benefactor when she becomes a successful author. She wins a scholarship and can support herself. Finally, she sells her novel and becomes successful. The benefactor at last reveals that he is Jervis Pendleton, whom she has known as a friend's uncle. Jervis

proposes. "We belong to each other now," she writes to him in her final letter (p. 303). And so Jerusha repays her rescuer by marrying him and making him happy. If all this sounds quite familiar, it is because Webster's novel has much the same plot as *Beulah*, and, although Jerusha at seventeen is older than the other orphans, she is included here to show how Wilson's rescue pattern and plot can reappear nearly sixty years later and be as successful as ever.

Although the domestic novelists used the rescue of a child more often than other writers did, novelists concerned with social issues sometimes used the convention to open their novels. Again, because the rescue so effectively captured the initial interest of the readers, it assured the writer an audience for his social views.

In 1875 Josiah Holland wrote a muckraking novel about the immoral business practices in New England mill towns. He begins the novel, *Sevenoaks: a Story of Today*, by introducing mill owner Robert Belcher, who has cheated and driven inventor Paul Benedict insane. Benedict is in the poorhouse with his small son Harry. Jim Fenton, a trapper and old friend of Benedict's, comes to town and sees the boy weeping. "He was thinly and very shabbily clad, and was shivering with cold. The great, healthy heart within Jim Fenton was touched in an instant."[13]

Holland varies the rescue pattern in that Fenton also has to rescue Harry's insane father from the poorhouse. They all go to live in the woods. Harry is not the main character of the novel and does not grow up in the book. Therefore, there is no need for a little girl to appear, and the full rescue pattern does not appear. But Harry does repay his rescue by recalling his father from insanity through prayer. When Jim Fenton fails to cure his friend with good food and clean air, he tells Harry that the boy's father is not getting better and Harry must pray.

> The boy was serious.... He had said his prayers many times when he did not know that he wanted anything. Here was a great emergency.... He... was the only one who could pray for the life of his father (p. 91).

After some concentrated effort by Harry, his father suddenly has a look "full of intelligence and peace" (p. 92). The little boy

through prayer has "fetched 'im" as Jim says (p. 93).

Another novel concerned with business ethics was the enormously popular *The Winning of Barbara Worth* (Harold Bell Wright, 1911). The book sold 1,635,000 copies by 1941.[14] Wright used two rescues of children to start his novel. The main rescue is clearly inserted only for initial interest. Jefferson Worth, a Colorado banker, and his party are traveling through the Mojave Desert when they find an abandoned wagon. Up ahead lies a dead woman. A four-year-old girl is toddling around the body, wailing, "Barba wants a drink."[15] "Jefferson Worth reached her first" (p. 43). Barbara has been rescued. She grows up to be a lovely young woman amid many advantages. Although she is the title character, she is not really the main focus of the novel which is concerned with political and financial machinations in the development of Colorado mines and towns. No other part of the rescue pattern is used. In the structure of the novel, Wright has no clear need for this rescue.

The second rescue of a child took place before the novel begins, but we learn while the men ride through the desert that ten-year-old Abe Lee (in Worth's party) was left an orphan in a mining camp and was taken up by an engineer known as the Seer. "He has been with me ever since," comments the Seer (p. 28). Again, the rest of the pattern is missing. Abe does become a valuable engineer and is a trusted employee of Jefferson Worth; but since Worth did not rescue him, it cannot be said that Abe ever repays his rescue as the pattern would dictate. Since Wright's novel is actually an investigation of business ethics, it seems clear that he is only using the rescue convention to get the novel going, and he must have felt such a start was important since there are two rescues of children in the opening pages.

The consistently bestselling author Gertrude Atherton used the child rescue to open her novel *Patience Sparhawk and Her Times* (1895).[16] Fifteen-year-old Patience is left an orphan when her drunken mother dies in a fire. Patience is taken in by Mr. Foord, an elderly gentleman of reduced fortune but much refinement. Because of his age, Mr. Foord sends Patience off to his half-sister Miss Tremont in San Francisco. Patience's social level has been raised and improved. Her moral surroundings are now beyond reproach. (Miss Tremont is a temperance leader.) Her educational opportunities are

numerous. Atherton's primary theme in the novel is woman's independent spirit and the degree to which she can properly exercise that spirit. Although Atherton used the rescue of a child to begin the novel, she did not allow the convention to control the ending of the book. She did, however, use another rescue pattern, the male rescuing the female from a dilemma, to end the novel. That novelists who were interested in social issues used even part of the convention demonstrates the appeal of the convention to readers.

Structurally, in the novels which used the whole pattern, the writer had a convention that gave a framework to whatever story he wished to tell. The rescue of a child opened the novel at a fast pace and held the reader's natural interest in the fate of a charming youngster. Since the child was moved to an improved environment, often a better social class, the writer was free to work out subsequent events in a setting more attractive than the original depressing surroundings. Most bestselling popular novelists avoided extensive discussion of social problems and since they wished to end the books happily, they needed to place the main characters in promising circumstances.

The rescue pattern, after moving the child to a better situation, puts him in immediate contact with the future sweetheart. The writer can begin the romantic plot at once—a plot that the readers confidently expected all domestic novels at least to provide. The romance was never settled until the end of the novel, so the writer using the rescue pattern had a book-length thread of interest in which to tangle other plot complications. The repayment part of the pattern was important to the novel's structure in that it rewarded the rescuer, affirmed the validity of the novel's opening event, brought the novel full circle, and finished off the original episode.

The rescue makes it possible for these children to become adults. What kind of adults are they? The qualities they display as adults can tell us something about the social and moral values of the readers. From a humanitarian standpoint, all children are worth rescuing. However, the rescued children in the novels usually make a definite contribution to society, further proving the importance of their rescues. Because these novels were so popular, we must conclude that the qualities the

children have as adults were considered desirable by a majority of readers.

All the children grow up to be moral, upright citizens. The chance to lead a good, honest life was the primary opportunity resulting from the rescue. Only two children, however, offered nothing more to society than good lives. In *Wyoming, a Tale*, Ruth Dinning grows up to be a charming young lady and finally marries the hero. And Harold Bell Wright's heroine Barbara Worth develops into a vibrant, beautiful young woman, who charms every male in the novel. It is probably significant that both writers here are male, and the children in the books are female. As we will see, these writers do not allow the male children rescued in their novels to lead merely good lives. But even as late as 1911, it was enough that a young lady be charming.

There was another way for young ladies to serve society— three of them married the men who took them from poverty. When Beulah agrees to marry Dr. Hartwell, he sighs, "At last, then, after years of sorrow, and pain, and bitterness, I shall be happy in my own home; shall have a wife, a companion, who loves me for myself alone" (p. 433). Beulah's material success is important as a contribution to society, but when she brings comfort to this lonely man that, too, is an important contribution. And until Flaxen in Garland's novel is ready to marry Bert, he wanders through the West, accomplishing nothing, amounting to nothing, accumulating nothing. With Flaxen as his wife, Bert is going to settle down and run a dray with his old partner Anson. The marriage to Flaxen will vastly improve his life. Another orphan turned writer, Jerusha in *Daddy-Long-Legs*, marries her benefactor and brightens his solitary, though wealthy, life. Her last letter says they are "both very, very happy" (p. 303).

The men are lonely—they need good women. Women can make a clearcut contribution by bringing both happiness and direction to men's lives. These three novels are dated 1859, 1892 and 1912 respectively. Obviously, this social value lasted through the years. It is also significant that these are all May-December unions. (Wilson, in fact, specialized in romances with substantial age gaps between the men and women. Beulah is seventeen years younger than Dr. Hartwell, and Edna Earl is twenty-two years younger than St. Elmo.) There is

no doubt in the novels about whether such matches are wise. In the world of the novels, such matches were very sensible.

The most consistent virtue expressed in the adult lives of these rescued children is that of becoming a hard-working, productive member of society. None of the characters grows up to be a criminal or vagrant. Not all, of course, were able to equal the achievements of Edna Earl (*St. Elmo*). She becomes an international religious scholar, widely respected and sought after. She literally wears down her health in trying to satisfy her eager public. Wilson's other heroine, Beulah, also becomes a famous writer, as does Jerusha in *Daddy-Long-Legs*. Gertrude Atherton has her independent heroine, Patience Sparhawk, become a successful writer. It is probably not surprising that the novelists chose writing as the professions of their heroines, but all the writers also stress how hard the women work and how successful they become. Until marriage takes them to another area of endeavor and a different kind of social service, the women work very hard in one of the few work situations open to the middle-class woman in the nineteenth century. The female writers, unlike the male writers, made certain that their heroines actively contributed to society before they went on to support the family structure by marrying.

Bacheller's child hero Willie (*Eben Holden*) grows up to be a writer for the New York *Tribune*. After being wounded in the Spanish-American War, Willie goes into politics. Since the basis of this novel is the depiction of good people leading good lives, Willie will contribute to society by bringing morality to politics. Serving in the war shows that he is a man who does his duty.

Although Harold Bell Wright allows Barbara Worth to grow up and contribute nothing but charm to the world, he does not allow the rescued boy in his novel to do so little. Without any formal training, Abe Lee becomes an engineer, and he is the standard in the novel against which Easterners are measured. Abe Lee can do almost anything. He figures out where to place irrigation channels, something the developers and pioneers desperately need. Later, he rescues valuable property and averts tragedy. When an Eastern engineer questions Lee's lack of formal training, banker Jefferson Worth snaps, "We have only one standard in the West, Mr.

Holmes. What can you do?" (p. 113).

As another kind of service, mid-century novels often used spiritual reform or guidance as the contribution by the rescued child. When *St. Elmo* begins, Edna Earl clearly has her work of redemption cut out for her. Since she develops into a religious scholar, she not only prays for the dark, tormented St. Elmo but also has long conversations with him about the Greek idea of self-improvement, the Coptic civilization, and the doctrines of Zoroaster. At last St. Elmo is redeemed from his life of depravity. "My precious Edna, no oath shall ever soil my lips again.... I loath my past life.... My Edna—my own wife, shall save me!" (p. 283). It is not until St. Elmo actually becomes a minister that Edna feels her work is complete, and she agrees to marry him. By saving St. Elmo from dissipation, Edna, of course, has saved a soul—always a worthy endeavor. Converting men from the evil ways was a common role for fictional heroines.

It might seem obvious that in a convention dealing with rescues, one way of becoming valuable to society is by more rescues. Jessee Holman in *The Prisoners of Niagara, or Errors of Education* has five-year-old William Evermont jump into the Potomac to rescue Zerelda Engleton. This rescue not only repays his own rescue but also establishes his courage. Many of the children demonstrate both moral and physical courage when they grow up.

Gertrude in *The Lamplighter* rescues her supposed rival in love. While at Saratoga, Gertrude has encountered her childhood sweetheart, Willie Sullivan. Not only has Willie apparently forgotten her, he is being very attentive to Isabel Clinton, a well-known flirt. Gertrude, of course, is crushed. "She wept as the broken-hearted weep" (p. 262). A few days later, the steamboat on which Gertrude is returning to New York City catches fire. Gertrude finds herself clinging to the same rope as Isabel Clinton. Another passenger comes to Gertrude's aid. She decides to save Isabel rather than herself because "Willie would weep for her loss, and that must not be" (p. 297). Isabel is rescued, and, fortunately, Gertrude is also picked up by a later rescue boat. At the end of the novel, Gertrude learns that her sacrifice would have been for nothing since Willie does indeed still love her. Her noble gesture, however, clearly shows a courage and greatness of spirit,

virtues that are invaluable to society. Chad Buford in *The Little Shepherd of Kingdom Come* rides sixty miles to save a childhood friend from being shot by Yankees. The ride is not only physically dangerous; but it demonstrates Chad's fine character since he is on the Union side, and the novel deals with divided loyalties. These particular rescues, then, emphasize personal courage and the concern for others that transcends selfishness.

Some of the children grow up and perform acts which reflect clear ideas of social justice, giving immediate benefits to society. Little Harry (*Sevenoaks; a Story of Today*) not only saves his father through prayer but he is instrumental in the final ruin of the villain Belcher and in the restoration of his father's business rights. Harry's youthful innocence influences Mrs. Dillingham, who exposes Belcher's shady financial records, subsequently ruining him. The rescue of a child here supports Holland's social purpose in writing. Holland's child needs rescuing because of the business corruption the novel says is pervasive in American life, and the child helps end that corruption at the end of the book. Also supporting justice, Abe Lee (*The Winning of Barbara Worth*) makes a spectacular ride to bring the payroll to the miners after the bank, controlled by corrupt interests, refuses to release the money. And Ben Blair, though wounded, holds off a lynch mob successfully, and so upholds law and order.

All these values—becoming upright citizens, being good wives, being hard working and productive, offering spiritual help, displaying physical and ethical courage, contributing to social justice—provide definite benefits to society. Readers continued to buy books that expressed such ideas, showing their support and acceptance of those values.

A primary social belief implicit in the rescue of a child is the idea that environment is the factor that determines one's development. The rescued children come from a variety of backgrounds. Barbara Worth is a nameless waif wandering in the desert; Flaxen is the daughter of Norwegian pioneers; little Willie (*Eben Holden*) is the son of a rich farmer. The backgrounds, however, are not as important as the environments to which the children are moved. Each new environment offers not only personal safety, but also an opportunity for the child to develop whatever talents he may

possess. Central to this development is education.

Education has an unquestioned value in the system of social beliefs revealed in these novels. In some cases, the rescue is based on an offer of education. Jerusha Abbott (*Daddy-Long-Legs*) is offered a college education by a trustee of the orphanage. The terms of her rescue are precisely stated as tuition, board, books, and $35 a month allowance. Jerusha is not in any physical danger but she is facing a life of drudgery. Her rescue consists entirely of the opportunity for an education, the only thing she needs to develop her writing talents. During her sophomore year in college, Jerusha wins a short story contest and is on her way to success.

In Fox's *The Little Shepherd of Kingdom Come*, Major Buford specifically asks Chad if he wants to go to school. "Chad's eyes lighted up. 'I reckon I would' " (p. 90). Augusta Evans Wilson includes education as an important element in the rescues in both her novels. Edna Earl is offered an education by Mrs. Murray so that she can become a teacher. And Dr. Hartwell offers Beulah Benton an education when he takes her home to his mansion. In spite of the insults she endures from Hartwell's sister, Beulah clings to her educational opportunity as the way to become self-supporting and make something of herself.

Even when education is not mentioned at the moment of rescue, the child usually is given an opportunity for schooling in his new environment. Barbara Worth is educated to be a refined, cultured young lady, the proper daughter of a banker. Ben Blair is educated to handle the business of running a ranch. William Evermont (*The Prisoners of Niagara, or Errors of Education*) does brilliantly in school. Even the two pioneer bachelors raising Flaxen believe in the value of education. She is sent to a city school when she is fourteen even though the men will be lonely without her. Willie in *Eben Holden* goes to school in town and then goes on to college. Patience Sparhawk has always been an avid reader. When she goes to San Francisco, she gets a good education. Gertrude in *The Lamplighter* is educated when she goes to live with rich Miss Graham after the lamplighter's death. In all the cases, a good education is the crucial factor in the child's development.

So important was education considered in the future prospects of a child that Holland's novel introduces this value

even though Harry does not grow up in the book. Harry Benedict is living happily with his father and his rescuer Jim Fenton in the woods. The healthful atmosphere of the outdoors is superior to the corrupt atmosphere of the city. Nevertheless, when a rich lawyer who is on a hunting trip offers to take little Harry to New York and send him to school, both Jim Fenton and Harry's father agree that the opportunity for an education cannot be turned down.

The result of all this education is that the rescued children develop into worthwhile and productive people. The qualities that make them worthwhile and productive come from their own efforts. The rescues give the children a chance to develop; the actual development is up to the child. The fact that the children do so well is a clear reflection of the democratic ideal of the self-made man. The respect for what a man can do is far greater than an appreciation of his blood lines. However, the democratic ideal becomes less strong when a potential marriage is involved. Several of the rescued children find their true birth revealed as upper class at the end of the novels. These revelations are all connected to potential marriages. The convention of the rescue of a child, however, reflects clear support for the belief that, given a fair chance, anyone can rise from obscurity on the strength of personal merit.

The rescue of a child contributed to the readers' image of an ideal world in two ways. First, it represented the idea of a positive good in action. In the ideal world all people possess and exercise a sense of right, a sense of human obligation, and a sense of moral values. They do good because they are good. The rescue of a child shows this kind of person in action. No one rescues in expectation of reward. The bond of common humanity is in operation.

The second ideal state reflected by the convention is in the fact that good action is repaid or rewarded in the present. Writers (and obviously the readers) rejected the idea of a good act going unappreciated or unrewarded. The rescuers never regret their actions, and all are pleased with the results.

How clearly the rescue of a child reflected these two ideal states is easily seen in Louisa May Alcott's *Rose in Bloom* (1876). Alcott did not use the rescue convention to structure her novel, and, in fact, its function in the novel is very slight—it is there only to show the factors of goodness and reward.

One day Rose meets her cousin Mac holding "a child of three—so pale, so thin and tiny, that looked like a small scared bird just fallen from the nest."[17] The child's mother has died in a hospital (Mac is studying medicine), and Mac has promised that he will look after the baby. But the job is rather difficult for a single young man. Rose is instantly enthralled with the idea of rescuing the child. "I'm going to take this child home; and, if Uncle is willing, I'll adopt her, and she shall be happy!" (p. 245). Alcott's two good people now have a special tie, and it is not long before they get their reward in love and marriage. Alcott certainly did not need the rescue to get two young people together, but the rescue is a nice way to again emphasize that ideal state—goodness exists and it is always rewarded.

These two ideals seem so important that popular novelists often used a situation in which the child is the one doing the rescuing, a variation of the convention. This variation did not have the developed structure of the full pattern for the rescue of a child, and worked to reflect only that goodness exists naturally in man (who is more naturally good than a child?) and that goodness will be rewarded. The rewards are usually tangible and often immediate.

One of the most popular domestic novels, *Ishmael* (E.D.E.N. Southworth, 1864), used a child as a rescuer. Ishmael Worth may be the most noble character in popular fiction. Southworth tells the reader over and over how good Ishmael is. "Reader! I am not fooling you with a fictitious character here. Do you not love this boy?"[18] When he is about twelve, a fire breaks out at Brudenell Hall. The two Middleton sons are trapped. Ishmael "dashed into the front hall and up the main staircase through volumes of smoke that rolled down and nearly suffocated him" (p. 222). He rescues the boys, and his reward comes at once. He is given an education and a chance to make something of himself. Demonstrating how closely education was believed to be linked with one's future, the old black schoolmaster, who has been tutoring Ishmael, exclaims, "Your everlastin' fortin's made, young Ishmael!" (p. 237). Eventually, Ishmael becomes a lawyer.

A rescue from drowning is used in Thomas Nelson Page's *Gordon Keith* (1903). Twelve-year-old Gordon is dragged from a lake by young Norman Wentworth. The two become lifelong friends, and years later Gordon effects a reconciliation

between Norman and his estranged wife. Perhaps even more crucial, Gordon slows a run on Norman's bank by delaying the line and making a deposit, thus impressing the lower class depositors who are trying to take their money out. "I have confidence enough in this bank to put my money here."[19] Norman's rescue of Gordon so many years before brings its reward when he least expects it.

Caleb Wright in 1845 (*Wyoming, a Tale*) also used the situation of a child doing the rescuing. The book opens with eleven-year-old Walter Henderson coming upon an Indian boy caught between some poles and apparently strangled. "Walter seized a rail, and placing one end of it between the poles, exerted a sufficient lever power to break away one of them" (p. 6). The Indian boy survives to become a great chief, and years later he saves Walter from torture and death during the battle of Oriskany. The Indian chief also gives Walter a packet at that time. "Keep it safely; its value some time hereafter may remind you of a friend" (p. 54). Walter's reward is complete when the packet reveals his sweetheart's respectable parentage and facilitates their marriage. The Indian here repays his own rescue quite handsomely and rewards Walter for his actions.

The ideal of what constituted a reward for the child who rescued someone was so well known that Mark Twain could make fun of it. In *The Adventures of Tom Sawyer* (1876), Huck Finn rescues the Widow Douglas who is about to become the victim of a robbery. Just as the pattern dictates, Huck gets an immediate reward. But Mark Twain does not present it quite as the domestic novelists would have:

> His sufferings were almost more than he could bear. The widow's servants kept him clean and neat, combed and brushed.... He had to eat with knife and fork; he had to use napkin, cup, and plate; he had to learn his book; he had to go to church; he had to talk so properly that speech became insipid.[20]

Huck endures his reward but three weeks and then runs away.

Mark Twain's cynical view notwithstanding, the American readers who bought the popular novels did believe that such a life was a reward. A supportive environment and a solid education were the foundation for a happy, useful—and successful—life. Further, by connecting the romantic plot to the rescue of a child, writers could show that everyone who

developed a useful, successful life would also develop a satisfying romantic relationship. The pattern for the rescue of a child implied that every child in America could succeed in all things. The reading public wanted to believe it.

Chapter III

The Rescue from Physical Danger

When the heroine of a popular nineteenth century novel found herself in a runaway carriage, she usually had little cause for despair. It was fairly certain that, in a matter of seconds, a handsome young man would rush forward and rescue her. The convention in which a female is rescued from physical danger by a male (both parties were invariably young and attractive) was almost a staple of the popular novel which contained any romantic story at all. Certainly the situation of the pretty young girl in danger and the strong, handsome young fellow rescuing her provided in itself a vicarious thrill for readers. But the rescue from physical danger was also a good way for writers to illustrate the idea of natural sexual roles and the concept that a man's worth was not based on his social level or inheritance alone, but also on his actions.

Although the pattern of the rescue from physical danger is not as clearcut as the pattern for the rescue of a child, the convention, with whatever twist the individual writer chose to give it, had as its basis the solid belief that woman is made to be rescued and man is made to rescue her. In Emerson Bennett's novel *The Forest Rose; A Tale of the Frontier* (1850), this belief is illustrated quite clearly when Bennett introduces the young lovers. Bennett explains that Albert loves Rose because "the object of his affections was physically weak and needed a strong arm."[1] Rose loves Albert because "she could look up to the being of her choice and feel in him a protector" (p. 11). Just to make sure that the reader doesn't miss the point, Bennett comments, "By a righteous law of nature, man loves what he can foster and protect; woman, what can cherish and protect her" (p. 11).

Popular writers were obviously using this idea of the man as natural protector when they included the rescue from physical danger in their romantic plots. The rescue provided an easy way for the writers to establish that this particular man was capable of protecting this particular woman. In a

35

very early American novel, *Monima or The Begger Girl* (Martha Read, 1802), Monima is rescued several times—from the workhouse, from a mugger, and from kidnappers—by an older man who always happens to be walking down the street at precisely the time Monima needs to be rescued. The novel's episodic plot continues until the man's wife dies, and he is free to marry Monima for no clearer reason than that he has rescued her.[2] The episodic, disjointed structure of most of the early novels rarely involved a more sophisticated use of the rescue from physical danger than as a moment of excitement. As popular writers began to develop more defined themes, the rescue from physical danger began to be useful in demonstrating other social attitudes and in adding significantly to the novels' structures.

If we use the social status of the rescuer as the basis for classification of the several patterns of this rescue convention, we can more easily examine how the rescues worked in the novels and what kinds of attitudes they seem to reflect. In a very popular pattern, the young man is on a social level which is inferior to the young lady's—or at least *appears* to be inferior. Because of this disparity in social class, there is no ordinary way for the hero and heroine to get together. The rescue is crucial in that it makes the heroine instantly aware of this man who has just saved her from a life-threatening danger; it establishes the hero's courage, strength, and disregard for himself, all of which then overshadow his low status; it places him in a position to prove his worth to the heroine's protective family; and it seems to indicate that this couple fits what Bennett described as the natural female and male roles of frailty and strength. The rescue from physical danger when the man is socially or financially inferior to the heroine tends to come early in the novel, and, therefore, it opens the way to a development of romance.

James Kirke Paulding's *The Dutchman's Fireside* (1831) illustrates this pattern of the rescue from physical danger. Sybrandt Westbrook is the son of a distant cousin of Catalina Vancour, daughter of a wealthy farmer. Sybrandt is not only very poor, he is so inept and awkward that his manhood is open to question. Here, the hero's heritage is no problem, but his economic status and social problems place him considerably below Catalina.

Catalina is somewhat amused by his awkwardness, and, in a gesture of charity, invites him on an island picnic with some friends. Fortunately for the future of Sybrandt's romance but, unfortunately for the picnickers, a violent storm comes up.

> This storm was for a long time traditionary for its terrible violence; and for more than half a century people talked of the incessant flashes of the lightning, the stunning and harsh violence of the thunder, the deluge of rain, the hurricane which accompanied it, the lofty trees... torn up by the roots....[3]

Sybrandt heroically guides their skiff through the waves when, suddenly, the boat capsizes. Catalina "became insensible the moment the accident occurred and would have quickly perished, had not Sybrandt swum into the edge of the turbulent whirlpool where she was floating, and brought her safely to the land" (p. 66). Sybrandt, battling violent waves to save Catalina from certain death, provides a rather spectacular rescue. In a moment, the rescue has scuttled any lingering questions about Sybrandt's manliness. Although Catalina's interest in Sybrandt has been kindled, her mother still wishes for a better match. Since Catalina is susceptible to her mother's pressures, she does continue to entertain other suitors. This rescue early in the novel has opened the door to romance, but it certainly does not settle all the issues or resolve all parental opposition. Sybrandt's jealousy and Catalina's uncertainty result in a misunderstanding, and Sybrandt goes off to trade on the Indian frontier for a year.

Most popular writers did not allow their lower status heroes to win their ladies after only one rescue. The first rescue early in the novel established the hero's real worth as greater than his social or financial status, but he needed to do more—often he needed to rescue more—before all obstacles to the match disappeared. In Sybrandt's case, he needed to rescue Catalina again.

When he returns from a year on the frontier (his rugged manliness is now thoroughly established), he finds that a drunken renegade Indian is lurking around the Vancour estate seeking revenge against Catalina's father. Sybrandt keeps watch and sees the Indian follow Catalina to a stream:

> He [Sybrandt] saw him look cautiously round in every direction;

> he saw him lay himself down and crawl on his belly, dragging his gun after him towards the edge of the precipice, that he might gain a full view of his victim below,—and he followed him noiselessly.... At length the Indian raised himself on his knee, cocked his unerring musket, and carried it to his cheek. In an instant it was snatched from his grasp.... Catalina, looking up, saw a sight that recalled all her tenderness and all her fears (p. 157).

Sybrandt and the Indian struggle at the brink of the precipice, and the renegade hurtles over the edge. Catalina faints, of course, but when she revives, all is settled. "Dearest Sybrandt, I can now see it all.... You were every night on the watch, guarding me—me—who was accusing you of spending them in gaming, riot, and seduction..." (p. 159).

This second rescue has erased all Catalina's doubts about Sybrandt's devotion and has established that he has the necessary vigilance and strength to protect her. Catalina's mother is still not happy over the young man's lack of fortune, and she sends Catalina off to Albany to visit a cousin. There, Sybrandt is ridiculed by Catalina's cousin and others as being too rustic. But Catalina remains faithful. "I'd rather be a happy wife than a titled lady" (p. 208). Sybrandt has to fight bravely in the French and Indian War before the two can finally wed, but at the end of the novel he can say, "You are mine then, Catalina, at last" (p. 286).

Sybrandt has to rescue twice to overcome thoroughly his low financial status. Jessee Holman's hero William Evermont (*The Prisoners of Niagara or Errors of Education*) has to rescue the girl more than once because of his own moral lapses which strip him of the status the first rescue gives him. William is the five-year-old orphan who plunged into the Potomac and rescued two-year-old Zerelda. Along with repaying his own rescue as a child, this rescue of Zerelda establishes his innate worth at an early age. Since he is immediately adopted and raised as Zerelda's cousin, he is on his way to establishing a social level that might be sufficient for a match.

But when William reaches his teens, he shows a lack of moral restraint and gets involved in sexual episodes, becoming "increasingly bold" with both mature women and young girls. By age seventeen, William is so dissipated that Holman begins to sprinkle the novel with miscellaneous rescues of young women to prove that William, although he does not sexually

protect young women, does physically protect them and so has not lost all sense of male chivalry. It is also made clear that William takes advantage of all the sexual opportunities that come his way, but he does not force helpless women into sexual situations. On a brief visit home, William saves Zerelda from a local Indian attack and partially re-establishes his moral standing in her eyes. Unfortunately, William has not yet truly reformed, and it is not long before he is once more seducing young women. The improved status that he gained from the second rescue is almost immediately lost. Holman continues to have his hero rescue young women from death and other terrible fates—continuing to prove that somewhere under William's sexual immorality is the proper masculine protectiveness.

Finally, Zerelda is once more taken prisoner by the Indians. William, who by this time is trying to straighten out his life by fighting Indians with a local regiment, sees Zerelda in the Indian camp. "I raised my eyes and beheld the female captive... it was Zerelda!" (p. 178). Just as Zerelda is about to be raped by an Indian, William rushes up, tomahawks the Indian, and carries the fainting girl away into the woods. They must travel through the woods for several days before reaching civilization. During that time, William demonstrates masculine strength over and over again. This rescue compensates for all William's sins and re-establishes his worth in Zerelda's eyes.

Although Holman's novel goes on through a seemingly endless maze of coincidence and threatened disaster, William's worth, moral strength and ability to protect Zerelda are no longer questioned by either Zerelda or her family. William's low birth is not forgotten but, rather, it seems to make his rescues even more impressive. Zerelda's comment at the end of the novel assures him of her love:

> "Your birth is an honor to the human name: that such merit, such innate nobility should arise from so low an origin. Oh, Evermont, I love you more dearly on account of your humble parentage; because I love you for yourself" (p. 335).

After this declaration of admiration and love by Zerelda, Holman closes the novel by clearing up his hero's mysterious heritage and revealing that he is really heir to a title. This

revelation of birth solves the mystery which began the novel. The novel's romantic plot, however, is built around William's three rescues of Zerelda.

An example of how powerful an obstacle social status can be to a romance occurs in E.D.E.N. Southworth's *Ishmael.* The hero, Ishmael Worth, has been proving his good character since he was a child. When he is about seventeen, he falls desperately in love with the beautiful and proud Claudia Merlin. Because of Ishmael's childhood rescue of the Middleton boys, he has been rewarded with an education. The education has improved his future opportunities but not his social status. He is living with his aunt, who is married to the overseer on Claudia's father's plantation. Ishmael's social level seems an insurmountable barrier. Southworth describes Claudia as "the most ingrained little aristocrat that ever lived.... so perfect an aristocrat that she was quite unconscious of being so" (p. 189). As a young girl, Claudia tells her uncle she will never marry "anybody but a lord!" (p. 195).

It is not, however, a lord who rescues her when she is trapped in a runaway carriage. "On rushed the maddened beasts towards the brink of the precipice!" (p. 338). Ishmael grabs the reins and turns the horses at the last minute, but the horses "threw him down and passed, dragging the carriage with them, over his prostrate body!" (p. 338). Claudia is safe, but Ishmael is half-dead—a condition which requires that he be taken to the Merlin house and nursed for many weeks. Thus, the rescue of Claudia brings Ishmael in close contact with her over a period of time, and she begins to return his love. Ishmael's rescue of Claudia impresses Judge Merlin, who feels the young man has unlimited potential. But Claudia's pride cannot bring her to overlook Ishmael's low birth. In an exchange with her father, Claudia stands firm:

> "There is nothing to prevent his becoming a gentlemen." [the judge says]
>
> "Oh yes, there is, papa!"
>
> "To what do you allude, my dear?"
>
> "To his—low birth, papa!"
>
> "His low birth? Claudia! Do we live in a republic or not?'

"Ishmael's parents were not respectable! His mother was never married!" (p. 375)

The judge is disappointed but he does not try to persuade Claudia further. It is noteworthy that the judge expresses the American ideal of social rise through personal merit. Claudia, however, adheres to the idea that birth determines a man's social status.

Now, the reader knows that Ishmael is not illegitimate. Therefore if Claudia's pride would let her overlook his apparent lack of respectable background, all would be right in the end. In several of the novels in this study, the young women do worry about the heroes' low birth. But Claudia is the only heroine who is so adamant about the problem of inequality in social class. Southworth is using Claudia's pride to prove a point. Although Ishmael has proved his worth to the others in the novel, Claudia will not relinquish her pride. In the sequel, *Self-Raised* (1876), Southworth shows Claudia regretting her foolish decision, but it is then too late. So here, Southworth uses the convention of the rescue from physical danger to show what a mistake a young woman can make if she ignores the obvious demonstration of nobility that a young man displays in such a rescue.

The difficulties of proving worth beyond one's social class in the popular novels were nothing to the difficulties of proving worth over one's race. However, James Fenimore Cooper, the first American bestselling novelist,[4] used the rescue from physical danger to demonstrate the nobility of a young red man as well as a young white man. Cooper's *The Last of the Mohicans* (1826) probably sold over 2 million copies in the United States alone.[5] The plot structure, as has often been noted, is based on capture/pursuit/rescue, capture/pursuit/-rescue. The sisters Cora and Alice Munro are the young ladies who are rescued, and the men engaged through most of the novel in rescuing them are led by Cooper's famous hero Natty Bumppo. The sisters are traveling to join their father, commander of Fort William Henry, when Cora catches the eye of the Huron Magua, and the continuing chase begins. In spite of the fact that several men are involved, and although the sisters are usually rescued at the same time, the reader knows that Major Duncan Heyward is rescuing Alice, and the Mohican Uncas is rescuing Cora. In one instance, a Huron

seizes Cora by her hair:

> He tore her from her frantic hold and bowed her down with brutal
> violence to her knees.... It was just then the sight caught the eye of
> Uncas. Bounding from his footsteps he appeared for an instant
> darting through the air, and descending in a ball he fell on the
> chest of his enemy.... They rose together, fought, and bled... the
> knife of Uncas reached his heart.[6]

Uncas is an Indian, so he does not really have any social status
in the white civilization. But his daring feats of rescue bring
him immediately to almost god-like stature:

> At a little distance in advance stood Uncas, his whole person
> thrown powerfully into view. The travelers anxiously regarded
> the upright, flexible figure of the young Mohican... there was no
> concealment to his dark, glancing, fearless eye, alike terrible and
> calm; the bold outline of his high, haughty features, pure in their
> native red; or to the dignified elevation of his receding forehead,
> together with all the finest proportions of a noble head.... such an
> umblemished specimen of the noblest proportions of man (p. 61).

Cora exclaims, "Who that looks at this creature of nature,
remembers the shade of his skin!" (p. 62). The fact that "an
embarrassed silence" follows this remark indicates that Cora
may forget the shade of Uncas' skin but the others will not. It is
revealed later in the novel that Cora has some black ancestry.
Although Cora and Uncas never learn of her heritage, Cooper
may be implying that Uncas feels an attraction to Cora and
she feels an affinity for him precisely because of her racial
make-up.

The pursuit and rescue pattern goes on, but in the last
desperate rescue of Cora, Uncas becomes reckless. He and Cora
are both killed before Natty can dispose of the villain Magua.
Cooper used the convention of the physical rescue here very
successfully. He presented a male of unquestionably lower
social status who, through daring rescues of the female,
reached an almost super-human level. That Uncas is also
recognized as a leader of his tribe adds to his glamor but does
little for his status in a white society. There is no doubt about
the respect that all the white characters have for Uncas. He is
described at various times as "fearless and generous looking"
(p. 61); as having "eyes that had already lost their fierceness,
and were beaming with a sympathy that elevated him far
above the intelligence, and advanced him probably centuries
before the practices of his nation" (p. 135); and as "the rising

sun" (p. 367). Cooper ended the novel with the tragic deaths of Uncas and Cora because he could not bring himself to use the rest of the rescue pattern and allow Cora and Uncas to marry. Thus, Cooper found himself in the position of having elevated Uncas somewhat through daring exploits but not enough to cross racial lines in marriage. Since Cora is racially mixed, a marriage would mingle three races, a prospect Cooper did not wish to present. The importance of a pure race is emphasized by Natty who lives with the Indians but often says that he is glad he has no Indian blood.

Cooper's contemporary, William Gilmore Simms, also wrote about brave and noble Indians, but he did not use them in his romantic situations. In Simms' novel *The Yemassee* (1835), the romantic plot involves Bess Matthews, daughter of a colonial minister, and her admirer Captain Gabriel Harrison. The problem here is that Harrison does not appear to do anything very substantial for a living, and Bess's father objects to him as a suitor. The reader, however, knows that Harrison is really the governor of Carolina, Lord Craven, and so there is no problem on either a social or financial level. Knowing that the reader will not worry about the appropriateness of the match, Simms builds his plot with adventure upon adventure all leading to Harrison's climactic rescue of Bess.

Bess is the ideal heroine for the rescue from physical danger. She is sweet, lovely, helpless and her sole function in the novel seems to be to provide an object for all the men in the book to rescue. She literally faints at every crisis. She is saved by the Indian Occonestoga when she comes upon a rattlesnake in the woods. "Insensibility came to her aid, and she lay almost lifeless under the very folds of the monster."[7] She is saved by her father when Indians attack their home. " 'God be merciful—oh! my father—oh! Gabriel, save me—Gabriel—Ah! God, God—he cannot—' her eye closed, and she lay supine under the knife of the savage" (p. 286). She is also saved from Indians by the villain Chorley, a pirate. "The terror was too great; for as she beheld the whirling arm and the wave of glittering steel, she closed her eyes, and insensibility came to her relief, while she sank down under the feet of the savage" (p. 291). Since Chorley has an immoral reason for rescuing her, she then needs to be saved from Chorley by her lover Harrison.

" 'Come to me, Gabriel—save me, save me, or I perish. It is I—thy own Bess—ever thine—save me, save me.' She fell back fainting with exhaustion and excitement" (p. 344). As Harrison shoots Chorley and then sweeps Bess out of the bay where she is in danger of drowning, we are told, "She was a child in his grasp, for the strength of his fearless and passionate spirit, not less than that of his native vigour, was active to save her" (p. 346). After such a rescue, it is no wonder that Bess' parents immediately abandon their opposition to Harrison. "It was not long ere she lay in the arms of her parents, whose mutual tears and congratulations came sweetly, along with their free consent, to make her preserver happy with the hand hitherto denied him" (p. 346). The discovery of Harrison's real identity smooths over any parental reservations about the marriage, but the rescue itself earns him Bess' hand in marriage. Certainly, Bess has proved that she needs someone like Harrison to protect her.

Since the readers knew that Harrison did not actually lack social status, Simms could build to the rescue at the end of the novel and resolve all parental objections at once. Most historical romance writers, however, continued to use the rescue as an early event in the romance. The authors at the end of the nineteenth century who wrote historical romances found the rescue pattern very helpful.

Charles Major's *When Knighthood Was in Flower* (1898) was an extremely popular historical romance. The *National Union Catalog* lists a seventeenth edition in 1899, and Hart says the novel sold over 200,000 copies before dropping off the bestseller lists in 1901.[8] The novel, based on the real romance of Henry VIII's sister Mary and Charles Brandon, has the two necessary characters for a good rescue from physical danger. The Princess Mary is of a very high status, and Charles Brandon, a captain in the guard, is definitely beneath her.

Mary teases and flirts with Brandon, but she is very much aware of the gap between them; and "the possibility of such a thing as a union with Brandon had never entered her head."[9] However, one night Mary is out alone with one of her maids visiting a soothsayer when she is attacked by political enemies from the court. Brandon, who has been following her out of concern for her safety, comes to the rescue:

It was but a moment till Brandon came up with the pursuers, who,

all unconscious that they in turn were pursued, did not expect an attack from the rear. The men remaining on horseback shouted an alarm to their comrades, but so intent were the latter in their pursuit that they did not hear. One of the men on foot fell dead, pierced through the neck by Brandon's sword, before either was aware of his presence. The other turned but was a corpse before he could cry out (pp. 141-42).

After she is safe again, Mary thinks about the situation:

> She still saw the great distance between them as before, but with this difference, she was looking up now. Before that event he had been plain Charles Brandon, and she the Princess Mary. She was the princess still, but he was a demi-god. No mere mortal, thought she, could be so brave and strong and generous and wise; and above all no mere mortal could vanquish odds of four to one (p. 167).

In thinking about their possible future, Mary actually puts it in marketing terms. Surely, he would "win glory and fortune, and then return to buy her from her brother Henry with millions of pounds of yellow gold" (p. 168). Mary obviously feels that Henry will not give up his sister for a mere rescue although the rescue is enough to make Brandon worthy in her eyes. Mary is right about her brother. There are many plot complications before Henry VIII agrees to the marriage. But the rescue settled the question in Mary's eyes, and at the end of the novel she weds her love.

Undoubtedly, the commoner proving that he could take care of the woman who is a member of royalty appealed to Americans proud of their democratic institutions during the century after the Revolutionary War. In Mary Johnston's historical romance *To Have and to Hold* (1900), the heroine is the English king's ward and is being pursued by the lecherous Lord Carnal. She flees to Jamestown, Virginia in 1621, on a shipload of brides for the settlers. The beautiful Jocelyn Leigh is almost immediately in need of rescue as a local ruffian attempts unwelcome liberties. Fortunately, Captain Ralph Percy, a Jamestown settler and therefore representative of the first pioneer stock in America, sees her struggling. "She struggled fiercely, bending her head this way and that, but his hot lips had touched her face before I could come between."[10] Ralph knocks the thug down and sends him off.

Jocelyn is a lady in difficulty. Ralph is attracted to her, so

she agrees to marry him because she needs protection from Lord Carnal. But she insists that it be a marriage in name only. "I appeal to your generosity, to your honor" (p. 36). Ralph assures her he is a gentleman—as heroes have to be. So the marriage here is actually part of the rescue. It is Ralph's role now to continue to protect her—and he has to fight off Lord Carnal on several occasions. He must also defy the direct orders of his king. At the end of the novel, Lord Carnal is horribly maimed by a panther and commits suicide. Ralph's continuing rescues of Jocelyn have moved her through the stages of gratitude and respect to love. She becomes Ralph's loving wife at the end of the novel. "With all my heart I love thee, my knight, my lover, my lord and husband" (p. 398). There is no doubt that Ralph is worthy of her and capable of protecting her. This novel had record sales for five months and sold nearly 250,000 copies.[11] The entire plot was based on the convention of the rescue from physical danger. The first rescue introduced the couple. The larger rescue—marrying to discourage Lord Carnal—required constant reinforcement throughout the plot until the danger was over. At the end, Jocelyn knows that Ralph's merits override his commoner status.

Another historical romance was the turn-of-the-century hit *Beverly of Graustark* (George McCutcheon, 1904). Beverly, a dynamic, fearless, and independent American girl, is on her way to visit her friend Princess Yetive of Graustark. Her coach drivers desert her, and she is stranded in the mountains with only a servant. They are picked up by mountain bandits who promise to guide them to Graustark. The leader of the band is Baldos the goat herder, who seems to be a cut above the others. That night, a mountain lion enters their cave and attacks Beverly. Baldos intercepts the beast. "The lion's gaunt body shot through the air. In two bounds he was upon the goat-hunter."[12] Baldos fights the animal off with a dagger and saves Beverly. She is impressed. "He's a man, if there ever was one. Don't let me hear you call him a goat puncher again," she tells her servant (p. 67). Again, the rescue proves the man's ability to protect the woman, and his status rises immediately because of his courage. Other adventures follow, and Baldos continues to prove courage, daring and resourcefulness. When at the end of the novel, he tells Beverly, "You will not give

yourself to the lowly, humble hunter," she answers "I will marry you, Paul. I love you" (p. 314). The fact that Baldos turns out to be Prince Dantan of Dawsbergen makes everything better at the end, but it was the rescue that won Beverly's admiration and then her love.

Although the writers of historical romances continued to have their heroines rescued from certain death—or worse—a trend seems to have developed around the turn of the century in which the convention continues to use a man of low social status and a woman of high status, but the rescue in the novel is from a physical danger of a more minor nature than earlier in the century.

In Owen Wister's novel *The Virginian* (1902), Molly Stark Wood, a teacher from an old Vermont family, is on a stage going to Medicine Bow, Wyoming when "two wheels sank down over an edge, [of the river bank] and the canvas toppled like a descending kite. The ripple came sucking through the upper spokes and... she felt the seat careen...."[13] Molly's predicament is eased when "a tall rider appeared close against the buried axles, and took her out of the stage on his horse so suddenly that she screamed... and found herself lifted down upon the shore" (p. 101).

This rescue is hardly life saving, but it fits the pattern by introducing the hero and heroine and sparking her interest and appreciation at once. "Miss Wood entertained... maidenly hope to see him again" (p. 103). Molly is very conscious of their differences in education and social status. She starts to improve the Virginian's education, giving him books to read while telling him that she could not love him because of social differences. But as "the slow cowpuncher unfolded his notions of masculine courage and modesty," Molly lets her class consciousness slip away (p. 348). Although she objects to the brutal frontier code of justice, she accepts his participation in it:

> By love and her surrender to him their positions had been exchanged. He was not now... her half-obeying, half-refractory worshipper. She was no longer his half-indulgent, half-scornful superior. Her better birth and schooling...had given way before the onset of the natural man himself. (p. 447-9)

The rescue here does not dispel any of the disparity in social

level, but it provides the opportunity for the Virginian to show his worth and earn Molly's respect.

Another novel of frontier justice was *The Lone Star Ranger* (1914) by Zane Grey, called one of America's five most popular writers in the first quarter of the twentieth century.[14] Grey used the rescue pattern to bring romance to his hero Buck Duane, a fugitive from a murder charge. Offered a pardon if he works under cover for the Texas Rangers, Buck is to investigate the dangerous town of Fairdale and its mayor Colonel Longstreth. Buck meets Longstreth's daughter Ray when he and the Colonel intercept a robber who is ripping Ray's dress off. Buck shoots the robber. "You saved my life," cries Ray, and the rescue pattern is underway.[15] Actually, Buck realizes that the Colonel's arrival probably saved Ray, but the rescue not only introduces him to a pretty girl, but puts him in a position to carry out his investigation. At the end of this novel, Buck's status is elevated because he has earned his pardon while Ray's status actually falls when her father is exposed as a crook.

In Thomas Nelson Page's *Gordon Keith* the hero rescues Alice Yorke when he finds her thrown from her horse and unconscious. Gordon carries her down the hill and revives her. Again, this physical rescue is not as dramatic as the rescues in the earlier novels or the historical romances, but it serves to demonstrate Gordon's inner worth. Gordon is from an old Southern family, but the Civil War ruined the family's fortunes. When he meets Alice, he is a poor and shabby schoolmaster; but Alice tells her mother firmly, "He is a gentleman" (p. 88). However, mother prevails and whisks Alice off to New York and a wealthy marriage. The rescue convinces Alice of Gordon's merit, but it does not impress Mrs. Yorke. By the time Gordon can improve his financial situation and prove himself in the business world, it is too late. Page's use of the first part of the rescue convention illustrates just how wrong Mrs. Yorke is in her opposition to Gordon only on financial grounds. Page does not emphasize the folly of opposition of grounds of finance as much as Southworth does the folly of opposition on grounds of birth, but he makes his point nevertheless.

In all these books, a young man of apparently inferior social status is given a chance to rescue a young lady and

thereby demonstrate his inherent nobility and courage. In a few novels, the writer uses the rescue from physical danger to break down an ideological difference between the young man and the girl's family. In those cases, it is not the social status but the political beliefs that separate the couple. Since the girl already loves the young man and since the social status is not a problem, the rescue does not act as introduction or an impetus toward upward social movement. In this situation, the hero rescues a relative of the heroine, someone who is opposing the match. The rescue is at the end of the novel and works as the only thing that can overcome the obstacle to the romance.

Clear examples of this use of the rescue pattern occur in Albion W. Tourgée's *A Fool's Errand* (1879) and John Fox Jr.'s *The Little Shepherd of Kingdom Come*. Tourgée's novel is concerned with Reconstruction in North Carolina. Yankee Republican Colonel Comfort Servosse buys a plantation, brings his family south, and becomes politically active. The focus of the novel is on Servosse and his political activities, including his anti-Klan and pro-black positions. However, Servosse does have a lovely daughter, Lily, who falls in love with Melville Gurney, the son of General Gurney, ex-Confederate officer. Both families oppose any thought of a match. Political strife continues, and an anonymous warning arrives, saying that the Klan intends to ambush Servosse on his way home from the railroad station. Lily is alone when the warning comes, but she knows that she must do something to save her father:

> Before the horse was saddled, Lily had donned her riding-habit, put a revolver in her belt... swallowed a hasty supper, scrawled a short note to her mother... and was ready to start on a night-ride to Glenville.[16]

Glenville is sixteen miles away, and Lily rides frantically. "I will save him. O God, help me! I am but a weak girl" (p. 277). Around a turn she rides right into a meeting of the Klan. Hiding, she eases away to a bend in the road where she sees "sitting before her in the moonlight, one of the disguised horsemen, evidently a sentry" (p. 282). Moving quickly, Lily

> shot like an arrow into the bright moonlight, straight toward the black muffled horseman. "My God!" he cried, amazed at the

> sudden apparition. She was close upon him in an instant. There
> was a shot; his startled horse sprang aside and Lily... was flying
> down the road toward Glenville (p. 282).

Lily reaches the train station and warns her father, saving him from ambush.

It would appear from this description that the rescue certainly must be credited to Lily, and she becomes a local heroine after the event. But we find that the sentry she shot was Melville Gurney, who recognized her as she rode past him. When the other Klan members reach him, he tells them that a rabbit startled him and he shot himself. So Melville supports Lily's ride and, in fact, prevents her from getting caught as she surely would have been without his help. Melville, of course, as a gentleman, cannot claim credit for himself, so a friend makes sure Servosse hears the whole story:

> "Melville Gurney's chivalry and presence of mind is what saved
> you—next, of course, to Miss Lily's heroism.... But if Melville
> Gurney had not put him off the scene... you would have had Jake
> Carver and the rest on you" (pp. 349-50).

Servosse responds, "My God! You are right! I had never thought of it in that way" (p. 350). Servosse immediately writes to Melville and thanks him. When Melville responds by asking if he may court Lily, Servosse answers, "You are entirely unobjectionable to me" (p. 355). Melville's participation in the rescue inspires not only a feeling of personal gratitude in Servosse, but also a realization that the young man is honorable and possesses a sense of justice. Since the Klan has now broken up and since Melville had not been deeply involved in its activities, the rescue erases all Servosse's objections. Lily still insists on waiting for General Gurney's approval—an approval which takes somewhat longer—before she and Melville can wed.

The rescue in this case has to surmount objections to the young man's fundamental beliefs, a far more difficult task than just giving him an opportunity to prove his good personal qualities. Fox's novel, set in Kentucky, contains much the same problem in that Chad, after being taken in as an orphan by Major Buford, has stunned all those close to him by joining the Union army. Chad loves Margaret Dean, and he no sooner

finds out that she loves him in return than the war breaks out, and his conscience directs him to join the Yankees. He leaves, having alienated Margaret's family. But later when Chad learns that Margaret's brother Dan is going to be shot as a guerilla, he rides a desperate sixty miles to try to reach the commandant and get a stay of execution. "Twenty-seven miles to go and less than three hours before sunrise..." (p. 272). As dawn comes, Chad arrives with the stay of execution at the same time the rebels are defeating the Union forces and freeing the prisoners. Chad's rescue was needed only if the rebels had not won the battle, but he got the stay of execution and completed his ride, thus symbolically rescuing Dan. When Dan is a prisoner at the end of the war, Chad nurses him back to health and brings him home. Because of these rescues, at the war's end Mrs. Dean greets Chad with warmth:

> "I owe my son's life to you, Captain Buford," said Mrs. Dean with trembling lip, "and you must make our house your home while you are here. I bring that message to you from Harry and Margaret. I know and they know now all that you have done for us and all you have tried to do" (p. 320).

All opposition is over, and Margaret is Chad's. He cannot take the offered happiness because of another rescue convention— the female rescuing the male. The point in both Fox's and Tourgée's novels is that a heroic rescue of a male relative of the young lady can crumble family opposition which is based on political differences. The young man has shown that he can overlook political considerations when the humanitarian need arises, and the family must do likewise.

In considering how this convention of the rescue from physical danger generally works in the novels, we should keep in mind that we are dealing with what were regarded as the natural female and male roles. Although some of the young women may have a bit too much pride, all of them are perfect examples of women who deserve to be rescued. However, when a writer uses a hero who is morally superior to the young lady, he seems to have difficulty in deciding where to place the rescue. One writer who specialized in strict moral issues was E. P. Roe, a Presbyterian minister. Roe's books were fantastically successful. Ten years after the first printing of *Barriers Burned Away* (1872), a "limited" edition of 100,000

copies sold out immediately.[17]

Roe's novel starts out by introducing Dennis Fleet, a poor young man trying to support a mother and two sisters by working as a porter in an art gallery. He falls in love with Christine Ludolph, the daughter of the gallery owner. "It should seem that circumstances brought the threads of these two lives near each other... the most impassable barriers rose between them.... She was the daughter of the wealthy aristocratic Mr. Ludolph; he was her father's porter."[18] Dennis does have an education but no wealth. He tells Christine, "I am sufficiently a democrat, Miss Ludolph, to believe that a man can be a man in any honest work." "And I, Mr. Fleet," she replies, "am not in the least degree a democrat" (p. 123).

Here is an obvious situation where we need a physical rescue to break down Christine's pride. But Roe's novel includes the fact that Dennis is a devout Christian, and Christine is an "unbeliever in God and religion" (p. 83). Dennis then is morally superior to Christine, and her conversion must take place before she is worthy of being rescued. In the novel, Dennis becomes a successful artist, so there is no financial barrier to the match. The barrier is Christine's lack of faith in God. Roe uses the rescue from physical danger at the end of the novel to push Christine into accepting the Christian faith.

When the Chicago fire breaks out, Dennis (while saving other people along the way) rushes to rescue Christine. "Can you save me? Oh, do you think you can save me?" "Yes, I feel sure I can," Dennis answers calmly (p. 368). While they desperately struggle to reach Lake Michigan ahead of the fire, Dennis performs one heroic feat after another, and Christine begins to think that "he was right and she was wrong" (p. 376). While the fire rages, the two huddle in Lake Michigan. By the time the fire subsides, Christine has been converted. She asks, "And can you still truly love me after all the shameful past?" "When have I ceased to love you?" Dennis replies, and all ends well (p. 433).

This rescue ends the novel. Dennis has already improved his financial status. The rescue proves that he is physically capable of caring for Christine. More important for Roe's theme, however, the rescue demonstrates the strength of Christian action and results in Christine's conversion, thus making her worthy of being rescued—and worthy of marrying

an honest Christian man.

It would seem that this question of whether the young lady was worthy of being rescued also bothered John Esten Cooke when he wrote *The Virginia Comedians or Old Days in the Old Dominion* (1854). Early in the novel, Beatrice Hallam is out sailing when she falls overboard:

> The young man in the skiff... seemed to have recognized the young woman—and uttering an exclamation which was drowned in the shrill blast, threw himself into the waves, and catching her half-submerged form as she rose, struck out with the ease of a practiced swimmer.[19]

The immediate result of this rescue is love. "Beatrice Hallam felt her face fill with blood, her heart throb: for the first time she had found the nature which heaven had moulded in the form of her own" (p. 91). The difficulty Cooke faced at this point was that, although Charles Waters is a poor farmer of "humbler class" (p. 90), Beatrice is an actress, placing her even lower on the social ladder. Cooke has used the rescue for introduction and to stimulate love, but there is a disturbing possibility that Beatrice may not be worthy of rescue—although we do know that she has been fighting off the immoral advances of Champ Effingham. This problem of the woman's worth may be one of the reasons Cooke soon reveals that Beatrice is really Charles' cousin. The revelation of birth allows Beatrice to give up the stage and makes the two young people of equal social status. To clearly emphasize the natural roles, now perfectly suitable, Cooke shows Beatrice being kidnapped by the lustful Champ. As they speed off in a coach, Charles follows. "He now felt the advantages of his country training—days and nights spent in hunting; his speed was scarcely less than that of the flying horse" (p. 310). Although wounded, this amazingly fast young man foils the abduction and rescues Beatrice. This second rescue serves to demonstrate that it is Charles who has the right to rescue Beatrice and that Beatrice is worthy of rescue. They are filling natural male and female roles.

By mid-century, most of the popular writers apparently used the convention of the rescue from physical danger as a quick way to demonstrate the inherent worth of the lower class hero so that he could begin to prove his abilities in other areas. Before that time, however, writers frequently had men rescue

women of their own class. The convention, then in its early stages, was used as a symbol of the divine correctness of these two people marrying. The young woman is being rescued by the man most suited to care for her. The fact that he is the one to perform the rescue seems to prove that he is the one fated to protect her for the rest of their lives.

Cooper uses this approach with the second couple in *The Last of the Mohicans*. Socially Major Duncan Heyward is a perfect match for Alice Munro. What Duncan must prove with his rescues of Alice is that he is capable of caring for her in the wilderness, the new American civilization. Since Alice trembles and faints at every crisis, there is no doubt that she needs someone to look out for her. Duncan learns from Natty how to survive in the wilderness and proves he can indeed protect Alice who is frequently referred to in the novel as a "child."

Alice may be more childlike than some other heroines, but it is this helpless female frailty which the rescue convention stresses when the writer uses a rescuer of the same social class as the woman. Emerson Bennett carefully explained feminine frailty and masculine strength in *The Forest Rose*. Bennett uses the rescue to illustrate this frailty and strength when Rose is captured by Indians. Albert rescues her and modestly explains, "It was from here I saw you, my own Forest Rose, a helpless prisoner; it was from here I aimed the deadly weapon to set you free; and it was from here I rushed exultingly to clasp you..." (p. 49).

When Rose is captured a second time, Albert vows, "I will either set her free, alone and unaided, or die in the attempt" (p. 63). Albert's role as a lover, then, is to rescue Rose, although it takes him nearly two years to find her before he can rescue her the second time. The plot of this adventure, combined with the opening statements about male and female roles and the two rescues, reinforce the idea that the right man must rescue the right woman.

Two early novels with highly improbable plots based almost entirely on coincidence use the physical rescue in the romantic situations merely to emphasize that these two young people are really right for each other. In Samuel Woodworth's *The Champions of Freedom, or The Mysterious Chief* (1816), George Willoughby rescues his childhood sweetheart

Catherine Fleming from a theater fire. In the confusion, Catherine does not realize George was the one who rescued her, and she allows Thomas Sandford to court her because he claims to be her rescuer. When he makes improper advances, she dismisses him. "The debt was cancelled, and she forbade him her sight."[20] She learns who really rescued her, and everything is straightened out. This mixup is important because it illustrates that, even as early as 1816, the idea had become established that a woman may assume that her rescuer is destined to be her suitor.

The other early novel is James McHenry's *The Betrothed of Wyoming* (1830) in which Henry Austin rescues Agnes Watson from Indians, and it is love at first sight. There are no obstacles to the match, and the pair become engaged. McHenry also has Henry dash to Agnes' aid at the end of the novel when the villain threatens a fate worse than death. This final rescue only affirms what the first rescue began—the right man has found the right woman.

The first dime novel, *Malaeska; the Indian Wife of the White Hunter* (1860) by Ann Sophia Stephens, is concerned primarily with the life of Malaeska. But Stephens uses a rescue from physical danger early in the novel for the purpose of establishing the proper roles of the young lovers Arthur Jones and Martha Fellows. The two have had a lover's quarrel, and Martha is walking alone in the woods when she is seized by Indians. "A dark form rushed from its covert in the brushwood, and rudely seized her, darting back into the wilderness" (p. 47). At once, Arthur rescues her. "That moment a bullet whistled by her cheek. The Indian... staggered back, and fell to the ground..."(p. 47).

Martha realizes instantly that this incident has settled the roles the two are to fill. "Oh, Arthur! dear Arthur, I am glad it was you that saved me," she cries (p. 48). When she apologizes for their earlier quarrel, Arthur forgives her with a "look that humbled her to the heart," and after they are wed, Martha never dares to "brave" that look again (p. 49). The rescue here shows Arthur's superior strength and reaffirms the natural roles, settling the question of who is in charge of the relationship.

One late example of the use of the rescue only to establish traditional roles is in Harold MacGrath's *The Adventures of*

Kathlyn (1914). This novel offers a collection of crises which are stunning in their frequency and intensity. Heroine Kathlyn Hare, an American girl, has a series of adventures in India, putting her almost continually at the point of death or at the mercy of the lustful Umballa. John Bruce, a socially acceptable, immensely capable, and very wealthy white hunter, rescues Kathlyn no less than eight times. Since there is no problem of unequal social levels or parental opposition, MacGrath seems to be using the physical rescue only to stress the inevitable coming together of this extraordinary young man and this extraordinary young woman. MacGrath praises Kathlyn's endurance. "An ordinary woman would have died from mere exhaustion."[21] John's strength impresses Kathlyn. "How strong he was," she sighs (p. 145). By the time John has rescued her eight times (and her father once), there is certainly no doubt that this is a match engineered by fate.

Since the convention of a young man rescuing a young woman from physical danger appears so continuously in popular fiction from the early novels to World War I, it seems obvious that readers enjoyed it. The convention often appears to reflect a definite belief that a young man of low social class may well demonstrate his inherent qualities of chivalry and courage through the rescue. Once the man shows his merit, he may start to rise in the world through his own efforts and finally win the young lady in marriage. Certainly this whole idea shows the American ideal of the self-made man who rises through his own resourcefulness.

In these novels, it is important that the young lady exhibit proper appreciation of all the values that the man has displayed in these rescues. No matter what is finally revealed about the young man's background, the young woman must always agree to marry him before she knows anything more about his ancestry. This acceptance of him proves her own solid moral foundation. Southworth's novel stresses over and over again that Claudia is condemning herself to a loveless life because she will not recognize the virtues displayed in the rescue as more appropriate to happiness than mere money and background.

However, a significant number of novels in this sample also use the plot conventions of the revelation of good birth or of concealed identity in the denouement of the romantic

situation. That so many writers felt it safer to equalize the social levels in a traditional way really indicates a doubt about the efficacy of mere deeds to equalize social levels. The revelation of good birth or high status may have created a sigh of relief among readers who felt just a bit uneasy about a nameless nobody marrying the banker's daughter.

Jessee Holman in 1810 clears up the question of William Evermont's birth at the end of *The Prisoners of Niagara or Errors of Education*. William's love, Zerelda, has already vowed that she loves him for himself and says his low birth makes his courage especially impressive. Suddenly William is revealed to be the son of Sir William Valindon. At once, this hero rises to a position in the aristocracy, making him much more suitable for the daughter of a wealthy merchant. The revelation of titled ancestry is particularly interesting in a novel in which the hero joins Washington's army in the Revolutionary War. Holman undercuts his own emphasis on democratic ideals with this story of William's birth.

A birth revelation halfway through the novel occurs in Fox's *The Little Shepherd of Kingdom Come*. As a young boy, Chad has been taken in by Major Buford. The Major suspects very soon that Chad may be the descendant of his grandfather's only brother who had been supposedly killed by Indians in 1778. But there is no proof, and he dismisses the idea. Although the major's friends and neighbors welcome the little boy, Chad reaches an age where his friendship with Margaret Dean causes her parents concern. "It was right that they should be kind to the boy... but they could not have even the pretense of more than a friendly intimacy between the two" (p. 173). Because of Margaret's parents' objections to him, Chad investigates in the mountains and finds that he is indeed related to the major. In spite of all the sterling qualities Chad the orphan had demonstrated up to this time, this revelation of birth puts him in a new and better position:

> It was then that the Major took Chad by the shoulders roughly, and with tears in his eyes, swore he would have no more nonsense from the boy; that Chad was flesh of his flesh and bone of his bone; that he would adopt him..... And it was then that Chad told him how gladly he would come, now that he could bring him an untarnished name (p. 177).

Soon after this incident, Chad is invited to Margaret's home for dinner when, only a few weeks before, her parents had preferred that she stay away from him.

E.D.E.N. Southworth conceals Ishmael's birth from the characters in the novel but not from the readers. Therefore, when Ishmael falls in love with Claudia Merlin, the readers could relax, knowing that the pair's social levels were really equal. Ishmael is the son of Nora Worth, who died after his birth. What the world does not know is that Nora was secretly married to rich Herman Brudenell, whose family owns vast estates in Maryland. Brudenell is wandering through Europe under the impression that he has provided for the boy. Since the characters in Southworth's novel do not find out the truth, however, Claudia's pride stands in the way of romance. Southworth comments that even if Ishmael's parentage were made known and cleared up, "Claudia Merlin, in her present mood of mind, would have died and seen him die, before she would have given her hand to one upon whose birth a single shade of reproach was even suspected to rest" (p. 370). The implications in this novel are complex. Southworth is clearly proving a point with Claudia's obstinacy. Although she admits to loving Ishmael, Claudia marries another solely because of a desire to enter aristocracy. Yet Southworth blunts the issue of love versus ambition because Ishmael is really well born. Perhaps Southworth felt that if Ishmael possessed a good name as well as all his virtues readers would be more upset at the mistake Claudia makes. The fact of Ishmael's birth does work to magnify Claudia's mistake, and in the sequel it makes her disappointment especially bitter. But that fact also reduces the importance of all Ishmael's sterling qualities, which he demonstrates through his actions.

Sometimes a writer uses a concealed identity to cover the fact that the young man's social level is equal to or better than the young lady's. Simms' novel *The Yemassee* has Lord Charles Craven, the governor of Carolina, masquerading as the trader Gabriel Harrison. The reader knows who he is, but Bess' parents do not, and they disapprove of Harrison. Pastor Matthews' attitude toward Harrison has "something of backwardness, a chilly repulsiveness in the manner" (p. 51). When Harrison rescues Bess at the end of the novel, her parents thankfully consent to the match. They are glad to have

someone who can protect her. "She is yours, Captain Harrison—she is yours! But for you,.. I dread to think, what would have been her fate" (p. 354). All the same, when Harrison reveals that he is really Governor Craven, there is an extra measure of relief in the pastor's shout of "gratification," and Bess has a "heart full of silent happiness" (p. 357).

In *Beverly of Graustark*, Beverly is very relieved when the goat herder Baldos reveals that he is Prince Dantan. Although she loves him and has agreed to marry him, Beverly has frequently wished Baldos were really a prince. Becoming a princess will be more fun and more respectable than becoming the wife of a goat herder. And, probably, rich American girls should not really marry peasants.

If we consider how many of the novels in this sample used the physical rescue between members of the same class and then how many others used the revelation of birth or identity to equalize the social classes of the lovers, we are left with only a few novels in which the writer depended entirely on the rescue and the future success of the hero to equalize the social levels. The exceptions include Roe, whose theme was the superiority of the Christian life over any social status, and Wister, whose theme was the superiority of Western rugged manliness over Eastern effete culture.

Although the heroines proclaim complete respect for the hero and vow true love, it is impossible to ignore the implications in the endings of these novels. If writers used other kinds of equalizers before the couple could marry, then readers must have felt more comfortable with these traditional signs of worth. This acceptance of the importance of birth reveals a lack of faith in the democratic ideal of a man proving himself through his actions. Since the convention of the child rescue seems to indicate a strong belief in individual development, we must speculate that readers felt less comfortable with this ideal in romantic situations. For marriage, readers seem to have wanted some traditional signs of acceptability and substance. There is no indication in popular novels that it is good birth that makes a character willing to rescue others. Often good Indians rescue white settlers; good people of the lower classes rescue others. It is in the romantic situations, apparently, that writers and presumably the readers felt just a bit uncomfortable when a

man's own achievements were the only criteria for marrying into the upper class. Another reason for the reluctance to rely on demonstrated merit may be the tradition that a woman may marry upward, but a man does not unless he is a fortune hunter.

In spite of this seeming preference for traditional proof of respectability, there are some definite social values reflected in the physical rescue situation. The further worthy qualities displayed by the young men after the initial rescue include such things as honesty, courage, fortitude and strength. There are two other specific areas in which the young men usually excel. The first is participation in war or support of country.

One of the ways in which Holman's hero makes up for his sexual immorality is by joining George Washington's army and proving his bravery under fire. McHenry's hero, Henry Austin, also fights in the Revolutionary War. Woodworth's hero George Fleming fights in the War of 1812. Both Cooper and Paulding involve their heroes in the French and Indian War, and, of course, Fox's hero joins the Union army during the Civil War. All these men serve faithfully, valiantly and prove themselves superior to their fellow soldiers. And, of course, the heroes all serve on the "right" side. The villains invariably serve on the opposite side or, worse, become renegades.

If we extend the term war to include any defense of one's country and its values, we can add other heroes to this list of warriors. Both Johnston's and Major's heroes support their kings even though Charles Brandon unadvisedly loves his king's sister and Ralph Percy unadvisedly loves his king's ward. McCutcheon's hero Prince Dantan is engaged throughout the novel in overthrowing evil, repressive Prince Gabriel and recovering his rightful place as ruler of Dawsbergen.

The western novel usually presents patriotism in a somewhat regional context. Both Owen Wister and Zane Grey involve their heroes in the defense of frontier law and order although, in each case, it seems that the hero's defense may jeopardize his romance. This defense of law and order is the precursor of support for the civilized structure of the country and is as important as serving in a war.

Indian fighting was also considered a highly patriotic endeavor. Simms' hero Lord Craven is in disguise because he is

investigating and trying to avert Indian uprisings in colonial Carolina. Bennett's hero Albert joins an old Indian fighter while he pursues his sweetheart Rose. It is interesting that Bennett explains that Albert is still "a high-souled, well-born, well-bred young man... who if he were a hunter of men, was rather so from powerful circumstances than from any natural inclination" (p. 69). The point is made that Albert kills Indians but does not scalp them. It is evident from the activities of all these heroes that a worthy young man does serve and support his country—and in an appropriately noble fashion, never sinking to the level of the enemy.

The other major area in which these young men excel is in their work or in earning a living. Heroes in American novels do not lead idle lives. Many are farmers. Cooper's and Major's heroes are in the military, and we also have such exotic occupations as white hunter and prince.

Southworth, Page, Roe and Wister all take their heroes from obscurity and poverty to great financial success. Ishmael becomes a successful lawyer, so honest that he will refuse a case if the client is in the least guilty. Page's Gordon Keith becomes a prominent engineer and then a mine owner. Wister's Virginian has purchased coal land and is planning future success. Roe's Dennis Fleet goes from being a clerk in an art gallery to being a respected artist. The details of these financial rises take up sizeable portions of the novels, showing that such delineation of movements from rags to riches were interesting.

Several of the heroes have yet to reach their full potential wealth at the conclusions of the books, but there is no doubt that such wealth will be realized. Paulding's Sybrandt Westbrook has just returned home from the French and Indian War. But since the uncle who adopted him has died, Sybrandt's inheritance offers possibilities for growth and success. Grey's hero earns a governor's pardon by breaking up the outlaw gang and, at the end of the novel, heads for a new life in Louisiana. Fox's hero heads west with no money but a "strong body and a stout heart" (p. 336). In none of these novels is there any hint that the reader needs to worry about the future. These men are strong and honest and will make their way in the world.

The only novel in which the hard work ethic is not stressed is in Holman's 1810 book. Since William is revealed to be a

titled young man, perhaps Holman felt his financial situation was strong enough. Most probably, the importance of titles was still strong enough in the early nineteenth century to ensure success for a young man having one.

The evidence of a strong emphasis on honest work in these novels shows that readers believed not only that the man must earn his own way in the world but also that he must be capable of supporting the woman he has rescued. The man must prove in the rescue that his character is worthy of the woman, and then he must prove himself capable of caring for her both physically and financially.

The female role is clear. She needs the man's protection. She needs to be rescued. Once rescued, she is the reward for the man's bravery, and she has a strong sense of the debt she owes the man. It is another internal contradiction in the rescue convention that while the man proves himself worthy of the woman, she and often her family think of the relationship as a "debt" she owes him. Catalina thinks often of what she owes Sybrandt. She turns down an admirer because of her feeling for Sybrandt. "I have reason to love him; he twice saved my life" (*The Dutchman's Fireside*, p. 217). Princess Mary tells Charles Brandon, "I owe you my life and more—and more a thousand times" (*When Knighthood Was in Flower*, p. 144). Bess' father gives her to Harrison immediately after she is rescued. "It was not long ere she lay in the arms of her parents, whose mutual tears and congratulations came sweetly, along with their free consent, to make her preserver happy with the hand hitherto denied him" (*The Yemassee*, p. 346).

The real attitude being emphasized is that the man has earned a reward, and the woman he rescues is the reward. When a young woman is rescued by a villain, the man usually makes immoral demands. These demands prove he is no gentleman, and there is no reward. But when the hero rescues and makes no demands, then the woman as reward becomes implicit in the situation.

The correctness of male dominance and female submission is given so much emphasis in the novels that the only conclusion we can draw is that readers accepted these roles without reservations. The contrast of feminine weakness and masculine strength leading to masculine dominance appears on all social levels. When the Princess Mary weds Charles

Brandon (now given a title by King Henry), the novel ends:

> ... this fair, sweet, wilful Mary dropped out of history, a sure token
> that her heart was her husband's throne; her soul his empire; her
> every wish his subject, and her will... the meek and lowly servant
> of her strong but gentle lord and master, Charles Brandon, Duke
> of Suffolk (p. 358).

And Jocelyn says at the end of *To Have and To Hold,* "With all my heart I love thee, my knight, my lover, my lord and husband" (p. 398). While Dennis is rescuing Christine during the Chicago fire, a ruffian enters the house. "Trembling and half fainting... she cried for Dennis and never did knightly heart respond with more brave and loving throb to the cry of a helpless woman than his" (*Barriers Burned Away*, p. 367). When Beatrice Hallam thanks Charles Waters for saving her life, his father tells her, "Oh, that's his place—you're a weak little thing, and couldn't be expected to take care of yourself" (*The Virginia Comedians,* p. 90).

This weakness, this frailty, this need to be rescued does not change in popular novels throughout the nineteenth century although the popular heroine does change. Late nineteenth century heroines were much more energetic than the earlier heroines. Bess Matthews does nothing but scream and faint in *The Yemassee* in 1835. Kathlyn Hare in *The Adventures of Kathlyn* in 1914 is a dynamo of activity. Kathlyn has a "gift" for soothing wild animals. At one point, she faces down a lion. Threats from tigers do not even worry her. "It seemed to her... that a film of steel had grown over her nerves" (p. 115). Her lover, John Bruce, admires her as a woman who "was of the breed which produces heroes" (p. 155). In spite of her obvious energy and strength, Kathlyn needs to be rescued eight times while she sighs over John's superior strength. Heroines may become fiery, but they still need to be rescued, and they respond just as the early heroines do, with complete submission to the man's strength. The woman's positions in relation to the men they are destined to wed do not change no matter what else may change in the figure of the young heroine.

The social attitudes reflected by the rescue from physical danger of a woman by a man are frustratingly inconsistent. On the one hand, the young man proves his worth by his daring

rescue. On the other hand, the writers often equalize the social classes through traditional means just in time to prevent the heroines from marrying beneath themselves. Both Page's and Southworth's novels specifically condemn the snobbery about finances or birth that the other writers seem to be bowing to, but Southworth's hero is also revealed as well born. The rescue seems to indicate that the woman is the automatic reward for the man's daring; he dominates through physical strength. Yet it is clear that financial success and the ability to support the woman are really crucial in securing the marriage. The man must prove his ability in these areas.

In spite of these apparent contradictions in the actual social attitudes readers held, the physical rescue does reflect a consistent ideal view of romantic situations. The right man will find the right woman and they will marry. The physical rescue is the test by which we know the ideal couple, the two fated to meet and love. The right man rescues the right woman. The fact that the rescue situation is often the introduction for the couple only intensifies this feeling of destiny in the rescue situation. The rescue in one moment brings together a woman who needs rescuing and a man capable of doing so. The traditional male and female roles are filled immediately, and the rescue seems to show a predestined coming together. In the ideal world, there are no mismatches. The physical rescue is so important in demonstrating which man is suited for which woman that a realist like William Dean Howells uses the convention to avoid a mismatch in his novel *Indian Summer* (1886).

In the novel, Theodore Colville, a forty-one-year-old publisher, is engaged to marry twenty-year-old Imogene Graham. Colville worries somewhat about the age difference, but he decides that it doesn't matter. While Colville, Imogene, Mrs. Bowen, her daughter Effie, and Reverend Morton are all out on a carriage ride, there is trouble with the horses:

> Mrs. Bowen's horses... reared at the sight of the sable crew [a herd of black pigs], and backing violently up-hill, set the carriage across the road, with the hind wheels a few feet from the brink of the wall.[22]

Colville begins to rescue all the women. "Jump, Mrs.

Bowen! jump, Effie! Imogene—" (p. 253). Mrs. Bowen and Effie jump, but Imogene refuses to let Colville rescue her. "The girl sat still, staring at him with reproachful, with disdainful eyes" (p. 253). She lets Reverend Morton pull her out of the carriage. Colville is hurt by the horses. During his subsequent recovery, Imogene tells her mother that she knows now that she likes Colville but does not love him. The engagement ends. The fact that Imogene will not allow Colville to rescue her makes it obvious that he is not the proper man for her. In fact, at the end of the novel, Colville realizes that Mrs. Bowen—who did let him rescue her—is the woman for him. Howells the realist does not go so far as to mate Imogene with Reverend Morton. The fact, however, that Howells uses the convention to reveal that Colville and Imogene are not destined for each other is a significant indication of how important the convention was and how well the readers understood it. In the ideal happy endings of the popular novels, the right man always gets the right woman.

The rescue convention is so clearcut that it can be used as a real life guide. A non-fiction guide for young women aimed at helping them establish romantic relationships with young men includes it. As we would expect, young women are told to be warm, understanding, chaste and adoring. In a chapter designed to give the young woman special advice on how to get the young man to propose marriage, the author recommends "The Rescue Method":

> This is the method used by so many novelists.... In these cases, if the girl will tactfully let the man know of her distress, it is exceedingly hard for him to refrain from comforting her, from trying to make it easy for her, from heroically and chivalrously relieving her of her burdens and taking them upon himself....[23]

This guide for young women was written in 1969 and was in its ninth printing in 1977. Contradictions in its patterns notwithstanding, the rescue convention in the romantic situation is one of our clearest guides to the history of male-female relationships in America.

Chapter IV

The Rescue from a Dilemma

Energetic Kathlyn Hare in Harold MacGrath's 1914 novel, *The Adventures of Kathlyn,* represents a changing emphasis in the American heroine. The change is manifested in an increased physical strength and an increased intellectual development. Early in the novel, Kathlyn singlehandedly captures a runaway lion—demonstrating a remarkable physical presence. She also evaluates John Bruce when she first meets him as a worthwhile man because he caught "her interest in the very fact that he had but little to say and said that crisply and well" (p. 21). That her ability to deal with lions is rare is obvious, but her intellectual appraisal of a man is also a change from early nineteenth century heroines. Early heroines were more apt to sigh over a man's muscles or manners than his intellect. MacGrath does not use these traits in Kathlyn to affect the course of the romantic situation in his novel or to develop a new approach to that situation. In fact, since Kathlyn is rescued from death eight times by Bruce, MacGrath is clearly placing his heroine securely in the traditional female mold. Kathlyn's personal qualities, however, do reflect the change in the popular heroine that began appearing in popular novels in 1875.

All areas of American life were undergoing radical shifts during the last quarter of the nineteenth century. Cities were being swollen by foreign immigrants and migration from the farms. The American frontier closed, and, with the Massacre at Wounded Knee in 1890, the last Indian resistance faded. Labor unions were increasingly violent in their demands. Religious groups, pressured by Darwinism and science, became more liberal and more involved in political and social matters. Politically, Americans were moving from a traditional belief in laissez-faire to a conviction that government should control and regulate. Reform movements developed, and muckrakers called for action to improve social conditions.

The options available to the American woman were also

changing. Several women's colleges opened after the Civil War and, by the end of the century, there were 25,000 students in 128 women's colleges. Work possibilities also expanded because of industrialism. By 1900 some five and a third million women worked outside the home.[1] The percentage of women actually participating in these expanding opportunities was relatively small, and the percentage of women actively in the feminist movement was even smaller; but the ripples of these shifts in attitudes about female roles reached sufficiently deep into the American culture so that at least some popular writers began to reflect the changing concept of the feminine character in their heroines. Cawelti points out that a sympathetic picture of the new woman gradually evolved:

> While the divorcee, the promiscuous, and the prostitute remained beyond the pale and were still usually allocated an unfortunate fate, they were often treated with considerable sympathy and understanding and sometimes were even allowed to take a role as secondary heroines until their tragic fate caught up with them. The official heroine, though still usually characterized by sexual purity, gradually lost much of her submissiveness and was even granted a certain degree of wildness.[2]

The reasons for these changes in the popular heroine stem from the beginnings of the women's movement in America. The Seneca Falls women's rights convention was held in 1848. In 1845, three years earlier, Margaret Fuller, editor of *The Dial*, quarterly magazine of literature, published *Woman in the Nineteenth Century*. In this book, she touched on most of the questions that would be important for feminists later. Central to her ideas is the rejection of the concept that some things are "natural" to women. "I would have Woman lay aside all thought, such as she habitually cherishes, of being taught and led by men. I would have her... dedicate herself to the Sun, the Sun of Truth, and go nowhere if his beams did not make clear the path."[3] Fuller expressed great faith in the ability of women to think for themselves and to handle responsibilities. "Women must leave off asking [men] and being influenced by them, but retire within themselves and explore the ground-work of life till they find their peculiar secret."[4] Marriage as an institution upset her because, traditionally, the woman was submissive to the man:

But that is the very fault of marriage, and of the present relation between the sexes, that the woman *does* belong to the man, instead of forming a whole with him.... Woman, self-centered, would never be absorbed by any relation; it would be only an experience to her as to man. It is a vulgar error that love, *a* love, to Woman is her whole existence; she also is born for Truth and Love in their universal energy.[5]

By the last quarter of the nineteenth century, the cumulative effect of the women's movement and the social, economic and religious upheavals in the United States appeared in the characters of heroines in popular novels. Because of these changing concepts of feminine roles and in spite of the unceasing popularity of the rescue from physical danger of the female by the male, another rescue convention appears in the popular novels written after 1875. This convention, tied to the new heroine, is the male's rescue of the female—from a dilemma.

The rescue from a dilemma involves the same components as the physical rescue—a woman in trouble and a man who gets her out of it. The dilemma, however, while it may be serious as a physical danger, requires that the man exhibit not muscles but intellect. The dilemma usually arises less suddenly than the physical danger, and it is more completely part of the entire plot structure. In most cases, the man and woman are on equal social levels, and the rescue occurs at the end of the novel. Since social status is not an issue, the rescue at the end of the novel saves the heroine from her trouble, ends the novel by resolving the problem, and secures the marriage of the couple. The man does not need to prove his social worth, but only that he is capable of caring for the woman.

Most important in the convention is that the reason for this dilemma often lies in the heroine herself. The new feminine qualities of independent thought and action are the very things that get the heroine into trouble. And she must be rescued from her dilemma by a man who is eminently qualified to resolve her problem, thereby proving, too, that he is eminently qualified to guide her through life—and further proving that she does not need independent thought and action if she has the right man for a husband. Margaret Deland gave the convention of the rescue from a dilemma full treatment in her novel *The Rising Tide* (1916). The heroine is twenty-five-

year-old Frederica Payton, a "new woman." Fred, as she is not
very subtly called, is in favor of birth control, women's suffrage
and labor reform. She smokes; she swears; she runs a rental
agency; she makes speeches to striking female workers; and
she has radical ideas about marriage. To old friend Arthur
Weston's comment that women should trust to chivalry, Fred
answers:

> "Thank you, I prefer to trust the ballot! 'Chivalry,' and women
> working twelve hours a day in laundries! "Chivalry,' and
> women cleaning spittoons in bear-saloons! "Chivalry,' and
> prostitution! No, sir! unless his personal interests are concerned,
> man's 'chivalry' is a pretty rotten reed for women to lean on!"[6]

Arthur is dismayed that she is so bold as to say it but must
admit the truth of what she says. When Fred talks about
marriage, there are obvious echoes of Margaret Fuller:

> "Of course, marriage generally hampers a woman. Perhaps
> because most of us are tied down to the old idea that it's got to be
> permanent,—which might be a dreadful bore! I suppose that's a
> hold-over from the time that we were chattels, and men taught us
> to feel that marriage was permanent—for us! They didn't bother
> much with permanence for themselves! But I admit that
> marriage—as men have made it, entirely for their own comfort
> and convenience, with its drudgery of looking after children—is
> stunting to women (p. 168).

Fred continues discussing her radical opinions and
scandalizes everyone in the novel. She gets into difficulty while
she is speaking to striking women at a rubber factory. A slight
disturbance breaks out. She tells a policeman "her opinion of
men in general and policemen in particular.... Fred punctuated
her remonstrances by putting an abrupt hand on his arm, and
instantly there was an unseemly scuffle" (p. 262). The result of
the scuffle is that Fred, her cousin Laura Maitland, and an
Italian worker all end up in jail. After some frantic phone calls,
Fred and Laura are rescued by Arthur Weston. Arthur takes
charge and arranges bail for them. He also promises to "patch
things up" so Fred and Laura won't have to go to court. Arthur
not only patches things up, he also persuades the press to
ignore the story of two society women in jail for fighting with
the police. He has quite effectively rescued Fred from the
possible results of her own folly.

The last element in the rescue pattern is that Fred must realize that Arthur is the man best fitted to guide her through life. He is already "the one person to whom she turned" in trouble (p. 276). When he tells her he loves her, she answers, "Well, I don't see any reason why I shouldn't marry you" (p. 285). This matter-of-fact answer is followed by, "You see we're friends; and you never bore me.... So—I will marry you, Arthur" (p. 286).

The rescue from jail helps Fred realize that she does not know everything, that a woman needs a man, and that faithful Arthur is perfectly suited to her. He is thoughtful, mature, and able to give her the guidance she needs. What the rescue from a dilemma taught Fred was that she could not effectively function outside the normal female role of dependence on a husband. Early in the novel, Arthur compares Fred to her cousin Laura:

> Laura was not so hideously truthful as Fred, and her conceit was not quite so obvious; yet she, too, was of the present—full of preposterous theories for reforming the universe! Her activities overflowed the narrow boundaries of domesticity, just as Fred's did; she went to the School of Design, and perpetrated smudgy charcoal-sketches; she had her committees, and her clubs, every other darned, tiresome thing that a tired man, coming home from business, shrinks from hearing discussed, as he would shrink from the noises of his shop or factory.... Yet Laura differed, somehow, from Fred; she was—he couldn't quite formulate it.... then the dim idea took shape: you could think of Laura and babies together, but a baby in Frederica's arms was an anomaly (pp. 38-39).

Fred's cousin, Laura Maitland, really embodies the limits that writers were willing to give to their heroines by World War I. Laura is intelligent and active but submissive to her husband. Her baby and husband remain the center of her existence. She tells Fred that "no woman really knew what life meant unless she had a baby" (p. 281). It is significant that Laura, too, must be rescued from jail because she was imprudent enough to be in a place where she was out of her natural role as wife and mother. In Laura's case, it was loyalty to Fred that put her into difficulty. Fred gets into trouble because she refuses to accept the traditional female position. She scoffs at Laura as a "slave" leading a "narrow" life (p. 276). But in spite of Fred's ideas about women's independence,

when her activities get her into trouble, she must call for help—
she must ask a man. The rescue from a dilemma does not lead
Fred into love precisely, but it leads her to an awareness that
Arthur is the man suited to her, the man she can depend on, the
man who should be her husband. By the end of the novel, after
the rescue, Fred is "snuggling" next to Arthur and planning for
a family of her own. Having made the realization about her
proper role, Fred shows no reluctance to enter it completely
once the decision is made. She, in fact, convinces Arthur about
the rightness of their union when he worries about the
difference in their ages. Fred's extreme opinions have been at
least somewhat eradicated by the rescue.

Another independent young lady is Patience Sparhawk in
Gertrude Atherton's *Patience Sparhawk and Her Times*.
Patience marries dashing, rich and very social Beverly Peele
because of an intense physical attraction. Unfortunately, the
attraction wears off, and there is nothing left in the marriage.
Beverly is not Patience's equal in intellect, culture or
sensitivity. "She persuaded herself that she loved him as much
as she could love any man, and she did her pathetic best to shed
some glimmer of spiritual light into a man who might have
been compounded in a laboratory, so little soul was in him" (p.
213). The situation becomes unendurable, and Patience leaves
her husband, a move which is necessary for her own happiness
but which is also scandalous. She goes to work for a newspaper,
causing more scandal.

When Beverly becomes ill, he persuades Patience to come
back and nurse him, although she knows that she should not
get involved with him again. She is overconfident of her ability
to deal with the situation. At the same time, she is imprudent
enough to express her hatred and contempt for her husband.
When her father-in-law reminds her of her duty to her husband,
Patience declares, "There is only one law for a woman to
acknowledge, and that is her self-respect." To Beverly, she
gasps, "Oh, how I hate you! I could kill you! I could kill you!" (p.
329). The two quarrel constantly over Patience's request for a
divorce. When Beverly dies suddenly from an overdose of
morphine, Patience is accused of his murder. She is sent to jail
amid high public indignation against a woman who had left
her husband and made shocking statements in the newspapers
about women's rights. There is no doubt that Patience needs to

be rescued:

> Her fine courage retreated, and mocked her. She had no wish to recall it. She longed passionately for the strong arm and the strong soul of a man. The independence and self-reliance which Circumstance had implanted, seemed to fade out of her; she was woman symbolised. No shipwrecked mariner was ever so desolate; for nothing in all life is so tragic as a woman forced to stand and do battle alone (p 394).

Her lawyer is Garan Bourke, a distinguished and brilliant attorney at the New York bar. Bourke struggles desperately to save her. By the time the trial ends, Bourke is no longer working for pay but for love:

> Is there any possible condition in which a man can appear to such supreme advantage as when pleading for the life of a fellow being, more particularly of a young and beautiful woman? How paltry all the time-worn rescues of woman from sinking ship and runaway horse and burning house. A great criminal lawyer standing before the jury box with a life in his hand has the unique opportunity to display all the best gifts ever bestowed upon man: genius, brain, passion, heart, soul, eloquence, a figure instinct with grace and virility.... She forgot her danger, forgot everything but the man.... As Burke finally dropped upon his chair, he turned to Patience. Their eyes met and lingered; and in that moment each passed into the other's keeping (pp. 445-46).

The jury votes guilty. There is a year of appeals which all fail. "I know, I know, that you will save me," Patience tells Bourke as she is taken to Sing Sing for execution (p. 454). The novel ends on a high moment of excitement. As Patience is being strapped into the electric chair, Bourke rushes in with the governor's stay of execution based on new evidence which Bourke managed to ferret out when everyone else had given up:

> Bourke had entered. He had followed the guard mechanically, neither hoping nor fearing until the far-reaching cheers sent the blood springing through his veins once more.
> He was neither clean nor picturesque, but Patience saw only his eyes. He walked forward rapidly, and lifting her in his arms carried her from the room.

THE END (p. 488)

The rescue ends the novel. Although the theme in much of the novel has seemed to be woman's independence, Patience has said that "however much she may reason, nothing can eradicate the strongest instinct in a woman—that she can find happiness only through some man" (p. 295). The problem the novel really deals with is the problem of a woman finding a man who is morally, physically, socially and intellectually suited to her. If she finds such a man, there is no need for independence. Garan Bourke is the man suited to Patience's needs. He has always been socially acceptable. The dramatic rescue here emphasizes that he has all the qualities she admires; he is the man who can handle all her problems.

In both Atherton's and Deland's novels, the independent young lady needs only the right man to be happy. The authors make it clear that the heroines are intelligent and perceptive and, therefore, an ordinary man will not do. But the rescue from a dilemma which has been created, at least in part, by the young woman's independent activities or opinions proves that there is a man who possesses the requisite intellectual strength and moral dependability. When that wisdom and dependability are present in the man, the need for the woman's independence diminishes rapidly. Both Atherton and Deland were consistently popular from the 1890s through the 1920s. As women writers, they seemed ready to explore the implications of some of the complaints of the feminists. As popular writers, however, they steadfastly delineated the basic belief of the public that bought the books—the best thing for a woman was a suitable marriage. The rescue convention offered a way to explore the problems and then resolve the issue of women's rights in a way to satisfy the readers' conceptions of proper feminine roles.

When the rescue from a dilemma appears in popular novels written by men, the heroine reflects some independent thought and action, but not the extreme positions shown by Fred and Patience. Initiative and drive, however, were beginning to be part of the popular heroine.

Southern writer George Washington Cable used the rescue from a dilemma in a novel with a heroine capable of shrewd analysis of her predicament and capable of making plans to help herself. In *The Grandissimes* (1880) the heroine is Aurora De Grapion, a beautiful, charming Creole widow. Aurora's

problem stems from the fact that her late husband gambled away their plantation to Agricola Grandissime, who then killed him in a duel. Now Aurora and her daughter are living in straitened financial circumstances, unable to pay the rent, unable to buy much to eat. "Oh! Clotilde, my child, my child! the rent collector will be here Saturday and turn us out into the street!"[7]

Cable here makes it clear that Aurora's dilemma is not of her own making. She is a discerning and intelligent woman, but in this novel of Creole life, her possibilities for action are severely limited. Aurora pins her hopes on her ability to get a man to rescue her—specifically, she wants rich, powerful and attractive Honoré Grandissime (a relative of the man who killed her husband) to rescue her. Since the Creole society frowns on a lady accepting financial gifts from a man not connected to her, Aurora's task is to entice Honoré into marriage. She is already attracted to him, but she is clearheaded enough to know that his wealth and power add considerably to his suitability as her husband.

This novel is an example of the rescue from a dilemma. Cable differs from the later novelists in that, while he gives Aurora all the intellectual capacity and determination of the later heroines, he does not make her at all responsible for her dilemma. And, particularly interesting, Aurora knows before the rescue takes place that Honoré is the man suited to rescue her. Later novelists make the rescue of the heroine and her realization that she has met the right man for her occur at nearly the same time.

Aurora explains her position to her daughter:

"My angel daughter," said Aurora, "if society has decreed that ladies must be ladies, then that is our first duty; our second is to live. Do you not see why it is that this practical world does not permit ladies to make a living? Because if they could, none of them would ever consent to be married. Ha! women talk about marrying for love; but society is too sharp to trust them, yet! It makes it *necessary* to marry. I will tell you the honest truth; some days when I get very, very hungry, and we have nothing but rice—all because we are ladies without male protectors—I think society could drive even me to marriage" (p. 255).

Aurora is concealing from her daughter the extent of her interest in Honoré, but the emphasis in this passage is clear, as

well as stunning coming from the pen of a Southern gentleman. It is society's rule that ladies must be ladies, and they must be protected by men. If women could decide, many of them would prefer to make a living rather than marry. Although, within the boundaries of a novel about Creole society, Cable can allow Aurora very little independent action, he does allow her a great deal of independent thought. And it seems to be a measure of his respect for those sentiments that Aurora utters them without losing a shred of her natural feminine charm and appeal. In most later novels, the women who say such things are portrayed either as awkward creatures without feminine charm or as desperately and ineptly trying to enter a man's world for which they are totally unfit.

Aurora proceeds with her plan, and Honoré becomes more and more enamoured of her. The day comes when she receives a document giving her back the plantation and a credit of $105,000. The note from Honoré reads, "Not for love of woman, but in the name of justice and the fear of God" (p. 261). She has been rescued from poverty. And, most important, Honoré has rescued her for reasons of justice, not for reward. This kind of rescue proves that he is a man of strength and honor—a contrast to her first husband. Aurora now has money and so does not need Honoré for support. But Cable uses the rescue to show that marriage to the proper man is best. When Honoré proposes, Aurora tells him that she knows he will be the best man she has ever known and lets him "clasp her to his bosom" (p. 339).

Another heroine in a popular novel whose dilemma is not actually her fault is Mildred Jocelyn in *Without a Home* (E.P. Roe, 1881). Mildred's father is addicted to morphine, and, when his business fails, the family rapidly sinks from a life of affluence to one of impoverishment in the New York tenements. Mildred, trying to help support her parents and three younger children, takes a job as a clerk in a shop. The work exhausts her and wears down her health. Roger Atwood, a young man from the country determined to make a success by studying law, is in love with Mildred, but she rejects him as unrefined and uncultured. As the daughter of a morphine addict, Mildred's social level is hardly high, but she feels that Roger is beneath her in upbringing. Roger is aware that

Mildred thinks he is "coarse and rough," and "a country lout," but he vows to prove otherwise.[8]

In this novel, the young lady actively dislikes the man destined to rescue her. Contrary to the general pattern that places the rescue from a dilemma at the end of the novel, Roe puts it here in the middle of the novel because Roger must not only prove his dependability, competence and wisdom but he must also break down Mildred's resistance to him as a man.

Mildred's dilemma is increased when she is falsely accused of stealing and is arrested. As she is taken to jail, she looks back "hoping, for the first time in her life, that Roger Atwood was near.... She now did justice to his sturdy loyalty" (p. 341). In jail, she is so desperate that she vows, "If he can clear my name... if he will rescue my loved ones... I will make any sacrifice that he will ask. I will be his loyal wife" (p. 343). Roger tracks down the true story—another girl was the thief—and Mildred is freed.

Mildred's mother urges her to accept Roger. "Roger is not, and never will be, a weak man" (p. 372). Mildred is aware of Roger's sterling character; in fact, when he offers to send her father to a sanitarium, she is stunned. Now he is "the man who had saved her from prison and from shame—far more: the man who was ready to give all he had to rescue her fallen father" (p. 382).

But, in spite of her new appreciation of Roger and in spite of her gratitude, Mildred cannot feel real love for him; she cannot marry him. She continues to battle poverty alone. Most of her family dies; she is left with the two youngest children and must support them. She decides to study nursing. "I want a career," she tells her pastor (p. 487). Her dilemma—being alone in the world with responsibilities—continues, now partly from her stubbornness in not allowing herself to love Roger. But when Roger is hurt while stopping a runaway carriage and brought to her hospital, her resistance to him crumbles:

> "Roger... I am a weak, loving woman. I love you with my whole heart and soul, and if you should not recover, you will blot the sun out of my sky. I now know what you are to me. I knew it the moment I saw your unconscious face" (p. 519).

What is interesting in this novel is that Roger rescues Mildred from a dilemma to establish his dependability and

strength, but he must also rescue someone from physical danger to excite her feminine emotions and wipe out her consciousness of the differences in their backgrounds. Roe apparently believed that a young woman would not be swayed to love by anything but a display of masculine muscle.

A novel with a plot completely structured around the rescue from a dilemma is James Oliver Curwood's *God's Country and the Woman* (1914). In the arctic north, six hundred miles from civilization, trapper Philip Weyman meets a beautiful girl dining alone in the wilderness. As if the meeting were not strange enough (she is using a tablecloth and serving canned lobster and boiled tongue), Josephine Adare immediately asks Philip to rescue her. "You would do a great deal for me? A great deal—and like—a man?"[9] When he assures her that he would, Josephine goes on, "And when you had done this, you would be willing to go away, to promise never to see me again, to ask no reward?" (p. 21). He promises to ask for no reward, although he is already inwardly assuring himself that she will be his if he helps her. She refuses to actually explain what her dilemma is. He must do what she tells him without knowing why:

> "I cannot tell you what my trouble is. You will never know.... If you fight for me, it must be in the dark. You will not know why you are doing the things I ask you to do.... Your one reward will be the knowledge that you have fought for a woman, and that you have saved her" (p. 33).

Since Philip is already in love with her (it took only two paragraphs), he agrees to ask no questions. Josephine wants him to return to her home and act as her husband. Her dilemma lies in her attempt to conceal the fact that her mother has given birth to a baby during her father's absence. Josephine is an independent, fearless young lady; she has concocted an elaborate plan to handle this problem; she deals forcefully with unsavory trappers and Indians; she conceals the truth from her father and directs her mother's actions. Certainly she is no fragile weakling. But she needs a man.

By the end of the novel, Philip has dealt with increasing complications, fought off renegades trying to blackmail Josephine, foiled her abduction, and burned the evidence against her mother. "Sweetheart, there is nothing more for me

to know.... I will tell Father George that it has been your desire to have a second marriage ceremony performed by him.... Are you ready, dear?" (p. 346). Although Josephine has admitted earlier that she loves Philip, she has steadfastly insisted that she will not marry him. When her dilemma has been solved by this man who has done much more than she originally asked of him, she capitulates to the inevitable. "You may call him in, Philip. I guess—I've got to be—your wife" (p. 347). The curious tone she uses to agree to the marriage is probably meant to indicate not her reluctance, but her realization of the inevitability of that union.

Although Curwood was a writer of manly adventure stories, the rescue from a dilemma appears more often in domestic novels or novels about social issues. Harold Bell Wright includes the rescue from a dilemma in his first novel, *That Printer of Udell's* (1903), and in his extraordinarily successful *The Winning of Barbara Worth*. In both books, Wright uses the rescue to stress not only the capability of the man, but also his moral integrity in a world of uncertain moral values.

In *That Printer of Udell's*, Dick Falkner is not on either the same social level or the same moral level as Amy Goodrich, daughter of a prominent merchant:

> Dick's heart ached as he thought of his own life and the awful barrier between them; not the barrier of social position or wealth; that he knew, could be overcome; but the barrier he had builded himself, in the reckless, wasted years.[10]

Dick makes up for his wasted years by becoming a solid citizen, diligent worker, and active Christian. Unfortunately, as Dick's moral character improves, Amy's degenerates. She develops a love of frivolity. Finally, she quarrels with her father and defiantly runs away from home in the company of a man. When the man makes immoral advances, she leaves him; but now she is alone in the big city (Cleveland). She is friendless and starving, finally ending up in a brothel. Amy is in this desperate position because she cannot find work and cannot take care of herself in the city. She discovers her utter helplessness.

Dick has been searching all this time for her. On her first

night in the brothel (before she actually engages in any work), a Salvation Army group comes to sing in the lobby. Amy sees Dick in the group and faints. " 'O God!' the young soldier who had prayed last, sprang forward" (p. 379).

Dick takes her out of the brothel and arranges for her to live with a farm family while she rebuilds her shattered health and her shattered moral values. The question at this point is not whether Amy will accept Dick, but whether Dick can overlook Amy's moral fall:

> He was forced to confess, in his own heart, that he loved her yet, in spite of the fact that their positions were reversed; that he was an honored gentleman, respected and trusted by all, while she, in the eyes of the world, was a fallen woman with no friend but himself (p. 385).

The rescue proves that Amy needs guidance. She knows that she needs to be taken care of. "Won't you tell me what is best to do? I have thought and thought, but can get no farther than I am now" (p. 417). There is certainly nothing left of any independence now. Dick is the man to do her thinking for her. When he proposes, her response is tinged with relief. "Oh Dick, I do love you. Help me to be strong and true and worthy of your love. I—I—have no one in all the world but you" (p. 428).

In this novel, Wright uses the basic pattern of the rescue from a dilemma. Amy's dilemma comes at least partly from her willful actions and from her thinking that she could handle her own life. The dilemma is serious. Dick's rescue proves he has the moral strength to guide her through life and that he has the moral strength to overlook her sins. By the end of the novel, the relationship has been placed in the traditional pattern of male dominance and female submission.

In Wright's other novel, *The Winning of Barbara Worth*, Willard Holmes rescues Barbara's father from a dilemma. This twist to the pattern probably parallels the late nineteenth century variation in the pattern of the rescue from physical danger when the man rescues a male relative of the young lady to resolve ideological conflict. In this case, the ideological conflict is between Eastern capitalist exploitation and honest Western development. Willard, an engineer for the Eastern company that is only interested in squeezing profit out of Colorado, at first supports the company efforts to bilk

Jefferson Worth. But as he falls in love with Worth's daughter Barbara, Willard realizes that he will need to show that he has the Western attributes of honesty, strength and integrity and that he has rejected the immoral capitalist goal of wealth at any cost before he will be worthy of her.

When Worth is threatened with ruin if he cannot get the payroll to his men, Willard joins Abe Lee in a desperate ride to bring the payroll. They fight off an ambush, but Lee is wounded and must stay behind in the desert while Willard continues the desperate ride. Although he is rescuing Worth from a dilemma, there is no doubt that Barbara is the focus of the rescue effort: "The steady rhythm of his horse's feet seemed to beat out the word: 'Barbara! Barbara! Barbara!' " (p. 416). Willard arrives just in time to prevent a riot, "his face haggard and drawn with pain," and slips off his horse at Barbara's feet (p. 431). He has proved that he possesses the qualities deemed important in the Western society of this novel and that he is a proper match for the spunky Western heroine. "It is my desert now; mine as well as yours," he tells her. "Oh, Barbara! Barbara! I have learned the language of your land. Must I leave it now? Won't you tell me to stay?" (p. 509).

Although Barbara herself does not get into a dilemma or express radical ideas, she is representative of the new dynamic heroine. Cawelti calls her "vigorous" with "purity and moral worth" and "courage."[11] She does go to the engineering sites with her father; she does live in primitive conditions amid constant danger of riot, flood or some other natural disaster; she does articulate the Western values. The man who wins her must prove his ability to guide her life based on her values.

The rescue from a dilemma functions in all these novels as a way to deal with the new independent heroine and the threat that she represents to traditional roles. There is a measure of relief expressed in the novels when the dilemma is resolved and the heroine can fill the traditional role as a wife to a suitable, respectable man. Since the popular heroine had begun to have independent opinions and since she no longer screamed and fainted at absolutely every crisis, the writers emphasized qualities in the hero other than physical strength. That this rescue convention is a way to conquer what appears to be a threat to stability offered by the new heroine can be seen through two major writers who use the rescue from a dilemma

specifically as a way to emphasize the inherent helplessness of woman regardless of any new opinions she might be expressing.

It is interesting that George Washington Cable, a Southerner, was able to allow his heroine some independent thought without downgrading her capacity as a woman. William Dean Howells, the Northern realist, presents a very dim view of woman's intellectual independence in *Dr. Breen's Practice* (1881). Dr. Grace Breen is a practicing physician, but Howells makes it clear that she does not have the true feminist radical philosophy. "She would not entertain the vanity that she was serving what is called the cause of women."[12] In an early discussion with her mother, Grace remarks, "A woman is reminded of her insufficiency to herself every hour of the day. And it's always a man that comes to her help" (p. 43). With this attitude, it is no wonder that Grace is shortly asking a male doctor to advise her about a case she doesn't know how to handle.

Dr. Rufus Mulbridge is intelligent, "incredibly gentle and soft... perfectly kind," and an excellent physician (p. 107). Grace's patient has a dangerous case of pneumonia, and Dr. Mulbridge pulls her through when Grace does not know what to do. In saving the patient, of course, he has saved Grace from her problem of being unable to handle the case. As a result of this rescue by Dr. Mulbridge, Grace decides to give up medicine because she feels inadequate for the profession. And, certainly, there is no more indecisive heroine in all fiction than Grace Breen as presented by Howells. At this point in the rescue convention, she should realize that Mulbridge is the man to guide her through life and perhaps help her in her work. In fact, when he proposes, he puts their relationship in those very terms. "I mean that I ask you to let me help you carry out your plan of life, and to save all you have done, and all you have hoped, from waste—as your husband" (p. 225). He explains: "You can't do anything by yourself, but we could do anything together" (p. 228).

Grace refuses his offer. She doesn't love him. She tells her mother that "The waste that I lament is the years I spent in working myself to an undertaking I was never fit for.... I like pleasure and I like dress; I like pretty things" (p. 234).

She promptly becomes engaged to Walter Libby, a nice

young man who owns several New England mills. "Oh," she tells him, "*nothing* is easy that men have to do!" (p. 249). Howells comments: "There are moments of extreme concession, of magnanimous admission, that come but once in a lifetime" (p. 249). Howells is using the convention of the rescue from a dilemma to create a rather devastating portrait of a woman trying to fill a man's job. Mulbridge here is offering the kind of marriage that a new woman ought to see as advantageous. But Grace opts for love and pretty things, just as, Howells implies, all women would. She needs to be rescued to realize her mistake in attempting to work in a man's field, but then she marries Walter, something that she could have done without any rescue situation if she had only had the sense not to stray out of her element in the first place.

Another elite writer who alters the pattern of the rescue from a dilemma is Henry James. In *The Bostonians* (1886), the dilemma that Verena Tarrent faces is the conflict between feminism and love. Added to the problem is the atmosphere of lesbianism that permeates the feminist movement in which Verena is the star speaker. Much of the novel deals with the struggle for Verena's affections between Olive Chanchellor, "unmarried by every implication of her being,"[13] and Basil Ransom, a "striking young man, with his superior beard, his sedentary shoulders, his expression of bright grimness and hard enthusiasm" (p. 5).

Verena's dilemma is that on the one hand she is crucial to the feminist movement and on the other, "she loved, she was in love—she felt it in every throb of her being" (p. 396). The larger dilemma that the reader sees is the struggle between natural and unnatural passions. Ransom is a Southerner with traditional views:

> He was addicted with the ladies to the old forms of address and of gallantry.... This boldness did not prevent him from thinking that women were essentially inferior to men, and infinitely tiresome.... He had the most definite notions about their place in nature, in society... (p. 197).

Olive wishes to devour Verena, to keep her from men such as Ransom:

> Olive wished more and more to extract some definite pledge from

> her; she could hardly say what it had best be as yet; she only felt
> that it must be something that would have an absolute sanctity
> for Verena and would bind them together for life (p. 113).

Verena's dilemma ends when Ransom arrives shortly before
she is to lecture and sweeps her away. But the novel ends with
James' ironic prediction:

> But though she was glad, he presently discovered that, beneath
> her hood, she was in tears. It is to be feared that with the union, so
> far from brilliant, into which she was about to enter, these were
> not the last she was destined to shed (p. 464).

James uses the pattern of the rescue from a dilemma but then
destroys the reader's confidence in the results. And Verena,
like Grace Breen, is swept away by love and acts finally in the
traditional female way, her feminist principles and the
importance of the movement slipping away. Howells presents
this reversion to traditional roles as good, but James, in this
novel about the feminist movement, seems to indicate that
there is peril in both the traditional and nontraditional roles.
Verena is not yet sufficiently independent to make reasoned
decisions about her life. She enters the feminist movement
because Olive dictates to her and exerts a powerful influence.
Then she yields to her feminine instincts, which are betraying
her into more misery.

It is probably not surprising that two male writers with
frankly feminist heroines are very hard on the value and
efficacy of the radical position. But the two female writers,
Atherton and Deland, with feminist heroines are equally hard
on the feminist principles. Deland is writing nearly thirty-five
years after Howells, and her view of feminine independence
remains much the same as his. The rescue from a dilemma in
all the novels, including those novels with less completely
feminist heroines, always proves that the woman needs male
protection and guidance. Since the rescue from physical
danger has been proving the inevitability of male dominance
since the beginning of the nineteenth century and since the
rescue from a dilemma continues to prove this inevitability,
even in the face of women's move for more independence and
intellectual respect, we must conclude that the traditional male
and female roles held an unchangeable value for the readers
throughout this long period.

One interesting point in the novels is that no one expects the rescue to take place more than the women themselves do. "Oh!" cries Grace Breen to Dr. Mulbridge, "surely you won't refuse to take the case!" (*Dr. Breen's Practice*, p. 102). When Verena is swept away by Basil Ransom at the moment she is to address a crowd of people, she tells her mother, "Mother, dearest, it's all for the best, I can't help it... let me go, let me go" (*The Bostonians*, p.461). When Fred is arrested, she immediately demands the right to telephone Arthur Weston. When Patience Sparhawk is arrested, she at once longs for "the strong arm and the strong soul of a man" (p. 394). Curwood's heroine, Josephine Adare, asks the first likely man she meets for help and says his reward will be that he aided a woman. Mildred Jocelyn hopes Roger Atwood will see her being led off to jail and come to her aid. When Amy Goodrich lapses into delirium, she calls for Dick to save her. And, of course, Cable's heroine, Aurora, plots from the beginning of the book to secure her own rescue.

This turning to men for rescue—it is presented as instinctual—effectively undercuts the image of women's independence and puts the heroine at once into the traditional female position. The rescue from a dilemma certainly appears to be a direct affirmation of the social value of marriage and the rightness of female submissiveness and male dominance. Dr. Mulbridge, the only man who offers marriage as a partnership for career and home, is rejected. In all the marriages, the man will be dominant. But these women who are entering a submissive position when they marry are still active, vital women. What do they do after they marry? There are not many specific answers in the novels, but we have a few hints. When Amy tearfully begs Dick to tell her what to do with her life, he advises her to do church work. "Write your father and tell him of your desire; that you cannot be content as a useless woman of society.... You will find many ways to be of use to others" (p. 418).

Grace Breen, who abandoned medicine in a wave of self-doubt, begins to volunteer her services to the children of her husband's mill hands. She does this work at her husband's suggestion: "She was not happy, indeed, in any of the aesthetic dissipations into which she had plunged, and it was doubtless from a shrewder knowledge of her nature that she had herself

that her husband had proposed this active usefulness" (p. 270).

When Fred agrees to marry Arthur Weston, she says she doesn't think she could be like Laura and let her husband and children surround her. Arthur "smiled in spite of himself. 'Nature is a pretty big thing, Fred; when you hold your own child in your arms—,' he stopped short. 'Life is bigger than theories' " (p. 285). The activities the women seem destined to fill their lives with remain within the traditional bounds— charity work and domestic duties. It is probably also significant that the husbands have to suggest these activities. Just as they have to rescue the women from their dilemmas, so, too, they must advise them even in such standard feminine pursuits as charity work and domestic life.

Although the rescues in the novels affirm traditional marriage, the hero in the rescue from a dilemma is given some special qualities to make him worthy of the woman who possesses intellect, spirit and moral strength. The men in this rescue pattern, more than in the rescue from physical danger, offer established wealth and social position, absolute dependability and security from all of life's dangers. In addition, they appreciate the unique qualities of the women they are about to marry. It is not the woman's frailty that appeals to them, but the spirit that she demonstrates by trying (futilely, of course) to make her way independently. Arthur Weston very much admires Fred's honesty and intelligence. She never bores him. Both Patience Sparhawk and Mildred Jocelyn work very hard to earn a living, and both excite the admiration of men when they do so. The heroines in Cable's and Curwood's novels pit their wits against men and win. And it is Verena's magnetic presence while speaking that captivates Basil Ransom.

The heroes in Atherton's, Deland's and Curwood's novels are considerably older than the young women, a fact which adds to their images of stability and which emphasizes that the heroines need an experienced hand at the helm. All the men are successful. Garan Bourke is a distinguished lawyer; Arthur Weston, a respected trustee of large estates; and Philip Weyland has proved successful in the frozen north as a trapper. By the time Mildred realizes she loves Roger Atwood, he is a wealthy lawyer. Grace Breen does not marry the man who rescues her, but the man she does marry owns prosperous mills

and takes her on a European tour as soon as they are wed. Honoré Grandissime is from one of the finest families in New Orleans and is very wealthy. Willard Holmes is an engineer with a wealthy background. Wright's other hero, Dick Falkner, has been elected to Congress as the novel ends. Only Basil Ransom lacks a base of stability and financial success—a lack which underscores James' ominous warning about Verena's future.

It is the hero's ability to handle the crisis that emphasizes his natural dominance over the heroine. However intelligent the heroine may be, it is the hero's skills and intellect that settle the problem. And again, as does the rescue from physical danger, the rescue from a dilemma shows the ideal view of male-female relationships: There is a man capable of caring for every woman; she has only to wait for him to appear. The rescue convention shows the idealistic belief that when a woman is in crisis, the right man will step forward to save her. If it is true that a man with all the proper qualities will appear, then clearly it is also true that there is no need for feminism.

When Patience Sparhawk says, "I refuse to admit that any human being has the right to control me," she adds at once, "When a man and woman are properly married, there is no question of authority or disobedience" (p. 327). Garan Bourke satisfies her imagination, "and he was the first man that ever had" (p. 414). These dynamic heroines need extraordinary men. But the rescue convention shows that these extraordinary men exist. The ideal marriage state requires complete affinity between man and woman—an affinity which is demonstrated by the rescue.

Marriage, believes Arthur Weston, is the "universal panacea" (The Rising Tide, p. 34). This statement in a novel aimed at women, written by a woman some seventy years after Margaret Fuller's document on feminism, seems to indicate rather decisively that, for readers of popular novels up to World War I, nothing much had really changed in what were desirable roles for men and women.

Chapter V

Woman Rescues Man

When a man rescues a woman in popular literature, whether from a physical danger or from a dilemma, the reward for his bravery or his wisdom is the woman he has just rescued—a prize. In fact, nearly all rescue situations provide the rescuer with some reward, tangible or intangible. Since the two major rescue conventions involving the male rescuing the female affirm traditional male dominance and female submission, a strong sense of divine inevitability pervades the novel's conclusion as the man and woman enter matrimony.

But what happens if the woman rescues the man? A quick answer is nothing very good. The popularity of the situation of the man rescuing the woman from either a physical danger or a dilemma would seem to indicate that a rescue pattern reversing the roles would simply add more useful plot variations to the patterns of the popular novel. Instead, however, the structure of the rescue when the woman aids the man becomes disjointed. The lack of structure probably reflects the uncertainty such a role reversal would cause in a society that stresses the values inherent in the convention of the man rescuing the woman.

The pattern of the rescue of a male by a female is consistent only when an Indian maiden saves a white man. When the rescuer is a white woman, the pattern for the convention becomes confused, and the purpose of the convention in the plot becomes vague. The convention no longer fits the plot of the novel in any effective way. This rescue pattern then, lacking a strong structure, fails to provide any sense of continuity in plot development or add any meaning to the novel's conclusion. Unlike the rescue of the woman by the man—which is integral to the overall plot and the conclusion—the rescue of a man by a woman is usually an odd insertion into the plot.

The convention then fails to substantiate the overall implicit value in all rescue conventions which is that there is

reward in the present for good deeds. The woman who rescues a man generally gets no reward. Her action has no decisive effect on any possible marriage and reflects no sense of clear social value in the rescue effort. Since it does not support the overall ideal of sexual relationships expressed in the situations of the male rescuing the female, the rescue of a man by a woman flounders in trying to reflect any other ideal values.

In this rescue situation, a woman saves a man from threatening death or disaster. She acts bravely and decisively, just as a man does in the other rescue situations. But there the resemblance ends. The woman's display of bravery is not rewarded. It is often not much appreciated. Moreover, examples of a woman rescuing a man from a dilemma seem to be extremely rare, if they exist at all. That situation requires the rescuer to be wiser than the rescued party. Presumably, a woman in popular fiction may be as brave as a man, but she is never smarter than a man, so it would be impossible for her to rescue him from a dilemma. With these problems in structure and purpose, the convention of the rescue of a male by a female seems a waste of time, and one would expect that popular writers would never have attempted to use it. But the convention appears with some frequency during the period of this study. It is, however, often so loosely integrated into the plot of the novel, so uncertain in its purpose and so apparently lacking in social value that the very ambiguity in the convention may tell us something about the social attitudes of the readers.

The most clearcut pattern in this rescue convention appears when an Indian maiden rescues a white man. The source of this pattern lies in the myth of Pocahontas. Leslie Fiedler explains the myth of Pocahontas as one of four which formed a view of the West as a region where white American males fled to escape civilization:

> The first [myth] is The Myth of Love in the Woods or the story of Pocahontas and Captain John Smith, which presumably occurred in 1607.... Most Americans do not know the story, however, even in the version of 1624, but only as recast by the sentimental imagination of the early nineteenth century, to which period the myth, therefore, effectively belongs.[1]

Fiedler goes on to say that the Pocahontas legend appealed particularly to popular writers:

> The Pocahontas legend, despite its connection with the American West, is one which left untouched the imagination of our classical writers; it moved chiefly the producers of popular entertainment in prose and verse, between covers and on the stage, from the close of the eighteenth century to the verge of our own time.[2]

Pocahontas, as a character, has appeared in countless fictional narratives, and it is fairly obvious that most of the lovely daughters of Indian chiefs in American fiction derive directly from her image. But Pocahontas herself was rewarded for her actions. She was properly married to an Englishman and presented at the court of King James. The fictional pattern based on Pocahontas does not include a reward. The popular writers were faced with what Fiedler terms "the bugaboo of miscegenation" which terrified Americans.[3] The popular writers, then, had the peculiar writing problem of using the framework of a popular legend with a built-in rescue situation but being unable to conclude the situation in any satisfactory way because of a very strong social taboo against miscegenation. The answer most writers turned to was death for the Indian maiden.

Susanna Rowson, one of the earliest of American novelists, used the Indian maiden and the rescue in her 1798 novel *Reuben and Rachel or Tales of Old Times*. The plot of this rambling tale goes from the fifteenth century in Wales to the eighteenth century in America. Reuben Dudley (whose father was part Indian) has been raised and educated in England. Orphaned and poor, Reuben comes to America in search of the American estates that would be his inheritance. He is captured by Indians. While a captive, he is asked to teach white culture to the lovely Eumea, the daughter of the chief.

The teaching activity goes on for five months until the Indians decide to kill Reuben. Eumea warns him. "Englishman, awake, get up; death and danger are at hand."[4] She spirits him out of the camp. Once past the guards, she "threw her arms around the neck of Reuben, bathed his cheek with her tears, pressed her cold trembling lips to his, and sobbing Adieu! returned to her restless bed to weep and pray for

his safety" (II, p. 347). Reuben flees through the woods but falls ill of a fever. Fortunately for him, Eumea was unable to control her emotions and has followed him. "Is it strange that I should follow you;... was it possible that Eumea could stay behind you and live.... I will follow you, my dear instructor, I will be your handmaid, and love and serve you to the last hour of my life" (II, p. 347).

She nurses him through his illness and leads him to safety. Eumea has saved the man from certain death. When they reach civilization, Reuben locates his inheritance and promptly weds Jessy Oliver, an English girl. Understandably, Eumea is upset. Looking wild and in a broken voice, she tells him, "Eumea will rest no more, know peace no more. I had raised a deity of my own, built an altar in my bosom, and daily offered the sacrifice of a fond, an affectionate heart.... Farewell, do not quite forget the poor, poor Eumea" (II, p. 360). She then drowns herself in the pond. Although Reuben does have Indian ancestry, he never entertains any romantic thoughts toward Eumea. Here, the miscegenation taboo seems somewhat linked to the degree of civilization the Indian may have. Reuben is, for all practical purposes, an Englishman. Eumea is a savage. In spite of her dying plea, Reuben probably will forget her immediately. The episode, while it possesses some sentimental appeal, has no significance in the plot of the novel.

Another Indian maiden driven to suicide appears in E.D.E.N. Southworth's *The Three Beauties, or Shannondale* (1851). Southworth was a lady who knew what the public wanted. As late as 1930, Street & Smith had ninety of her books in print.[5] This novel was a domestic tale set in the Shenandoah Valley. It is a mark of how appealing the Pocahontas legend must have been that Southworth, finding no practical way to get an Indian into her plot, inserted an episode in which an old priest tells the legend of Lover's Leap. In this tale, Englishman Colonel Clinton is thrown by his horse while on a fox hunt. He lands in a forked tree projecting out the side of a precipice. He is rescued from this dangerous position by the fabulously beautiful Indian queen Lulu. "Her form was tall and majestic, but beautifully proportional. A small, but regal head.... Her eyes were large and dark, full of liquid fire, fierce and soft..."[6] The beautiful Lulu rescues Colonel Clinton, sets his broken arm and nurses him back to health. She also falls madly in

love. "She left her Indian crown; she left her glorious heritage of independence, of love, of worship, and of power, and followed like a slave the footsteps of her chosen master" (p. 30). Of course Clinton tires of Lulu. On the day of his marriage to another, Lulu sings her death song, jumps off the cliff and drowns. The only reason Southworth could have had to include this story was that the tale of an Indian maiden rescuing a white man was so popular that including it automatically enhanced the novel's appeal whether or not it enhanced the novel's coherent structure.

The Indian maidens do not seem to be able to judge the quality of the men they fall in love with. Malaeska, the heroine of the first dime novel, *Malaeska; The Indian Wife of the White Hunter*, is married to William Danforth, whom we first meet as he is flirting with a white girl. Later, William's comment to Malaeska about his son reveals his lack of feeling for his Indian family. "It's a pity the little fellow is not quite white" (p. 33). However, when Danforth is being chased by Indians, he is very glad that Malaeska is there to hide him and convince his pursuers that he is not at home.

She saves his life—and is rejected immediately. Since William is being hunted and must leave the territory, she assumes that she will go with him. But William "had never thought of introducing her as his wife among the whites" (p. 38). His pride and his fear of "scorn," "disgrace," and "degradation" cause him to leave her behind. Malaeska bows her head in submission and accepts his decision. She remains faithful in her devotion to this man. Later, when she finds him dying after an Indian skirmish, she comforts him and looks forward to joining him in the great hunting grounds. Malaeska's story continues through painful trials and tribulations. She is rejected by her son when he is young. And, years later as a grown man, he kills himself on learning that she is his mother and that he has Indian blood. Malaeska dies stretched over her son's grave. Stephens calls her "the heartbroken victim of an unnatural marriage" (p. 251). And certainly, Malaeska's whole story is about the awful consequences of marrying outside one's race.

Catherine Sedgwick, sometimes called the first domestic novelist,[7] used the Indian maiden in her novel *Hope Leslie or Early Times in The Massachusetts* (1827). In this novel, fifteen-

year-old Magawisca is working in the Fletcher household as a
servant. Indians attack, led by her father the chief, and capture
the fourteen-year-old Everell Fletcher. In true Pocahontas
fashion, Magawisca comes to the rescue just as Everell is about
to be chopped up by her father. As the chief raises his blade,
Magawisca "screamed 'Forbear!' and interposed her arm."[8]
The blow severs her arm. "Stand back!" she cries, "I have
bought his life with my own. Fly, Everell—fly" (I, p. 136). He
escapes to England.

Seven years pass and Everill returns to America. He does
remember Magawisca and tells his servant, "Yes, Digby, I
might have loved her—might have forgotten that Nature had
put barriers between us" (II, p. 52). The barriers, which are
endlessly discussed in this novel, are race, religion and culture.
Magawisca has never been willing to convert to Christianity;
she is always referred to as a savage. Everell's remark about
the possibility of love is probably more sentimental than
realistic. In any case, now he is in love with his cousin Hope
Leslie.

Everell does repay his rescue when Magawisca is seized
and thrown in jail for being a witch. Everell and Hope contrive
a disguise which enables her to sneak out of prison. Magawisca
slips away in a boat, clutching a locket containing a lock of
Everell's hair. Magawisca fares better than most Indian
maidens since she is alive, even if maimed, and has some
satisfaction in the fact that Everell repaid her rescue by
rescuing her in turn. Few other Indian maids had that
satisfaction.

Two novels by popular writers of masculine adventure
stories imply that the Indian maid's true reward came when
she died to preserve the man's life. Jack London's novel *Smoke
Bellew* (1912) is set in the Klondike. The hero, Smoke Bellew, is
prospecting when he and his partner Shorty are taken captive
by some Indians led by a white man named Snass. Of course,
Snass has a lovely daughter, Labiskwee, whose mother was
French, English and Indian. Labiskwee thinks of herself as
English and tells Smoke over and over that she is white. "I am
English and I will never marry an Indian—would you?"[9] She is
soon in love with him. "I love. We are white, you and I" (p. 348).
Labiskwee takes Smoke's love for granted, and he does not
correct her since she is his only means of freedom.

Shorty escapes, but Smoke is watched too closely to get out

of camp. Happy in her love, Labiskwee still realizes that Smoke wants to go back to the white world. Because she loves him, she rescues him. "I have thought much. The hunger for the world would come upon you, and in the long nights it would devour your heart" (p. 358).

She makes a cache of supplies outside camp and sneaks him past the guards. Then she leads him on the dangerous trail west. Unfortunately, they get lost, and after a month their food runs out. "Smoke and Labiskwee knew their danger. They were lost in the high mountains and they had seen no game" (p. 364). They survive the "white death" because Labiskwee knows they must cover up with furs until the dangerous mist passes. They struggle west without food. Finally, Labiskwee is lying in a stupor, helpless. She is dying. With her last bit of strength, she puts a pouch in Smoke's hand. When he opens it, he finds a "tiny flood of food" (p. 380). She has saved her rations for him. He eats and gets enough strength back to continue on to safety. Labiskwee literally starved herself to rescue him.

A similar situation takes place in Stewart Edward White's *The Silent Places* (1904). White wrote some fifty books—all masculine adventure stories. In this one, Dick Herron and old Sam Bolton are sent out by the Hudson Bay Company to track down and bring in for punishment an Indian who has not paid for his outfit. Before they leave, Dick notices a lovely Indian maiden in the tribe which is trading at the post. Dick pays her some compliments, which mean little to him but which cause May-may-gwan to fall desperately in love with him. When the two men set out on their journey, she trails after them. Dick is furious. "She'd hinder us, and bother us, and get in our way, and we'd have to feed her—we may have to starve ourselves— and she's no damn use to us. She can't go. I won't have it."[10]

The men try threats and pleading, but she will not turn back. She pathetically trails after them, stumbling through the woods, over streams and up mountains. She helps with chores but gets no gratitude from Dick. When Dick breaks his leg, May-may-gwan faithfully cares for him and tends the camp alone for three months while Sam goes off to hunt for food. Without May-may-gwan, the men might not have been able to survive. Sam is grateful, but Dick is not. He remains "profoundly indifferent to the girl" (p. 167). He is really more than indifferent; he is hostile.

May-may-gwan's major rescue effort comes when Dick and Sam have lost the trail of the renegade and have no idea which way to go. Everything seems hopeless. But May-may-gwan goes off with a passing Indian and sleeps with him so he will tell her which way the renegade has gone. When she finds out what the white men need to know, she kills the Indian to cover their trail. Her efforts save them from returning to Hudson Bay post in defeat and also help them establish their own position in the frozen north. Although Sam is grateful, Dick still ignores her. She tells Sam that it is enough "that I am near him... that I can raise my eyes and see him breaking trail" (p. 222).

Finally, in the territory known as the Barren Grounds, they are out of food and starving. Sam is too weak to go on. If they cannot find the renegade in the next day, they will have to give up and try to make it back to the post. Dick pushes blindly forward with the one remaining dog. May-may-gwan totters after him. He beats her; she still follows. He kills a fox and shares it with the dog, ignoring the starving girl; she still follows him. When she collapses in the snow, he leaves her. But a belated attack of conscience sends him back.

Poor May-may-gwan thinks that his return means he loves her. "Oh Jibiwanisi, I am yours, yours, yours! You are mine. Tell me" (p. 284). 'I am yours,' Dick lied steadily; 'my heart is yours, I love you' " (p. 285). She dies happy, promising to wait for him at the border of the "next land." At that moment, the renegade staggers up, snowblind. So the delay occasioned by the Indian maiden's death keeps Dick in the right spot long enough to capture the renegade. He manages to get Sam back to the post, and they are rewarded for their valiant effort. May-may-gwan, who secured their success with her sacrifice, is dead. One more sacrificial Indian maiden—one more unrewarded rescue.

Even a devotee of the Pocahontas legend should be appalled by the truly pathetic story of this girl's devotion and the insensitive treatment she receives from the man she loves. White, however, was extremely popular; the book was a bestseller. So we must assume that the story of the Indian maiden's rescue effort and sacrifice remained as appealing in 1904 as it had been in Rowson's story of 1798.

A book by Basil King (*The Wild Olive*, 1910) contains an

exception to the very rigid pattern of the convention when an Indian maiden is rescuing a white man. In King's novel, Norrie Ford, a fugitive from a death sentence (he is innocent, of course), is fleeing through the Adirondacks when a beautiful girl appears in the woods and beckons to him. She leads him to a remote cabin where she brings him food and conceals him from the posse prowling the area. She refuses to tell him her name or much about herself. He does, however, see "the hint of dark eyes flashing with an eager, non-Caucasian brightness—eyes that drew their fire from a source alien to that of any Aryan race."[11] The beautiful girl does tell him at last that she is the daughter of a Virginian and the wife of a French Canadian. "I believe," she says, "she had a strain of Indian blood" (p. 43). The girl is illegitimate, but her father provided handsomely for her before he died, and now she is very wealthy. Her guardian is Judge Wayne—the man who sentenced Norrie to death.

When the girl decides that the time has come for Norrie to move on, she leads him through the woods to Lake Champlain. She has hidden a boat there filled with provisions. She provides luggage, a ticket on a steamer for Ireland, and a wallet filled with money. She has worked out a route for him to take to Canada, and, furthermore, she provides him with a false identity. She has not only saved him from death but she has given him ample means to start a new life. Norrie is grateful but does remark several times that she is not his type of girl.

Years pass. Norrie travels to Argentina and makes a success in business there. He also becomes engaged to lovely Evelyn Colfax, the niece of his boss. King tells us that all this while the girl Miriam Strange was waiting for Norrie to return. "If he never came, she would rather go on waiting for him— uselessly! Her heart was listening for a call" (pp. 163-64). Miriam and Norrie finally meet again at a society dinner party in New York. Coincidentally, Miriam is an old friend of Evelyn's. When Miriam tries to tell Norrie that nineteen-year-old Evelyn is too young for him (he is thirty-two), he thinks she wants "payment of a long standing debt" (p. 191). Miriam is horrified that he thinks so. She insists that her fears for his marriage are based on Evelyn's immaturity. When Norrie reveals his past and starts an attempt to clear himself, Evelyn sticks by him at first but then can't stand the strain and breaks

the engagement. In the meantime, Miriam rescues Norrie again when she agrees to marry a long-time admirer, Charles Conquest, a brilliant lawyer who promises to defend Norrie if Miriam will marry him. At the end of the novel, when Norrie has been cleared of the old murder charge, he realizes that he loves Miriam. "You'd be committing a sacrilege against yourself—if you married anyone else but me" (p. 326). Conquest, when told the whole story, releases Miriam, and she and Norrie are free to wed.

Miriam is the only Indian woman to be rewarded with the love of the man she rescues. The setting in this novel is not on the frontier, but in the drawing rooms of New York. The time is contemporary. Miriam is Indian only in her ancestry not in her culture. She has money, and King has presented her character as intelligent, morally strong, and respected by everyone. She is definitely not a savage. A jaded reader might wonder if this remarkable woman is getting much of a reward in Norrie, but the readers who put this novel on the bestseller lists of 1910 were not such cynics.

When the rescue convention used an Indian maiden rescuing a white man, readers must have known what to expect. But when a white woman did the rescuing, the convention became less consistent. It was used in a few novels where the hero is socially beneath the heroine. In these cases, the heroine has started out showing very undemocratic feelings about the man's social position. If the heroine is overly conscious of her own social superiority, the reader begins to wonder if she is worthy of the stalwart hero. No matter how important social status may have been, the ideal of social mobility remains rooted in democratic principles, and heroines were not supposed to exhibit undemocratic values.

In Mary Johnston's *To Have and To Hold*, Jocelyn Leigh is being rescued by Ralph Percy, who has married her to protect her from Lord Carnal. Since Jocelyn insists on a marriage in name only and since Ralph must fight off Lord Carnal several times and defy the direct orders of the king, the reader begins to wonder if Jocelyn is worth all this effort. When Ralph is arrested on a charge of piracy and brought before the Virginia governor on trial, Jocelyn proves her worth by rescuing him.

She asks permission to speak and makes an eloquent plea for his release. "A pirate! [We were] prisoner to the pirates, and

out of that danger he plucked safety for us all" (p. 257). To convince the governor, Jocelyn asks Lord Carnal to tell the truth about the incident. He agrees—if she will kiss him. Jocelyn loathes the man, but she makes the sacrifice for Ralph. Ralph is cleared, and the governor apologizes. "Captain Percy, I beg to apologize to you for words that were never meant for a brave and gallant gentleman" (p. 260). Jocelyn's sacrificial gesture to save Ralph convinces the reader that she is indeed worthy of this brave man. Even more important, the rescue proves that she loves him.

The Princess Mary, in Charles Major's *When Knighthood Was in Flower*, must convince the reader that she is worthy of Charles Brandon after she fails to rescue him from the Tower. After Brandon's rescue of Mary, he is clapped into the Tower by King Henry on two charges of murder. Since Brandon killed the man in defense of Mary, she has a clear moral obligation to save him. But Mary is a spoiled princess, who doesn't want the king to know that she was out the night Brandon rescued her. So the reader waits in suspense and Brandon waits in the dungeon while Mary procrastinates. Finally, a loyal friend negotiates Brandon's release. Mary is now in the position, as far as the reader is concerned, of being superior to Brandon socially and inferior to him morally.

She and Brandon elope, but they are intercepted; Brandon goes back to the Tower. This time Mary proves she has a conscience. She pleads with the king, her brother. "Take my life and spare him—spare him!" (p. 296). The sacrifice Henry demands is that she marry aging Louis XII of France. She agrees and so rescues Brandon from the Tower. Now the reader knows that Mary's moral strength is worthy of Brandon, who has risked everything for his love. After Louis dies, Mary and Brandon can marry.

Another lady who must prove her inner worth is Molly Stark Wood, heroine of Owen Wister's *The Virginian*. Molly is descended from one of the finest New England families. "Had she so wished, she could have belonged to any number of those patriotic societies of which our American ears have grown accustomed to hear so much" (p. 90). Molly's character has been formed by pride. Although she seems to love the Virginian, she feels that he is beneath her and is too conscious of their different educational and social backgrounds to accept

him. She is planning to leave Wyoming when, during a ride, she finds the Virginian wounded by Indians. Molly tries desperately to revive him and get him back to safety:

> She tore strips from her dress and soaked them, keeping them cold and wet upon both openings of his wound.... She built another fire.... Meanwhile, she returned to nurse his head and wound.... Then she poured her brandy in the steaming cup, and, made rough by her desperate helplessness, forced some between his lips and teeth.... "Listen, friend," said she. "Nobody shall get you, and nobody shall get me" (pp. 327-29).

She does rescue him. During his convalescence, she realizes how much she loves him. The rescue proves to the reader that Molly is not as heartless as she has seemed and that she does love the Virginian. Her inner worth is greater than her pride.

These three women are proving their moral worth to the reader, not to the hero. The hero is already in love. But until the moment when the woman rescues the hero, the reader has not been certain that she possesses the good character such a man deserves. The women in these novels are also repaying their own earlier rescues by these men.

Another young lady who repays her own rescue is Ray Longstreth in Zane Grey's *The Lone Star Ranger*. Ray had been saved by Buck Duane from a robber's attack. Buck is working under cover for the Texas Rangers, investigating Ray's father, Colonel Longstreth. One night, he is trapped when the Colonel returns unexpectedly to his study. Buck dashes through the house to Ray's room. She conceals him. "They might shoot you before you got away. Stay. If we hear them, you can hide. I'll turn out the light. I'll meet them at the door. You can trust me" (p. 296). When her father knocks at the door, Ray tells him she is going to bed, saving Buck from detection.

Ray's rescue of Buck not only repays her own rescue but also proves that she does not have the criminal inclinations of her father. She has begun to suspect that her father is a criminal, and in concealing Buck, she chooses the morally right position.

These young ladies all marry the men they rescue—but not as a result of that rescue. When the male rescues the female from physical danger or a dilemma, the rescue provides the

impetus to a romance, culminating in marriage. The young woman and her family begin to appreciate the man's superior character, and he is in a position to prove that he is capable of caring for the woman he rescued, that he is the right man for her. The rescue by the female does not work in these ways. The four men rescued in the situations just described are already in love with the women. If there are doubts about the worth of the women, they belong to the reader. Since a woman is never required to be the man's support, there is nothing further to prove there, and no sense of inevitability attends the rescue event. The purpose of the rescue convention here is only to establish the woman's moral character for the reader.

In other novels where the writer uses the convention of the female rescuing the male, the purpose is less clear. Melissa, the mountain girl in John Fox's *The Little Shepherd of Kingdom Come*, rescues Chad twice—once at the beginning of the novel when they are both youngsters in school and once at the end of the novel when they are grown up. In the first episode, Chad is being bullied at school because he is a stranger. Melissa comes to his aid. "You wouldn' dare tech him if one of my brothers was here, an' don't you dare tech him again, Tad Dillon" (p. 39). Her eye "spoke with the fierce authority of the Turner clan and its dominant power for half a century," and the bullies slink away. Chad is grateful although he is too embarrassed to say so. On the way home, he wishes a wild-cat would leap into the road so he could fight it and save her.

The second time Melissa rescues Chad is during the Civil War while Chad is with the Union forces. Melissa in the mountains hears that a rebel guerilla is planning to ambush and kill him. During a raging storm, she makes her way down the mountains to Chad's camp to warn him. But she slips away before he can return with the sentry to thank her. As a result of being out in the rain, Melissa gets pneumonia. She did not expect to be rewarded for her rescue because she has always known that Chad can never be hers. Melissa is illegitimate. For a while, Chad thought that he too was illegitimate, but he knew that the question of his birth was not as difficult for him as the question of her birth was for Melissa:

> It came with a shock to Chad one day to realize how little was the tragedy of his life in comparison with the tragedy in hers, and to

learn that the little girl with swift vision had already reached that truth and with sweet unselfishness had reconciled herself. He was a boy—he could go out in the world and conquer it, while her life was as rigid and straight before her as though it ran between close walls of rock as steep and sheer as the cliff across the river (p. 155).

Melissa can gain nothing from her rescues of Chad. Her stigma of illegitimacy bars her future as effectively as their race bars the Indian maidens.

Fox may have included Melissa's rescue effort in his novel for sentimental effect. There seems to be no clear reason for George Barr McCutcheon to use the rescue convention in *Jane Cable* (1906). The hero Graydon Bansemer enlists in the army and goes to the Philippines during the Spanish-American War. While there, he becomes the protector of beautiful refugee Teresa Velasquez. When he is wounded, his love, Jane Cable a volunteer nurse, cares for him. Teresa describes to Jane how she saved Graydon's life while he was grappling with a Filipino. "I seized a pistol that was lying near me and fired; the Filipino fell."[12] Teresa says that she loves Graydon, but because he loves Jane, she is leaving. This rescue situation is only a brief episode in the plot. We do not even see the rescue; Teresa describes it to Jane in a few sentences. The rescue episode really serves no structural purpose in McCutcheon's novel.

The purpose of the rescue of a man by a woman in James McHenry's *The Betrothed of Wyoming* seems to be only a warning that a woman should not rescue a man. Isabella Austin is in love with ruthless Tory John Butler. When he is imprisoned, she deceives the jailer and rescues Butler. Butler, however, shows neither gratitude nor love toward his rescuer. Isabella took a grave risk at the time of the rescue, but her risk is far reaching. The other characters feel sorry for her. Butler ignores her. Finally, Isabella goes insane. She is accidentally killed during a battle—a pathetic mad figure—a woman scorned. The young lovers in this novel are Henry Austin and Agnes Watson whose romance began when Henry rescued Agnes from an Indian attack. Isabella's failure to win love with a rescue while her brother Henry does win love with a rescue probably shows the root of the issue: it is not natural for women to rescue; it *is* natural for men to rescue.

This lack of naturalness made the convention awkward to

handle. Just how awkward it could be is evident in the ridiculous plot of Oliver Wendell Holmes' *A Mortal Antipathy* (1885). In trying to set up the rescue situation as plausible, Holmes introduces the heroine, eighteen-year-old Euthymia Tower, as a dynamo of feminine strength:

> While all her contours and all her movements betrayed a fine muscular development, there was no lack of proportion, and her finely shaped hands and feet showed that her organization was one of those carefully finished masterpieces of nature....[13]

Euthymia handles dumbbells "too heavy for most of the girls" (p. 41). She also performs daring feats on the trapeze and rows on the crew of her college.

The hero of this novel is Maurice Kirkwood who has a special problem. When he was two years old, Maurice was accidentally tossed over a balcony by his lovely seventeen-year-old cousin. The result of this accident is that Maurice has an extreme antipathy to lovely young women. If he is in the presence of a young woman, he has a seizure and faints. Holmes speculates that a rescue by a young woman will counteract the accident caused by a young woman, and Maurice will be cured of his antipathy. In order to set up this situation, Holmes has forced his heroine and hero to switch traditional sexual qualities. The result is that the reader feels disjointed; his expectations are askew. It is difficult to see Maurice as a hero at all.

Maurice gets typhoid fever. While he is recovering, his house catches on fire. He is too weak to flee the flames. "He tried to call for help, but his voice failed him, and died away in a whisper..... he sank back upon the pillow, helpless" (p. 264). Of course, Euthymia dashes into the burning house to rescue him. She picks Maurice up and carries him out "as easily as if he had been a babe" (p. 274). And as Holmes predicted, Maurice is cured of his antipathy. "You must not leave me," he tells Euthymia. "You must never leave me. You saved my life. But you have done more than that..." (p. 282).

It is easy to see why this novel never made the bestseller list. Aside from other ludicrous aspects in structure and development, the hero and heroine do not reflect any of the reader's common expectations for such characters. And while Euthymia has a certain attractive quality in her healthy

animal strength, Maurice, in his helplessness, has no appeal at all. The novel is useful here to show the difficulties writers faced in trying to set up a rescue of the man by the female. The rescue from physical danger with inverted sexual roles not only lacks appeal, but also lacks verisimilitude. The difficulty lay in the writers not being able to fit the situation into the novel's structure so that it was integral in the overall plot and so that it reflected the value system of the novel and that of the readers who would buy the book. The writers who used the convention with the Pocahontas myth had the advantage of using a situation that readers expected to be a passing episode in the life of the hero, not crucial to his future domestic happiness.

The cultural importance of the traditional sexual roles is clear in a novel in which the young lady tries but *fails* in her rescue effort. Robert Montgomery Bird introduces the lovers in *The Hawks of Hawk-Hollow* (1835) when Catherine Loring tries to rescue Hyland Gilbert. Hyland falls out of a tree into the river rushing over a fall. Catherine "did not pause.... she ran down to the rocks that led to the base of the fall and rushed into the water."[14] She grips the body, but he is too heavy and she can't pull him to safety. Fortunately, at that moment a passing stranger jumps in and rescues Hyland.

Catherine fails in her rescue effort, but she, in fact, wins in a way that few of the other women do. Hyland falls in love with her at once. He responds just as the women do when the men succeed in rescuing them. "So heroic!" he says, "instead of committing me to my destiny, with a pathetic scream, to run at once to my assistance, like an angel, rather than a woman!" (I, p. 135). Catherine's heart is right, but her strength is inadequate. She, therefore, fills the proper female role. Hyland adores her. "Such an admirable creature! so gentle, and yet so firm! so frank, yet so modest! so merry, yet so dignified" (I, p. 153). It is simply not woman's role to rescue successfully. In failing, Catherine has proved her womanly qualities, and Hyland loves her for those qualities.

To emphasize doubly the principle being expressed here, Bird sets up a physical rescue for Hyland at the end of the novel. Hyland rescues Catherine from a forced marriage when he interrupts the ceremony in a dramatic fashion and carries her away:

... a young man... rushed into the circle and displayed to the eyes of the bride the features of the younger Gilbert. She uttered a scream... crying with tones as wild and imploring as his own, "Oh,... save me!" and fell into a swoon (II, p. 64).

The implications in the way Bird used both the convention of the female rescuing the male and the convention of the male rescuing the female from physical danger are clear. In failing to rescue, Catherine proves her womanliness. In rescuing, Hyland proves his masculinity. The traditional roles of the two lovers are maintained. The reader is in familiar territory.

The social values reflected in the convention of the female rescuing the male are revealed as much in the awkwardness with which writers used it as in any effectiveness it may have had. As Fiedler said, it is obvious that, appealing as the myth of Pocahontas was, writers could not reward these women with the love of the men they rescued. The rescue situation in general cannot elevate someone above his race and its level in the society. The rescue could not elevate Cooper's Uncas sufficiently to allow him to marry Cora Munro, and it cannot elevate these Indian maidens enough to wed the white men they rescue—even though, like Cooper's Uncas, the maidens are Indian royalty. The only Indian woman to succeed in the way we might expect is Miriam Strange in *The Wild Olive*. And Miriam as a character has virtually nothing in common with the other Indian women.

Of the seven Indian women, one is a queen and four are the daughters of chiefs. Considering the good matrimonial possibilities such young women would have, it is difficult to see exactly what appeal these young men had for them. Five of the seven are indifferent or even cruel to the women. The implication seems to be that any white man is more desirable as a mate than an Indian. And having once loved a white man, the Indian maiden is unable to accept an "inferior" Indian.

Malaeska demonstrates this concept when she refuses to wed a chief. She has returned to her tribe after her son has been taken away by his white grandfather. Her husband is dead, and she is alone. The women of the tribe wish to kill her, but she is saved by a chief. The chief had once loved her and now proposes again. "Malaeska, my wigwam is empty; will you go back?" (p. 140). She refuses because she expects to meet the husband who deserted her in the happy hunting grounds.

Instead of marrying a chief and beginning a new life, Malaeska lives a lonely isolated existence on the edge of white civilization until she dies. And it is noteworthy that Stephens ignored the reward pattern in the chief's rescue of Malaeska to make this point of lifelong devotion to the faithless white man.

None of the Indian maidens is allowed to do the practical thing—shrug off rejection by the ungrateful clod she rescued, find some likely brave, and produce several strapping children. The Indian maidens in the novels of Rowson and Southworth commit suicide when they are rejected. Stephens' heroine pines away. Sedgwick's heroine sails off to a lonely future. When London and White kill off their Indian maidens, they make the women happy to die so that the unworthy objects of their affection can live. White, in fact, stresses May-may-gwan's happiness as she dies hearing Dick say his first kind word to her—a lie.

The two primary social attitudes that seem to be paramount in the rescue of a white man by an Indian maiden are an absolute belief in white supremacy and an appreciation of complete female submission. The figure of the Indian maiden rescuing and serving the white man she loves shows both concepts in bold relief. The sensitivity of the reader of today may be horrified by the picture of May-may-gwan tottering through the snow after the man who ignores her, but obviously, the readers of 1904 did not react that way.

It is easy, too, to sympathize with Melissa in Fox's novel, but she dies as surely as the Indian maidens die. Melissa is illegitimate and would bring the man down socially just as the Indians would. Clearly, a man is not expected to give up any social status for love. These women have the insurmountable barriers of race or birth—romance is not possible.

The situation of the female rescuing the male does reflect some positive democratic values. Although it is good to be a member of the upper class in these novels, it is not acceptable to be too proud of it. The heroines in the novels of Johnston, Major and Wister are too proud. They need to show that they have the right moral instincts and that they truly love the men who have already rescued them. The rescue convention is useful for showing that the woman is capable of an unselfish act and is not really tied to undemocratic views of social levels.

Perhaps the most important social attitude reflected in this

rescue convention is that women must not be too obvious in expressing their love. The Indian maidens are very frank in their affections. May-may-gwan may seem like an extreme case, but the others are equally intense in their devotion. Southworth's Lulu gives up her queen's crown to follow Colonel Clinton, and Rowson's Eumea follows Reuben away from her tribe. None of these maidens is asked to come—each unabashedly follows, pleading for love and affection, offering to serve until she dies.

London's heroine is leading Smoke Bellew to safety, but she is equally obvious in her affections. "Her glances were love glances; every look was a caress" (p. 349). Sedgwick's Magawisca adores Everell. "She had done and suffered much for him, and she felt that his worth must be the sole requital for her sufferings" (II, p. 126). When she sails off, she takes a lock of his hair. Malaeska accepts insult and desertion in "humble submission" and remains loyal to her worthless husband (p. 38).

But it is not only the Indian maidens who display their love too conspicuously. The mountain girl Melissa in Fox's novel is devoted to Chad from childhood on. When Chad thinks of the two girls in his life, he thinks "Melissa was the glow-worm that, when darkness came, would be a watch-fire at his feet—Margaret, the star to which his eyes were lifted day and night" (p. 152). Unlike Melissa, Margaret does not reveal her love for Chad until he first reveals his. When Melissa is dead, Mother Turner tells Chad that Melissa had "fought his battles so fiercely that no one dared attack him in her hearing" (p. 334). The dead girl has preserved his footprint in the mud outside the cabin door, and she died with his name on her lips. Unlike most of the men, Chad feels guilty about not returning Melissa's love. He decides not to go back at once to Margaret in the valley. He "would send Margaret word, and she would understand" (p. 336).

Chad's appreciation of Melissa's emotions is rather exceptional. Most of the men ignore the woman's love or else deliberately reject her. McHenry's Isabella Austin is driven to madness by Butler's rejection and his pursuit of other women. She has no appeal for him once she displays her love. And Teresa Velasquez gives up her love for Graydon saying, "Dios, how I loved him! I would have gone through my whole life with

him!" (*Jane Cable*, p. 256).

Six women do marry the men they rescue. Of those six, the Princess Mary (*When Knighthood Was in Flower*), Jocelyn Leigh (*To Have and To Hold*), Molly Stark Wood (*The Virginian*), and Ray Longstreth (*The Lone Star Ranger*) all know before the rescue takes place that the men love them. Although the reader knows Miriam Strange loves Norrie Ford, Miriam never reveals her affection to Norrie until he first acknowledges his love (*The Wild Olive*). Holmes' heroine, Euthymia, does not meet Maurice until she rescues him, but he had already noticed her—although he could not speak to her because of his antipathy. The social value in these rescues is clear. Men must pursue, and women must wait. And the woman who does not wait loses her appeal.

Women are not rewarded for rescuing men the way men are rewarded for rescuing women. The female rescue does not excite the interest of the male, establish the woman as an appropriate mate, or create a sense of inevitability about the union. The fact that eight of the fifteen women die probably means that the writers, unable to reward them, could only envision death as the next logical step. Indeed, since in the ideal state there is one man for every woman, there is little else to do but die when one's love is not returned.

The rescue effort itself, accompanied by obviously displayed affections, totally demolishes the traditional values of women—weakness, shyness, modesty and helplessness. The rescue then displays none of the qualities that make a woman appealing. Therefore, the ideal of relationships between the sexes is expressed only in the male rescue of the female. The ambiguous use of the rescue convention as applying to women rescuing men shows that the popular writers could find no consistent way to use the situation to structurally reinforce the social values in the novels. What the rescue of the male by the female does seem to prove overwhelmingly is that she shouldn't have done it.

Chapter VI

The Ideal of the Rescue

The rescue convention in popular novels written before World War I always produced excitement and tension. Fiction is littered with rescues from both the dreadful dangers and the petty annoyances of life. The four rescue patterns examined here, however, not only produce excitement and interest but also embody the main elements of the system of social values held by the reading public before World War I. In *The Popular Book*, James D. Hart insisted that the popular writers were those who understood the public's beliefs and were able to incorporate those beliefs into fiction:

> Literary taste is not an isolated phenomenon.... Books flourish when they answer a need and die when they do not.... There are many books whose popularity relates to a most subtle blending of appeals to ...needs of the public. Yet, in some way or another, the popular author is always the one who expresses the people's minds and paraphrases what they consider their private feelings.[1]

Hart felt that the result was "a dynamic interplay of reader, writer, and the times in which both lived."[2] The value of the rescue convention for us lies in what it reflects about those readers, writers and times.

All the rescue patterns embody two major ideals: good actions and rewards. The rescue situation shows that good exists and that it is an active force. The result is reward to the good person who has acted. Although none of the rescuers asks for reward —it is a criterion of goodness that the deed is done for its own sake—all the rescuers get rewarded. The sole exception to this ideal is the woman who rescues a man in a potentially romantic situation. In this exception lie social values that are obviously so crucial that they override the ideal that is present in all other rescue patterns. The reward for most of the rescuers, however, is in the present. This ideal state of good actions and reward in the present reflects the world as the readers wanted to believe it existed.

109

Beyond the ideal state, the four rescue patterns show social values which have varying degrees of importance. The most important social value seems to be rooted in the consciousness of class that filters through all the rescue patterns and the attendant plot situations.

The rescue itself presents moral worth in action, unattached to any considerations of birth or class. The democratic ideal of the self-made man, the rise from obscurity on merit, and the equal possibilities for all who have a decent start in life are all, apparently, the basis for the rescue convention. Yet we see that this democratic ideal is the gloss that covers the rescue pattern. The democratic ideal works well in the rescue of a child. The orphan develops into an exemplary citizen when rescued and given a fair start in the world. Although most of the children are orphans when they are rescued, they do come from varying backgrounds. Patience Sparhawk's mother was a promiscuous drunkard. Barbara Worth's parents were wealthy Easterners. Little Gertrude in *The Lamplighter* has been abandoned in the street. Young Ben Blair sees his mother die while his drunken father berates her. Chad Buford in *The Little Shepherd of Kingdom Come* is a sturdy young mountaineer trying to make his own way. The range of background implied in these examples is important in the overall value being expressed by the rescue of a child. No matter the background, the child, once rescued, is brought up in an atmosphere that nurtures the best qualities he possesses. And the respect and success he attains in adulthood come entirely from his own achievements and merits.

But when marriage enters the picture, the democratic ideal of individual merit begins to weaken. Although the man's rescue of the woman from physical danger opens the doors to a rise in social status, the rescue effort and the man's subsequent success cannot fully overcome a low or questionable birth. Marriage is simply too intimate a connection. The popular writers fell back on the convention of the revelation of upper class birth or true identity in order to avoid actually allowing a lower class character to marry an upper class character. It seems obvious that, while readers supported the democratic principle of individual worth, when it came to marriage, they wanted the traditional reassurance of good birth. Fox's *The Little Shepherd of Kingdom Come* shows this split in the ideal.

The orphan Chad attains a high degree of respect and admiration based on his own attributes of courage, integrity, intelligence, moral character and honesty. But when Chad falls in love with the plantation owner's daughter, Fox has to clear up the question of his birth before the romance can continue.

The act of rescue cannot elevate the young man far enough to wed the rich young lady. The consciousness of social class is heightened when the potential romantic situation involves someone who is not white. Blacks and Orientals do not usually appear as major characters in the novels. So the race question centers on the Indian. The American Indian, as noble savage, presented fictional possibilities for excitement and pathos that popular writers could not overlook. But when the noble Indian appears in a rescue situation with romantic possibilities, there are problems. Since most Indians are in novels with frontier settings, the race question is compounded by the problem of radically different cultures. No matter how noble, the savage remains a savage. The Indian maidens have the double handicap of being savage and of failing to comply with traditional female reticence. They are punished on both counts. The fact that death for the Indian was most often chosen by the writer as the solution to the romantic problem may well reflect the final answer to the Indian problem that was being acted out in nineteenth-century America.

The issue of religious differences between the man and the woman usually does not appear. In some cases, the man or woman must give up godless ways and accept the path of Christianity before the marriage can take place. St. Elmo has to give up his life of dissipation before Edna Earl will marry him. Christine Ludolph must accept God before she is worthy of Dennis Fleet (*Barriers Burned Away*). But the romantic problem of the Christian and the Jew or the Protestant and the Catholic was not a situation popular writers were interested in. The absence of such a problem in the romantic plots probably means that for the public it was unthinkable that such a problem would arise.

The popular novelists saw no difficulty in matches with foreigners—the foreigners were always titled. The novels firmly support the value of a definite social hierarchy. The relief expressed when birth or identity was revealed shows how

pressing an issue social class was when linked with marriage. No one is more relieved than Beverly when the goatherder she has agreed to marry turns out to be Prince Dantan (*Beverly of Graustark*). For Americans before World War I, the democratic ideals mingled strangely with a traditional belief in the values of social class. When marriage was involved, class became the deciding factor.

The second important reflection of social values comes in the traditional sexual roles, supported strongly in these popular novels. The rescue patterns in which the reward is present are the man's rescue of the female from physical danger or from a dilemma. The overwhelming value expressed in these patterns is that man must be dominant and woman must be submissive. These roles will lead to happiness. A violation of these roles, as when the woman acts aggressively and reveals her love (when she rescues a man), will lead to unhappiness. In the rescue from a dilemma, even the most feminist heroines realize the rightness of the traditional roles. When Patience Sparhawk is in deep trouble, she yearns for "the strong arm and the strong soul of a man" (p. 394). Every woman in popular fiction longs for a strong man to guide her, and every man looks for a helpless woman he can protect and care for. The late nineteenth-century novels with independent heroines allowed some exploration of woman's position, but the rescue pattern cleared the way for the solid social value of male dominance and female submission. The man's reward for rescue was the woman. The woman who rescued got no reward. The message is plain.

The two rescue patterns in which men rescue women also reveal attitudes about age and accomplishment. The rescue of a female from physical danger always is performed by a young man. The rescue from a dilemma usually is handled by an older man. There are obvious practical considerations in this division. It is not as easy for a forty-five-year-old to stop a runaway carriage as for a twenty-year-old. But the implication in this division is in what society expects at a certain age. The rescue from physical danger generally opens the way to romance. What the man must do next is start his upward climb to financial success. He has used his brute strength; now he must use his head. But the rescue from a dilemma relies on wisdom and stability in the rescuer. This man is at an age

when society expects that he has developed these qualities. He no longer needs brute strength.

These two men symbolize the process of success. A man begins to make his way in the world through his natural physical strength, and he is regarded as successful when he can handle his affairs with his brains. Only the writers of male adventure stories continued to stress physical strength in the older man.

The degree of possible financial success was considerable. Men worked their way up to wealth and professional positions. They did not settle for mediocre jobs and modest income. The men who rescued women from dilemmas were usually quite wealthy. The ideal state lay in great wealth and a powerful position.

It is noteworthy, too, that although the older man is considered a candidate for romance, there are few older women in the romantic arena. A man's value increases with age and mounting financial success. A woman's value fades with age. All the May-December unions are presented as advantageous to both parties. The young woman gets substantial security. The older man gets renewed vigor in his empty life. The social attitude toward marriage, then, was that marriage was an exchange. In spite of all the romantic trappings that might attend the event, the men brought financial security and the women provided beauty and charm.

The consciousness of class and the consciousness of correct male and female roles are the two paramount social values shown in these rescue patterns. There are, however, several other social values distinctively presented. One is the value of hard work. The rescued children work hard when they grow up. In the rescue from physical danger, the young man works hard to prove that he can support the young woman he has already proved he can protect.

Hard work is a positive value to the society. It is also a positive value to the person working. In these novels, hard work brings success. No one toils hopelessly—unless he has terrible moral lapses that drag him down. The rescue situation provides the opportunity, and the hard work brings the success. A good moral life will support the person through hard times or hard work. While Dennis Fleet toils night and day to get ahead, he staunchly resists the allure of alcohol (*Barriers*

Burned Away).

Along with hard work, education is a definite value. One of the major benefits the orphan receives when he is rescued is the chance for a good education. Although Huck Finn may not have appreciated the values implicit in education, the other orphans did. A great part of the future success is based on the education that opened the doors. The young ladies who become renowned authors all have to have the educational opportunities necessary to expand their perceptions of the world. Edna Earl spends most of her time studying in the library and emerges as a religious scholar of international repute (*St. Elmo*). It was through education that the American ideal of the self-made man could be reached.

Other definite social values lay in service to the community. Men were expected to serve their country. Most heroes either were just out of the military, were about to enter the military, or had been in the military for a time. Along with military service, heroes were expected to fight corruption in business. This corruption was a social problem that gained attention in fiction after the Civil War. Wright's novel *The Winning of Barbara Worth* concentrates on corruption as represented by Eastern capitalists. The hero must reject and fight these forces before he is worthy of the heroine.

And in all the rescuers and all the children who are rescued is manifested the attribute of courage. The act of rescue, with its accompanying risks, requires courage. Even more, the future activities of these characters require courage—physical and moral. Chad Buford joins the Union Army because of his moral convictions (*The Little Shepherd of Kingdom Come*). When he becomes a lawyer, Ishmael Worth refuses to take a case if his client is not truly innocent.

The rescue itself brings out the finest qualities of mankind. The fictional patterns in the novels supported a network of social values that gave substance and purpose to the readers' lives. The value of past popular literature lies in its ability to give us a window to the past so that we can see those values of daily life as well as the hopes and dreams of people in another time. John Cawelti bases his belief in the importance of popular fiction on those very grounds:

> It may be that, when he most powerfully embodies the thoughts

and feelings unique to a particular period, the artist is, at the same time, creating something that, by virtue of its special relation to its own times, cannot attain more than an ephemeral place in the history of culture. The ability to express the spirit of the moment may not be as important an artistic characteristic as the appeal to universal human concerns in a lasting way; nonetheless, I have come to believe... that this is a distinctive kind of artistry worth studying in its own right.[3]

Leslie Fiedler, discussing the bestselling epic of the nineteenth century, *Song of Hiawatha,* warns that "a nation which expurgates from its anthologies those great bad poems it has loved... is a nation with only half a memory."[4]

The popular novel shows us the spirit of the moment. And it is apparent that the rescue convention is a major component in those novels. The rescue could be used to express both the ideal values and the actual values of the times. For these reasons alone, the rescue convention would be prominent.

But the rescue convention offered something more. It expressed an ideal state even beyond the factors of good action and reward. The rescue expresses an ideal of intense desirability—the ideal that the possibility of rescue exists. No matter the danger or dilemma, we can be rescued. What's more, we *will* be rescued.

In Simms' *The Yemassee* Pastor Matthews shouts "God be praised!" when Harrison rescues Bess (p. 344). Many prayers and thanks were directed to God when rescues took place. But the reason the rescue was so satisfying as a convention was that it was performed by human beings. The rescue was that splendid overthrowing of a seemingly omnipotent fate—a new chance—a glorious possibility.

For the readers the ideal world contained rescue, rescue from both the awful crises and the numbing "quiet desperation" of life. That "damned mob of scribbling women" and all the other popular writers knew what readers wanted—they wanted to be rescued.

Appendix

The following are plot synopses of the popular novels used in this study.

Alcott, Louisia May. *Rose in Bloom.* 1876.

Rose Campbell, now twenty, is back from her European tour and preparing to take her place as heiress to a fortune. Rose has a philanthropic nature and does much charity work. Her first love is her cousin Charlie, but he is beginning to drink too much at parties. Charlie is killed in a fall from a horse. Rose continues her philanthropic work and adopts an orphan brought to her by her cousin Mac. Eventually Rose and Mac grow to love each other and marry.

Atherton, Gertrude. *Patience Sparhawk and Her Times.* 1895.

Young Patience Sparhawk is taken in by elderly Mr. Foord after her drunken mother dies in a fire. Patience is sent to San Francisco and lives with Miss Tremont, a temperance leader. Eventually Patience meets rich, dashing Beverly Peele. There is an intense physical attraction between the two, and they marry. The marriage is a mistake, and Patience leaves her husband to become a newspaper reporter. Beverly becomes ill, and Patience returns to nurse him, while pleading for a divorce. When he dies from an overdose of morphine, she is accused of his murder. Garan Bourke, a brilliant lawyer, defends Patience and falls in love with her. She is convicted and sentenced to die, but Bourke rescues her at the last moment when he uncovers fresh evidence.

Bacheller, Irving. *Eben Holden.* 1900.

Eben Holden, an itinerent farm worker, takes care of young orphaned Willie. They settle at the farm of David Brower, and Willie grows up to marry Hope Brower and work on the New York *Tribune.* Later Willie goes into politics. Eben lives to a peaceful old age and dies.

Bennett, Emerson. *The Forest Rose; A Tale of the Frontier.* 1850.

In the Ohio River valley in 1789 Albert Maywood loves Rose Forester. Rose is captured by Indians. Albert and trapper Lewis Wetzel pursue and rescue her. Unfortunately, the Indians recapture her, and Albert must rescue her again before they can wed.

Bird, Robert Montgomery. *The Hawks of Hawk-Hollow.* 1835.

In Delaware during Revolutionary War times, the members of the Gilbert family, once feared and hated by neighbors, are reported to be dead. The family estate is owned now by Colonel Falconer, an old enemy of the Gilberts. The youngest Gilbert, disguised as a painter, returns to the territory and falls in love with Catherine Loring after she tries unsuccessfully to rescue him when he falls into the river. After much political maneuvering—Hyland is a patriot, unlike his Tory family—Hyland rescues Catherine from a forced marriage. All ends well when Hyland is revealed to be the son of Colonel Falconer.

Cable, George Washington. *The Grandissimes.* 1880.

There has been a long family feud between the aristocratic Creole families the Grandissimes and the De Grapions. Lovely widow Aurora De Grapion is living in poverty in New Orleans with her daughter Clotilde because her husband lost their plantation gambling with old Agricola Grandissime and then was killed in a duel. She carries on a calculated plot to win the love of Honoré Grandissime. He returns the plantation to her for the sake of justice and then reveals his love. They wed and the feud ends.

Cooke, John Esten. *The Virginia Comedians or Old Days in the Old Dominion.* 1854.

Aristocrat Champ Effingham becomes enamoured of actress Beatrice Hallam. She rejects him, but he continues his lustful pursuit. In the meantime Beatrice is rescued from drowning by Charles Waters, who is revealed to be her cousin. Beatrice and Charles fall in love, but Champ continues his pursuit. Finally, Champ kidnaps Beatrice and Charles rescues

her although he is wounded by Champ, who flees to Europe. Charles and Beatrice wed and live happily. Champ finally returns from Europe, a reformed man.

Cooper, James Fenimore. *The Last of the Mohicans.* 1826.
Hawkeye and his Indian companions, Chingachgook and Uncas, escort the sisters Alice and Cora Munro to Fort William Henry to join their father. The villainous Huron Magua lusts after Cora and pursues them. After being captured and then rescued, the girls arrive at the fort. Unfortunately, they are captured again during the massacre of Fort William Henry. Hawkeye, the Indians, and Duncan Heyward, Alice's betrothed, manage to rescue Alice, but, according to Indian law, Cora remains Magua's prisoner. Uncas leads a last desperate rescue attempt, but both he and Cora are killed.

Cummins, Maria, *The Lamplighter.* 1854.
Eight-year-old orphan Gertrude is taken in by Trueman Flint, the kindly lamplighter. After he dies, she goes to live with rich Miss Graham. She grows up to love her childhood playmate, Willie Sullivan. While visiting Saratoga, Gertrude fears that Willie loves Isabel Clinton. In a boat disaster, Gertrude nobly rescues her supposed rival from the burning boat. She later finds out that Willie still loves her. She also discovers her long lost father, now a rich merchant.

Curwood, James Oliver. *God's Country and the Woman.* 1914.
In the frozen arctic, trapper Philip Weyman meets beautiful Josephine Adare who asks him to help her. She wants him to pose as her husband so that she can convince her father that she is married and has a child. Actually, she is trying to conceal the fact that the child is her mother's. Philip agrees and masquerades as Josephine's husband. He foils an attempt to blackmail the women, and destroys the evidence against Josephine's mother. The child dies. Phillip and Josephine wed when everything is settled.

Deland, Margaret. *The Rising Tide.* 1916.
Frederica Payton is a young woman who believes in all the feminist positions and supports women's suffrage. She is

active in that cause and in labor disputes. Demonstrating her belief in equality, she proposes to Howard Maitland, but he rejects her. He admires her but loves her more conventional cousin Laura. Fred's confidence in the feminist belief in equality is shaken. It is shaken further when she is arrested and thrown into jail for fighting with the police during a labor strike. Old friend Arthur Weston gets her out of jail, and Fred realizes that he will make the best husband for her. She further realizes that her feminist positions are too extreme and must be modified.

Fox, John Jr. *The Little Shepherd of Kingdom Come.* 1903.
  Orphan Chad Buford is taken in by the Turner family in the Kentucky mountains. On a trip to Lexington, he gets lost and meets Major Buford who takes him in and provides him with an education. They discover that Chad is really the descendant of a relative of the major's. Chad loves Margaret Dean, but they are estranged when he joins the Union Army during the Civil War. After the war, they reconcile. On a visit to the mountains, Chad finds that Melissa, also adopted by the Turners, has died as a result of the pneumonia she got while warning him about an ambush. Melissa's evident love for him disturbs Chad, and he decides to forego his own happiness for a while and head west to start a new future.

Garland, Hamlin. *A Little Norsk or Ol' Pap's Flaxen.* 1892.
  Settlers Bert Gearheart and Anson Wood take in a five-year-old orphan they name Flaxen. The girl grows up happily with the bachelors. When she is fifteen, she marries a boy from town and leaves them. Bert has fallen in love with her and heads west after the marriage. Flaxen has a child but grows to hate her worthless husband. When her husband leaves town because of debts, Anson comes to stay with Flaxen, and they are a happy family with Anson acting as grandfather. Bert returns when Flaxen's husband dies, and he and Flaxen wed.

Grey, Zane. *The Lone Star Ranger.* 1914.
  Buck Duane kills a man in a fight and becomes a fugitive. He joins an outlaw camp when he meets a girl who has been forced to stay there and work. Buck and Jennie escape, but they are tracked down, and Jennie is killed. His failure to rescue

Jennie haunts Buck, and he agrees to work under cover for the Texas Rangers in exchange for a pardon. He begins to investigate Colonel Longstreth, major of outlaw-infested Fairdale. He falls in love with Longstreth's daughter, Ray, and she saves him from detection. When Longstreth is at last exposed as corrupt, Buck and Ray wed and go to Louisiana to build a new life.

Holland, Josiah G. *Sevenoaks; a Story of Today.* 1875.

Robert Belcher is a corrupt mill owner in a New England town. He has stolen the proceeds of several inventions of Paul Benedict and driven him and his small son Harry to the poorhouse. Trapper Jim Fenton rescues both Harry and his father. Benedict eventually recovers his healthy mind. Belcher continues his ruthless business practices until he is exposed by Mrs. Dillingham, a social dilettante who is the sister of Benedict.

Holman, Jessee L. *The Prisoners of Niagara or Errors of Education.* 1810.

As a baby, William Evermont is rescued from Indians by a trapper who gives him his name. Growing up with a farm family, William is miserable and asks a passing gentleman to be his father. The gentleman agrees, and William goes to live with Major Hayland, after first rescuing the major's niece, Zerelda, from the Potomac River. William grows up and is educated, but he becomes sexually promiscuous when he is fifteen and wastes his time in sexual escapades. Finally, he settles down and joins the Indian fighters. After rescuing Zerelda from Indians, William discovers he is the son of Sir William Valindon. He and Zerelda marry.

Holmes, Oliver Wendell. *A Mortal Antipathy.* 1885.

Maurice Kirkwood comes to live in Arrowhead Village, a New England town. The townspeople do not understand why the young man does not mingle with the young ladies. Maurice gets typhoid and tells the doctor treating him that he has an antipathy to young women because his female cousin dropped him over a balcony when he was a baby. Holmes speculates at length whether such antipathy could be cured by a young woman who saved Maurice instead of injuring him. When a

fire in his home breaks out, Maurice is rescued by Euthymia Tower, a strong, athletic young lady. Maurice loses his antipathy, and he and Euthymia wed.

Howells, William Dean. *Dr. Breen's Practice.* 1881.

Dr. Grace Breen becomes a physician because she is disappointed in love. Now, as a young doctor, she discovers that she is completely inadequate as a physician. She must get the assistance of Dr. Rufus Mulbridge to save her first patient. Grace decides to quit medicine and rejects Mulbridge's offer of marriage and a joint practice. She decides women should not try to do men's work. She marries Walter Libby, who is rich and can give her pretty things.

Howells, William Dean. *Indian Summer.* 1886.

Theodore Colville, an American publisher, goes to Florence for a vacation and becomes engaged to Imogene Graham, who is twenty years his junior. Imogene is staying with Evalina Bowen, a widow with a young daughter. Colville worries about being older than Imogene, but he decides it doesn't matter. While on a carriage ride, Imogene refuses to jump into Colville's arms when the carriage teeters on the brink of a precipice. She realizes at that moment that she does not love Colville, and she breaks the engagement. Colville subsequently realizes that he loves Evalina Bowen, who has been waiting patiently for him to reach that decision.

James, Henry. *The Bostonians.* 1886.

Olive Chancellor, a radical feminist, hears lovely Verena Tarrant speak and realizes that the young woman has a gift for swaying audiences. She enlists Verena in the feminist cause and takes her into her own home, urging her to promise that she will never marry. Olive's cousin, Basil Ransom, who has come to Boston from Mississippi, becomes enamoured of Verena and courts her. There is open hostility between Basil and Olive as each struggles for control over Verena. On a night Verena is to speak, Basil appears and sweeps her away, out of the feminist cause and into marriage.

Johnston, Mary. *To Have and To Hold.* 1900.

Ralph Percy, a Jamestown settler, meets a young lady who

has just arrived on a bride ship. Jocelyn Leigh, the king's ward, has fled to America to escape marriage to Lord Carnal. Ralph marries Jocelyn to protect her. Lord Carnal arrives in Jamestown and continues his pursuit of Jocelyn. When a message arrives from the king ordering Jocelyn back to court and Ralph to face arrest, the couple flee. They run into pirates, but Ralph manages to take command of the band. When he refuses to fire on a British ship, the pirates mutiny, and Ralph and Jocelyn are picked up by the British. Ralph is on trial facing charges of piracy when Jocelyn eloquently pleads for his life and saves him. Lord Carnal is maimed by a panther and commits suicide. Ralph and Jocelyn are free to return to England with the king's pardon.

King, Basil. *The Wild Olive.* 1910.

Norrie Ford is a fugitive in the Adirondacks, having escaped jail waiting execution on a murder charge. He meets a beautiful girl who hides him in a cabin, feeds him and arranges for his escape to Canada. She refuses to reveal her name, so he calls her the Wild Olive. Ford eventually reaches Argentina where he becomes successful in business and falls in love with lovely, young Evelyn Colfax. On a business trip to New York, he meets Miriam Strange at a party and realizes that she is the Wild Olive. Miriam is a friend of Evelyn's and tries to tell Norrie that his proposed marriage is a mistake. In an effort to clear himself of the old murder charge, Ford reveals his true identity. Miriam promises to marry an admirer, attorney Charles Conquest, if he will defend Ford. Conquest does clear Ford, but Evelyn becomes hysterical and breaks the engagement when Ford must return to jail for a time. Ford then realizes that he really loves Miriam. Conquest releases Miriam, and she and Ford can wed.

Lillibridge, William Otis. *Ben Blair, The Story of a Plainsman.* 1905.

Wealthy rancher Rankin takes in orphan Ben Blair after his drunken father disappears and his mother dies. Twelve years pass. Ben is a young man and in love with neighbor Florence Baker. Florence decides to move to New York with her mother so that she can meet eligible men of the upper social class. Rankin is killed one night by a rustler who turns out to be

Tom Blair, Ben's father. Ben hunts his father down and takes him to jail where Ben is wounded while stopping a lynch mob. He discovers evidence that he is really Rankin's son, but he destroys it because the dead man had not wanted it known. Ben goes to New York, and Florence realizes she loves him.

London, Jack. *Smoke Bellew.* 1912.

Smoke Bellew quits his job as an editor on a San Francisco newspaper and heads for the Klondike for adventure. He has many brushes with death and takes up prospecting. While on the trail with a partner, Smoke is captured by a band of Indians led by a white man named Snass. Smoke's partner manages to escape, but Smoke is too closely guarded. Snass has a daughter, Labiskwee, who falls in love with Smoke and helps him escape. They travel west to freedom, but their food runs out, and they grow weak. As Labiskwee dies from starvation, she gives Smoke her food ration that she had saved for him. The food gives him enough strength to reach safety.

McCutcheon, George Barr. *Beverly of Graustark.* 1904.

Beverly Calhoun is the daughter of a Southern senator. She decides to visit her friend, Princess Yetive of Graustark. While she is traveling through the hills to reach the kingdom, her drivers desert, and her coach is seized by mountain bandits. The bandit leader is Baldos, a goatherder. Baldos saves her from an attacking mountain lion, and Beverly feels he possesses nobility beyond his lowly station in life. She finally reaches the capital of Graustark to find there is war with evil Prince Gabriel of Dawsbergen. There is much political turmoil before Prince Gabriel is overthrown and Baldos reveals he is really Prince Dantan, the rightful ruler of Dawsbergen. Although Beverly had already agreed to marry him, she is thrilled that Baldos has turned out to be a prince.

McCutcheon, George Barr. *Jane Cable.* 1906.

Jane Cable is the daughter of railroad tycoon David Cable. Cable's wife never told her husband that she had adopted the girl while he was out West. James Bansemer, an unscrupulous lawyer, arranged the adoption. Now Jane is in love with Graydon Bansemer, the lawyer's son. Bansemer has been involved in numerous shady dealings over the years, and he is

now under heavy pressure. Because Jane's mother has refused his advances, the lawyer reveals Jane's adoption in public. Graydon still wants to marry Jan, but she refuses since they do not know her parentage. Finally, while in jail, Bansemer reveals her upper-class birth, and Jane and Graydon wed.

MacGrath, Harold. *The Adventures of Kathlyn.* 1914.

Kathlyn Hare goes to India in search of her father Colonel Hare, who has disappeared after being named heir to an Indian kingdom. The villain Umballa has put the colonel in prison and plans to take over the country by marrying Kathlyn after she is crowned queen as her father's heir. Kathlyn undergoes a series of harrowing adventures while she resists marrying Umballa and tries to find her father. She is rescued frequently by white hunter John Bruce. In the end, her father is freed; Umballa is killed; and Kathlyn and Bruce are wed.

McHenry, James. *The Betrothed of Wyoming.* 1830.

Settlers in the territory near the Susquehanna River welcome the Austin family in 1776. The Austin party had rescued Mary Watson and Agnes Norwood from Indians. Agnes and Henry Austin become engaged. Also in the party is Tory renegade John Butler, loved by Isabella Austin who rescued him from prison. The turmoil of the Revolutionary War comes to the settlement. Henry joins the colonials while Butler continues his guerilla activities. Isabella goes insane because Butler rejects her, and she is killed during a battle. Henry arrives with the militia just as Butler is about to kill Agnes' father and friends.

Major, Charles. *When Knighthood Was in Flower.* 1898.

Princess Mary, sister of Henry VIII, falls in love with Charles Brandon, a captain of the guard. They elope but are captured, and Brandon is sentenced to die. In order to save him, Mary agrees to marry aging Louis XII of France. She wears out the old king with strenuous activities and long hours. When he dies, Mary is free to marry Brandon.

Page, Thomas Nelson. *Gordon Keith.* 1903.

Gordon Keith is the son of Southern General Keith. After

the war, the family has lost all its money, and Gordon becomes a teacher. He falls in love with Alice Yorke, but her mother opposes the match because of Gordon's poverty and takes Alice to New York. Gordon rises to being a successful engineer, but Alice has married a wealthy, older man. She and Gordon remain friends. Although Alice later becomes a widow, she and Gordon never resume their romance. Gordon becomes a wealthy mine owner and finally falls in love with Lois Huntington whose father bought the Keith plantation. The two wed after Gordon has prevented panic in banking circles.

Paulding, James Kirke. *The Dutchman's Fireside.* 1831.
Sybrandt Westbrook loves his aristocratic cousin Catalina Vancour. After he rescues her from drowning and from a renegade Indian, Catalina returns his love. In spite of her mother's opposition, Catalina remains true to Sybrandt who becomes a scout for Sir William Johnson in the French and Indian War. Sybrandt is reported killed in battle. His unexpected return, wounded but not dead, is cause for joy, and he and Catalina marry.

Read, Martha. *Monima or The Beggar Girl.* 1802.
Monima Fontanbleu works as a seamstress to support herself and her aged father. She cannot find enough work and they are close to starving. Madame Sontine is jealous of Monima's beauty and exerts great effort to destroy her by putting her in the poorhouse or shipping her to Africa. Monsieur Sontine, however, continually rescues Monima from his wife's perfidy. Finally, Madame dies, and Monima weds Monsieur Sontine.

Roe, Edward Payson. *Barriers Burned Away.* 1872.
Dennis Fleet must support his two sisters and mother after the death of his father. He goes to work in an art gallery as a porter and, through hard work, rises to chief clerk. He falls in love with the owner's daughter, Christine Ludolph. However, Christine rejects him because of the difference in their social classes. Further, she is not an active Christian as he is. During the great Chicago fire, Dennis rescues her, and she accepts the Christian faith. Dennis is now a famous artist, and the two are wed.

Roe, Edward Payson. *Without a Home.* 1881.

The Jocelyn family goes from wealth to poverty as Mr. Jocelyn's business fails and he becomes addicted to morphine. Mildred Jocelyn is loved by Roger Atwood, a young man from the country trying to make his way in the city. In spite of her family's poverty, Mildred remains conscious of Roger's uncultured background, and she cannot accept him. Even when he rescues her from a jail sentence by clearing her of a charge of theft, Mildred can feel only gratitude. She becomes a nurse. When Roger, now a rich lawyer, is hurt while stopping a runaway carriage, Mildred realizes that she loves him, and they are wed.

Rowson, Susanna. *Reuben and Rachel or Tales of Old Times.* 1798.

The adventures of a family are traced from the fifteenth century in Wales to the eighteenth century in America. The final episode deals with the twins Reuben and Rachel. Rachel marries secretly to protect her husband's fortune. When he goes off to America, she follows and at last they are able to live as man and wife. Meanwhile, Reuben has been searching for proof that he is the heir to an American estate. He is captured by Indians. The daughter of the chief falls in love with him and rescues him, leading him to civilization. Reuben discovers the proof he needs to claim the estate, weds an English girl, and the Indian maiden commits suicide. Reuben and Rachel, however, are happy in the new world.

Sedgwick, Catherine M. *Hope Leslie or Early Times in The Massachusetts.* 1827.

William Fletcher takes his two orphaned nieces, Hope and Faith Leslie, to his home in New England. There is an Indian raid and Everell Fletcher and Faith Leslie are taken captive. Through the intervention of the chief's daughter, Magawisca, who loves him, Everell escapes, but Faith remains a prisoner and eventually marries an Indian. After living in England for seven years, Everell returns to New England. He is in love with Hope Leslie although he is engaged to Esther Downing. Magawisca is arrested and tried as a witch. Everell and Hope manage to rescue her from jail, and she goes away, still in love with Everell. Esther releases Everell, and he and Hope marry.

Simms, William Gilmore. *The Yemassee.* 1835.

Lord Charles Craven, governor of Carolina, is posing as cavalier Captain Gabriel Harrison in order to investigate potential Indian uprisings. He is in love with Bess Matthews, but her father opposes the match. After Craven rescues Bess from a pirate, her father consents to their marriage. Craven reveals his identity, and the couple are wed.

Southworth, E.D.E.N. *Ishmael or In the Depths.* 1864.

Ishmael Worth is believed to be illegitimate because his mother died without revealing her secret marriage to wealthy Herman Brudenell, who has gone to Europe. As a youth, Ishmael rescues the two sons of James Middleton from a fire and is rewarded with an education, which starts him on the way to success. Ishmael falls in love with rich Claudia Merlin, who loves him but will not consider marriage to anyone who is socially beneath her. Ishmael becomes a lawyer, and Claudia marries Lord Vincent. In the sequel, *Self-Raised or From the Depths* (1876), Ishmael's real parentage is revealed, and he rescues Claudia from her husband's plot to kill her. However, Ishmael no longer loves Claudia, and she bitterly regrets her mistake.

Southworth, E.D.E.N. *The Three Beauties, or Shannondale.* 1851.

In the Shenandoah Valley, widow Margery Summerfield lives with her daughter Imogene and niece Winny Darling. Winny is in love with her tutor Edgar Ardenne. They elope, but they sink into poverty and finally starvation. Edgar leaves, and Winny returns to Imogene with her baby daughter. Imogene is unhappy because she has fallen in love with the priest, Father Vellemont. Finally, matters are straightened out. Edgar returns to Winny, and Father Vellemont is released from his vows to marry Imogene.

Stephens, Mrs. Anna Sophia. *Malaeska; The Indian Wife of the White Hunter.* 1860.

Malaeska is married to William Danforth, who deserts her after she saves him from Indians. Later, she finds him dying after an Indian battle. He tells her to take their son to his parents in Manhattan. The grandparents welcome their

grandson but insist that Malaeska conceal the fact that she is the mother and act as a servant in the house. After several years, Malaeska flees with her son to the woods, intending to return to her people. The boy, however, wishes to return to his grandfather, and she allows the grandfather to take him away from her. She spends the rest of her life living on the edge of white civilization. When she meets her grown son at last, she tells him that she is his mother. Horrified, he commits suicide, and Malaeska dies on his grave.

Tourgée, Albion W. *A Fool's Errand.* 1879.

Comfort Servosse moves to North Carolina after the Civil War and buys a plantation. As an ex-Union officer and an active Republican, Servosse makes many enemies. His daughter, Lily, falls in love with Melville Gurney, a Southerner. Both families oppose the match. After Melville helps Lily rescue her father from a Klan ambush, Servosse withdraws his objections to the marriage. Melville's father, however, does not consent to the marriage until a year later when Servosse dies.

Twain, Mark. *The Adventures of Tom Sawyer.* 1876.

Tom Sawyer, a young boy in a Missouri town near the Mississippi River, lives with his Aunt Polly. Tom has a variety of adventures with his friend Huckleberry Finn. Tom and Huck see Injun Joe kill the town doctor, and they tell the authorities. While on a school picnic, Tom and Becky Thatcher are lost in a cave where Tom sees Injun Joe's hideout. Tom and Becky are rescued, but Injun Joe dies in the cave. Huck is taken in by the Widow Douglas.

Webster, Jean. *Daddy-Long-Legs.* 1912.

Jerusha Abbott, the oldest orphan in the orphanage, is sent to college by a trustee who wishes to remain anonymous. He only requires that Jerusha write to him once a month about her progress. Jerusha does well at college. She meets Jervis Pendleton, her roommate's uncle, and he becomes very important to her. Jerusha begins to write fiction and sells a story. She wins a scholarship and pays her own way at school. By the time she graduates from college, she is writing a novel. Jervis proposes and reveals that he is her benefactor. The two are wed.

White, Stewart Edward. *The Silent Places.* 1904.

Dick Herron and old Sam Bolton are sent by Hudson Bay Company to catch a renegade Indian who has not paid for his outfit. Before they leave the fort, Dick pays some compliments to an Indian girl, May-may-gwán, who falls in love with him and follows the men through the wilderness. The men cannot make her turn back. Although she helps them find the renegade's trail and does the chores, Dick is abusive and hostile to her. Finally, they are without food. May-may-gwán dies in the snow from starvation just as the renegade Indian staggers up snowblind. Dick and old Sam make it back to the fort and are hailed as heroes.

Wilson, Augusta Evans. *Beulah.* 1859.

Beulah Benton and her sister Lilly are orphans. Lilly is adopted, but Beulah is hired out as a nursemaid. When Lilly dies of scarlet fever, Dr. Guy Hartwell is so touched by Beulah's grief that he takes the girl in and gives her an education. Beulah becomes a teacher and insists on supporting herself instead of living an idle life as Hartwell wishes her to. She becomes a famous writer, and in the end agrees to marry Hartwell, who has declared his love.

Wilson, Augusta Evans. *St. Elmo.* 1867.

Orphan Edna Earl is on her way to find work in a factory in Columbus, Georgia, when there is a train wreck, and she is injured. Mrs. Murray, a wealthy widow, takes her in and offers to give her an education. Mrs. Murray's son is the dissipated and brooding St. Elmo. Edna studies and develops into a religious scholar. She and St. Elmo have long philosophical discussions about religion. Edna writes scholarly works and gains an international reputation. She refuses to marry St. Elmo until he reforms. He finally becomes a minister and they marry.

Wister, Owen. *The Virginian.* 1902.

Schoolteacher Molly Stark Wood comes to Wyoming and meets the exciting cowboy called the Virginian. While the hero deals with local rustlers and evil men, Molly decides that she can never love a man who is socially beneath her. When she

rescues the Virginian from an Indian attack and nurses him back to health, however, Molly comes to appreciate his natural heroism and innate moral strength. After a shootout with the villain Trampas, the Virginian and the schoolteacher marry.

Woodworth, Samuel. *The Champions of Freedom, or The Mysterious Chief: A Romance of the Nineteenth Century Founded on the Events of the War Between the United States and Great Britain which terminated in March, 1815. 1816.*
Major Willoughby lives near Lake Erie in 1809 with his son George and daughter Amelia. George is in love with their neighbor Catherine Fleming. He goes to Harvard to study and makes the acquaintance of Thomas Sandford, a dissipated young man. George rejects a life of dissipation. Angry, Sandford tries to seduce Catherine as revenge. After many harrowing episodes, Sandford is killed, and Catherine and George are reunited.

Wright, Caleb. *Wyoming, A Tale.* 1845.
Pioneers in northern Pennsylvania rescue an Indian boy from accidental hanging. The boy, called Hanger, stays with the John Henderson family for a while and then leaves. Ten years later in 1775, the family is torn apart when Walter Henderson joins the colonials and Charles Henderson joins the British. Walter loves Ruth Dinning, the daughter of a Tory. When Walter is captured by Mohawks, he is saved from death by a renowned chief, who reveals he was the boy called Hanger. After being a prisoner of the British and escaping, Walter is reunited with Ruth at the close of the war.

Wright, Harold Bell. *That Printer of Udell's.* 1903.
Dick Falkner, a young printer, gets a job at George Udell's shop after virtually every solid citizen and Christian in town has turned him down. Dick has been dissipated in the past but knows now that Christianity is the best way to live. He loves Amy Goodrich, daughter of a rich storeowner. Amy is forbidden to see Dick because he is socially beneath her. She runs away to the city but cannot take care of herself and ends up in a brothel. On her first night there, Dick arrives with a Salvation Army group and saves her from entering a life of sin. Amy's brother has developed gambling debts, and Dick saves

him from disgrace. In spite of Dick's help, Amy's father still opposes the match. But the couple reject his authority and wed. Dick goes off to Washington as a congressman.

Wright, Harold Bell. *The Winning of Barbara Worth.* 1911.

While in the Colorado desert, banker Jefferson Worth rescues a little girl whose parents have died. Barbara grows up to be a charming and intelligent young lady. While her father is involved with business deals to develop the irrigation possibilities in the desert, Barbara falls in love with Willard Holmes, an engineer for the corrupt Eastern firm trying to cheat Jefferson Worth. After Willard proves his morality by rejecting the corrupt company and helping Barbara's father, he and Barbara can wed.

Notes

Chapter I

[1]James D. Hart, *The Popular Book* (1950; rpt. Berkeley, Calif.: Univ. of California Press, 1963), p. 93.

[2]Caroline Ticknor, *Hawthorne and His Publisher* (Boston: Houghton Mifflin Co., 1913), pp. 141-142.

[3]Russel Nye, *The Unembarrassed Muse: The Popular Arts in America* (New York: Dial Press, 1970), pp. 29-31.

[4]Abraham Kaplan, "The Aesthetics of the Popular Arts," *Journal of Aesthetics* (1964), p. 356.

[5]Hart, p. 285.

[6]Nye, p. 4.

[7]John Cawelti, "The Concept of Formula in the Study of Popular Literature," *Journal of Popular Culture*, 3 (1969), p. 388.

[8]Cawelti, p. 390.

[9]Quoted in Hart, p. 208.

[10]John Fox, Jr., *The Little Shepherd of Kingdom Come* (1903; rpt. New York: Grosset & Dunlap, n.d.), pp. 269-77. All further references to this work appear in the text.

[11]Beadle & Co., introd. *Malaeska; The Indian Wife of the White Hunter* by Ann Sophia Stephens (1860; rpt. New York: The John Day Co., 1929), n.p. All further references to this work appear in the text.

[12]Kaplan, p. 361.

Chapter II

[1]Augusta Evans Wilson, *Beulah* (1859; rpt. New York: Grosset & Dunlap, 1900), p. 43. All further references to this work appear in the text.

[2]Hart, p. 118.

[3]Augusta Evans Wilson, *St. Elmo* (1867, rpt. New York: Grosset & Dunlap, n.d.), p. 31. All further references to this work appear in the text.

[4]Maria Cummins, *The Lamplighter* (1854, rpt. London: George Routledge and Sons, Ltd., n.d.), p. 9. All further references to this work appear in the text.

[5]Jessee L. Holman, *The Prisoners of Niagara or Errors of Education* (Frankfort: William Gerard, 1810), p. 46. All further references to this work appear in the text.

[6]Caleb Wright, *Wyoming, a Tale* (New York: Harper & Brothers, 1845), p. 29. All further references to this work appear in the text.

[7]Hamlin Garland, *A Little Norsk or Old Pap's Flaxen* (New York: D. Appleton and Company, 1892), p. 10. All further references to this work appear in the text.

[8]William Lillibridge, *Ben Blair, The Story of a Plainsman* (Chicago: A.C. McClurg & Co., 1905), p. 32. All further references to this work appear in the text.

[9]Nye, p. 36.

[10]Irving Bacheller, *Eben Holden* (Boston: Lothrop Publishing Co., 1900), p. 8. All further references to this work appear in the text.

[11]Frank Luther Mott, *Golden Multitudes* (New York: Macmillan Co., 1947), p. 214.

[12]Jean Webster, *Daddy-Long-Legs* (1912, rpt. New York: The Century Co., 1915), p. 14. All further references to this work appear in the text.

[13]Josiah G. Holland, *Sevenoaks; a Story of Today* (1875; rpt. Upper Saddle River, New Jersey: The Gregg Press, 1968), p. 39. All further references to this work appear in the text.

[14]Mott, p. 232.

[15]Harold Bell Wright, *The Winning of Barbara Worth* (Chicago: The Book Supply Co., 1911), p. 43. All further references to this work appear in the text.

[16]Gertrude Atherton, *Patience Sparhawk and Her Times* (1895; rpt. Toronto: The Macmillan Co. of Canada, 1910). All further references to this work appear in the text.

[17]Louisa May Alcott, *Rose in Bloom* (1876; rpt. New York: Grosset & Dunlap, 1927), p. 242. All further references to this work appear in the text.

[18]E.D.E.N. Southworth, *Ishmael or In the Depths* (1864; rpt. New York: A.L. Burt Co., 19—), p. 203. All further references to this work appear in the text.

[19]Thomas Nelson Page, *Gordon Keith* (1903; rpt. New York: Charles Scribner's Sons, 1905), p. 481. All further references to this work appear in the text.

[20]Samuel Clemens, *The Adventures of Tom Sawyer* in *The Family Mark Twain* (1876; rpt. New York: Harper & Brothers Publishers, 1935), p. 433. All further references to this work appear in the text.

Chapter III

[1]Emerson Bennett, *The Forest Rose: A Tale of the Frontier* (1850; rpt. Athens, Ohio: Ohio University Press, 1973), p. 11. All further references to this work appear in the text.

[2]Martha Read, *Monima or The Begger Girl* (New York: printed by P.R. Johnson for I.N. Ralston, 1802), p. 227. All further references to this work appear in the text.

[3]James Kirke Paulding, *The Dutchman's Fireside* (1831; rpt. New Haven, Conn.: College & University Press, 1966), p. 64. All further references to this work appear in the text.

[4]Hart, p. 82, and Nye, p. 22.

[5]Mott, p. 74.

[6]James Fenimore Cooper, *The Last of the Mohicans* (1826; rpt. New York: New American Library, 1962), p. 132. All further references to this work appear in the text.

[7]William Gilmore Simms, *The Yemassee* (1835; rpt. Boston: Houghton Mifflin, Riverside Edition, 1961), p. 141. All further references to this work appear in the text.

[8]Hart, p. 199.

[9]Charles Major, *When Knighthood Was in Flower* (1898; rpt. New York Grosset and Dunlap, n.d.), p. 120. All further references to this work appear in the text.

[10]Mary Johnston, *To Have and To Hold* (Boston: Houghton Mifflin and Co., 1900), p. 21. All further references to this work appear in the text.

[11]Hart, p. 199.

[12]George Barr McCutcheon, *Beverly of Graustark* (1904; rpt. New York: Grosset and Dunlap, n.d.), p. 63. All further references to this work appear in the text.

[13]Owen Wister, *The Virginian* (1902; rpt. New York: The Macmillan Co., 1904), p. 101. All further references to this work appear in the text.

[14]Nye, p. 54. Nye cites Winston Churchill, Zane Grey, Harold Bell Wright, Gene Stratton-Porter, and Mary Roberts Rinehart as the most popular writers in the first quarter of the twentieth century.

[15]Zane Grey, *The Lone Star Ranger* (New York: Harper & Brothers 1914), p. 238. All further references to this work appear in the text.

[16]Albion W. Tourgée, *A Fool's Errand* (1879; rpt. New York: Harper & Row, 1966), p. 272. All further references to this work appear in the text.

[17]Hart, p. 121.

[18]Edward Payson Roe, *Barriers Burned Away* (1872; rpt. New York: Dodd, Mead & Co., 1892), p. 82. All further references to this work appear in the text.

[19]John Esten Cooke, *The Virginia Comedians or Old Days in the Old Dominion* (1854; rpt. New York: D. Appleton and Co., 1883), p. 87. All further references to this work appear in the text.

[20]Samuel Woodworth, *The Champions of Freedom, or The Mysterious Chief: A Romance of the Nineteenth Century founded on the Events of the War Between the United States and Great Britain which terminated in March, 1815,* 2nd ed (New York: Charles N. Baldwin, 1818), I, p. 182. All further references to this work appear in the text.

[21]Harold MacGrath, *The Adventures of Kathlyn* (Indianapolis: The Bobbs-Merrill Co., 1914), p. 94. All further references to this work appear in the text.

[22]William Dean Howells, *Indian Summer* (1886; rpt. Bloomington, Indiana; Indiana University Press, 1971), p. 253. All further references to this work appear in the text.

[23]Helen Andelin, *The Fascinating Girl* (Santa Barbara, Calif.: Pacific Press Santa Barbara, 1969), p. 295.

Chapter IV

[1]William Charvat, "Literature as Business," in *Literary History of the United States: History,* ed. Robert E. Spiller, et al. (London: The Macmillan Co., 1963), p. 956.

[2]John Cawelti, *Adventure, Mystery, and Romance* (Chicago: Univ. of Chicago Press, 1976), p. 278.

[3]Margaret Fuller Ossoli, *Woman in the Nineteenth Century and Kindred Papers Relating to the Sphere, Condition and Duties of Woman,* ed. Arthur B.

Fuller (Boston: Roberts Brothers, 1874), p. 119.

[4]Ossoli, p. 121.

[5]Ossoli, pp. 176-77.

[6]Margaret Deland, *The Rising Tide* (New York: Harper & Brothers Publishers, 1916), p. 141. All further references to this work appear in the text.

[7]George Washington Cable, *The Grandissimes* (1880; rpt. New York: Hill and Wang, 1957), p. 131. All further references to this work appear in the text.

[8]Edward Payson Roe, *Without a Home*. Vol. II of *The Works of E.P. Roe* (1881; rpt. New York: P. F. Collier & Son, 1902), p. 90. All further references to this work appear in the text.

[9]James Oliver Curwood, *God's Country and the Woman* (1914; rpt. New York: A.L. Burt Co., n.d.), p. 21. All further references to this work appear in the text.

[10]Harold Bell Wright, *That Printer of Udell's* (New York: A.L. Burt Co., 1903), p. 109. All further references to this work appear in the text.

[11]Cawelti, *Adventure*, p. 278.

[12]William Dean Howells, *Dr. Breen's Practice* (Boston: Houghton Mifflin Co., 1881), p. 15. All further references to this work appear in the text.

[13]Henry James, *The Bostonians* (1886; rpt. New York: The Modern Library, 1956), p. 18. All further references to this work appear in the text.

Chapter V

[1]Leslie A. Fiedler, *The Return of the Vanishing American* (New York: Stein and Day, 1968), pp. 50-51. Fiedler cites four myths as the foundation of the American concept of the West: *The Myth of Love in the Woods, The Myth of the White Woman with a Tomahawk, The Myth of the Good Companions in the Wilderness,* and *The Myth of the Runaway Male.*

[2]Fiedler, p. 64.

[3]Fiedler, p. 70

[4]Susanna Rowson, *Reuben and Rachel or Tales of Old Times* (Boston: Manning & Loring, 1798), II, p. 346. All further references to this work appear in the text.

[5]Mott, p. 142.

[6]E.D.E.N. Southworth, *The Three Beauties, or Shannondale* (1851: rpt. New York: Hurst & Co., n.d.), p. 27. All further references to this work appear in the text.

[7]Helen Waite Papashvily, *All The Happy Endings* (New York: Harper & Brothers Publishers, 1956), p. 41.

[8]Catherine M. Sedgwick, *Hope Leslie or Early Times in The Massachusetts* (1827; rpt. New York: Harper & Brothers, Publishers, 1855), I, p. 136. All further references to this work appear in the text.

[9]Jack London, *Smoke Bellew* (New York: The Century Co., 1912), p. 343. All further references to this work appear in the text.

[10]Stewart Edward White, *The Silent Places* (New York: McClure, Phillips & Co., 1904), p. 97. All further references to this work appear in the text.

[11]Basil King, *The Wild Olive* (New York: Harper & Brothers, 1910), p. 31. All further references to this work appear in the text.

¹²George Barr McCutcheon, *Jane Cable* (New York: Dodd, Mead & Co., 1906), p. 254. All further references to this work appear in the text.

¹³Oliver Wendell Holmes, *A Mortal Antipathy* (1885; rpt. Boston Houghton Mifflin and Co., 1892), p. 41. All further references to this work appear in the text. Holmes' primary concern in this novel was human psychology and unorthodox ways to solve psychological problems. Although Holmes probably was not interested in traditional male-female relationships, his novel is useful here because it uses the pattern of the physical rescue with role reversal. The awkwardness of such a role reversal is evident in the characterizations of the hero and heroine.

¹⁴Robert Montgomery Bird, *The Hawks of Hawk-Hollow* (Philadelphia: Carey, Lea, & Blanchard, 1835), I, p. 100. All further references to this work appear in the text.

Chapter VI

¹Hart, p. 285.
²Hart, p. 285.
³Cawelti, *Adventure,* p. 300.
⁴Fiedler, p. 77.

Bibliography
Novels

Alcott, Louisa May. *Rose in Bloom*. 1876; rpt. New York: Grossett & Dunlap, 1927.

Atherton, Gertrude, *Patience Sparhawk and Her Times*. 1895; rpt. Toronto: The Macmillan Co. of Canada, Ltd., 1910.

Bacheller, Irving. *Eben Holden*. Boston: Lothrop Publishing Co., 1900.

Bennett, Emerson. *The Forest Rose; A Tale of the Frontier*. 1885; rpt. Athens, Ohio: Ohio Univ. Press, 1973.

Bird, Robert Montgomery. *The Hawks of Hawk-Hollow*. 2 vols. Philadelphia: Carey, Lea, & Blanchard, 1835.

Cable, George Washington. *The Grandissimes*. 1880; rpt. New York: Hill and Wang, 1957.

Cooke, John Esten. *The Virginia Comedians or Old Days in the Old Dominion*. 1854; rpt. New York: D. Appleton and Co., 1883.

Cooper, James Fenimore. *The Last of the Mohicans*. 1826; rpt. New York: New American Library, 1962.

Cummins, Maria. *The Lamplighter*. 1854; rpt. London: George Routledge and Sons, ltd., n.d.

Curwood, James Oliver. *God's Country and the Woman*. 1914; rpt. New York: A.L. Burt Co., n.d.

Deland, Margaret. *The Rising Tide*. New York: Harper & Brothers, 1916.

Fox, John Jr. *The Little Shepherd of Kingdom Come*. 1903; rpt. New York: Grosset & Dunlap, n.d.

Garland, Hamlin. *A Little Norsk or Ol' Pap's Flaxen*. New York: D. Appleton and Co., 1892.

Grey, Zane. *The Lone Star Ranger*. New York: Harper & Brothers, 1914.

Holland, Josiah G. *Sevenoaks; a Story of Today*. 1875; rpt. Upper Saddle River, New Jersey: The Gregg Press, 1968.

Holman, Jessee L. *The Prisoners of Niagara or Errors of Education*. Frankfort: William Girard, 1810.

Holmes, Oliver Wendell. *A Mortal Antipathy*. 1885; rpt. Boston: Houghton Mifflin and Co., 1892.

Howells, William Dean. *Dr. Breen's Practice*. Boston: Houghton Mifflin Co., 1881.

———. *Indian Summer*. 1886; rpt. Bloomington, Indiana: Indiana Univ. Press, 1971.

James, Henry. *The Bostonians*. 1886; rpt. New York: The Modern Library, 1956.

Johnston, Mary. *To Have and To Hold*. Boston: Houghton, Mifflin and Co., 1900.

King, Basil. *The Wild Olive*. New York: Harper & Brothers, 1910.

Lillibridge, William. *Ben Blair, The Story of a Plainsman.* 5th ed. Chicago: A.C. McClurg & Co., 1905.

London, Jack. *Smoke Bellew.* New York: The Century Co., 1912.

McCutcheon, George Barr. *Beverly of Graustark.* 1904; rpt. New York: Grosset & Dunlap, n.d.

———. *Jane Cable.* New York: Dodd, Mead & Co., 1906.

MacGrath, Harold. *The Adventures of Kathlyn.* Indianapolis: The Bobbs-Merrill Co., 1914.

McHenry, James. *The Betrothed of Wyoming.* 2nd ed. Philadelphia: principal booksellers, 1830.

Major, Charles. *When Knighthood Was in Flower.* 1898; rpt. New York: Grosset & Dunlap, n.d.

Page, Thomas Nelson. *Gordon Keith.* 1903; rpt. New York: Charles Scribner's Sons, 1905.

Paulding, James Kirke. *The Dutchman's Fireside.* 1831; rpt. New Haven, Conn.: College & Univ. Press, 1966.

Read, Martha. *Monima or The Beggar Girl.* New York: printed by P.R. Johnson for I.N. Ralston, 1802.

Roe, Edward Payson. *Barriers Burned Away.* 1872; rpt. New York: Dodd, Mead & Co., 1892.

———. *Without a Home* in *The Works of E.P. Roe.* 1881; rpt. New York: P.F. Collier & Son, 1902.

Rowson, Susanna. *Reuben and Rachel or Tales of Old Times.* 2 vols. Boston: Manning & Loring, 1798.

Sedgwick, Catherine M. *Hope Leslie or Early Times in The Massachusetts.* 1827; rpt. New York: Harper & Brothers Publishers, 1855.

Simms, William Gilmore. *The Yemassee.* 1835; rpt. Boston: Houghton Mifflin, 1961.

Southworth, E.D.E.N. *Ishmael or In the Depths.* 1864; rpt. New York: A.L. Burt Co., 19-.

———. *The Three Beauties or Shannondale.* 1851; rpt. New York: Hurst & Co., n.d.

Stephens, Mrs. Ann Sophia. *Malaeska; The Indian Wife of the White Hunter.* 1860; rpt. New York: The John Day Co., 1929.

Tourgée, Albion W. *A Fool's Errand.* 1880; rpt. New York: Harper & Row Publishers, 1966.

Twain, Mark. *The Adventures of Tom Sawyer* in *The Family Mark Twain.* 1876; rpt. New York: Harper & Brothers Publishers, 1935.

Webster, Jean. *Daddy-Long-Legs.* 1912; rpt. New York: The Century Co., 1915.

White, Stewart Edward. *The Silent Places.* New York: McClure, Phillips & Co., 1904.

Wilson, Augusta Evans. *Beulah.* 1859; rpt. New York: Grosset & Dunlap, 1900.

———. *St. Elmo.* 1867; rpt. New York: Grosset & Dunlap, n.d.

Wister, Owen. *The Virginian.* 1902; rpt. New York: The Macmillan Co., 1904.

Woodworth, Samuel. *The Champions of Freedom, or The Mysterious Chief: A Romance of the Nineteenth Century Founded on the Events of the War Between the United States and Great Britain which terminated in March, 1815.* 2 vols. 2nd ed. New York: Charles N. Baldwin, 1818.

Wright, Caleb. *Wyoming, A Tale*. New York: Harper & Brothers, 1845.

Wright, Harold Bell. *That Printer of Udell's*. New York: A.L. Burt Co., 1903.

_____ *The Winning of Barbara Worth*. Chicago: The Book Supply Co., 1911.

Critical Sources

Andelin, Helen. *The Fascinating Girl.* Santa Barbara, Calif.: Pacific Press Santa Barbara, 1969.

Benschoten, Virginia van. "Changes in Best Sellers Since World War One." *Journal of Popular Culture,* I, No. 4 (1968), 379-388.

Bode, Carl. *The Anatomy of American Popular Culture 1840-1861.* Berkeley: Univ. of California Press, 1959.

Bristed, John. *The Resources of the United States of America.* New York: James Eastburn & Co., 1818.

Brown, Herbert Ross. *The Sentimental Novel in America 1789-1860.* Durham, N.C.: Duke Univ. Press, 1940.

Browne, Ray B., Marshall Fishwick, and Michael T. Marsden. *Heroes of Popular Culture.* Bowling Green, Ohio: Bowling Green Univ. Popular Press, 1972.

Cawelti, John F. *Adventure, Mystery, and Romance.* Chicago: Univ. of Chicago Press, 1976.

_____."The Concept of Formula in the Study of Popular Literature." *Journal of Popular Culture,* 3 No. 3 (1969), 381-390.

_____. "Notes Toward an Aesthetic of Popular Culture." *Journal of Popular Culture,* 5, No. 2 (1971), 255-268.

Charvat, William. "Literature as Business," in *Literary History of the United States: History.* ed. Robert E. Spiller, et al. 3rd ed. London: The Macmillan Co., 1963.

Cowie, Alexander. *The Rise of the American Novel.* New York: American Book Co., 1948.

_____ "The Vogue of the Domestic Novel 1850-1870." The *South Atlantic Quarterly,* 51, No. 4 (1942), 416-424.

Fiedler, Leslie A. *Love and Death in the American Novel.* New York: Dell Publishing Co., 1969.

_____. *The Return of the Vanishing American.* New York: Stein and Day, 1968.

Fishwick, Marshall and Ray B. Browne, eds. *Icons of Popular Culture.* Bowling Green, Ohio Bowling Green Univ. Popular Press, 1970.

Gans, Herbert J. *Popular Culture and High Culture: An Analysis and Evaluation of Taste.* New York: Basic Books, 1974.

Garrison, Dee. "Immoral Fiction in the Late Victorian Library." *American Quarterly,* 28, No. 1 (1976), 71-89.

Gowans, Alan. *The Unchanging Arts: New Forms for the Traditional Function of Art in Society.* Philadelphia: J.B. Lippincott Co., 1971.

Hackett, Alice Payne. *Fifty Years of Best Sellers, 1895-1945.* New York: R.R. Bowker Co., 1945.

Hammel, William M., ed. *The Popular Arts in America.* 2nd ed. New York: Harcourt Brace Jovanovich, 1977.

Hart, James D. *The Popular Book.* 1950; rpt. Berkeley: Univ. of California Press, 1963.

Hockey, Dorothy C. "The Good and the Beautiful, A Study of Best

Selling Novels in America, 1895-1920." Diss. Case Western Reserve, 1947.

Hofstadter, Beatrice K. "Popular Culture and the Romantic Heroine." *The American Scholar*, 30, No. 1 (1960-61), 98-116.

Kaplan, Abraham. "The Aesthetics of the Popular Arts." *Journal of Aesthetics* (1964), 351-364.

Loshe, Lillie Deming. *The Early American Novel*. New York: Columbia Univ. Press, 1907.

Madden, David. "The Necessity for an Aesthetics of Popular Culture." *Journal of Popular Culture,* 7 (1973), 1-13.

Mott, Frank Luther. *Golden Multitudes*. New York: Macmillan Co., 1947.

The National Union Catalog Pre-1956 Imprints. London: Mansell, 1974.

Nye, Russel. *The Unembarrassed Muse: The Popular Arts in America*. New York: The Dial Press, 1970.

Orians, G. Harrison. "The Censure of Fiction in American Romances and Magazines 1789-1810." *PMLA,* 52, No. 1 (1937), 195-214.

Ossoli, Margaret Fuller. *Woman in the Nineteenth Century and Kindred Papers Relating to the Sphere, Condition, and Duties of Woman*. ed. Arthur B. Fuller. Boston: Roberts Brothers, 1874.

Papashvily, Helen Waite. *All The Happy Endings*. New York: Harper & Brothers Publishers, 1956.

Perkins, Frederic C. "Free Libraries & Unclean Books." *Library Journal* 10, No. 12 (1885), 396-399.

Petter, Henri. *The Early American Novel*. Columbus, Ohio Ohio State Univ. Press, 1971.

Reynolds, Quentin. *The Fiction Factory, or From Pulp Row to Quality Street*. New York: Random House, 1955.

Rosenberg, Bernard and David Manning White, eds. *Mass Culture: The Popular Arts in America*. Glencoe, Ill.: The Free Press, 1957.

Satterwhite, Joseph N. "The Tremulous Formula: Form and Technique in *Godey's* Fiction." *American Quarterly*, 8, No. 2, (1956), 99-113.

Smith, Henry Nash. "The Scribbling Women and the Cosmic Success Story." *Critical Inquiry* 1, No. 1 (1974), 47-70.

Van Doren, Carl. *The American Novel 1789-1939*. New York: The Macmillan Co., 1940.

Wasserstrom, William. *Heiress of All the Ages: Sex and Sentiment in the Genteel Tradition*. Minneapolis: Univ. of Minnesota Press, 1959.

Western, Richard D. "Genres & Teaching: Uses of Formula Fiction." MMLA Convention, St. Louis. 5 Nov. 1976.

Ziff, Larzer. *The American 1890s, Life & Times of a Lost Generation*. New York: Viking Press, 1966.

Index